The Local Politics of Global English

The Local Politics of Global English

Case Studies in Linguistic Globalization

Selma K. Sonntag

LEXINGTON BOOKS
Lanham • Boulder • New York • Toronto • Oxford

LEXINGTON BOOKS

Published in the United States of America
by Lexington Books
An imprint of The Rowman & Littlefield Publishing Group, Inc.
4501 Forbes Boulevard, Suite 200, Lanham, Maryland 20706

PO Box 317
Oxford
OX2 9RU, UK

British Library Cataloguing in Publication Information Available

Library of Congress Cataloging-in-Publication Data
Sonntag, Selma K.
  The local politics of global English : case studies in linguistic
globalization / Selma K. Sonntag.
     p. cm.
  Includes bibliographical references and index.
  1. English language—Political aspects—Case studies. 2. Language
policy—United States—Case studies. 3. Language policy—South
Africa—Case studies. 4. Language policy—France—Case studies. 5.
Language policy—India—Case studies. 6. Language policy—Nepal—
Case studies. 7. Globalization—Case studies. I. Title.
  PE2751.S65 2003
  420—dc21   2003013194

ISBN 0-7391-0597-3 (alk. paper) — ISBN 0-7391-0598-1 (pbk. : alk. paper)

Printed in the United States of America

♾™ The paper used in this publication meets the minimum requirements of American
National Standard for Information Sciences—Permanence of Paper for Printed Library
Materials, ANSI/NISO Z39.48–1992.

To Bob and Yasmine

Contents

Acknowledgments

The most enjoyable part of writing a book such as this is conducting the field research. In my case, most of the field research consisted of interviewing and talking to fascinating and knowledgeable people involved in language policy and language debates. Those I interviewed were generous with their time and knowledge, and I am indebted to all of them.

The list of Bretons to whom I want to acknowledge my gratitude is particularly long. Foremost is Mr. Fañch Broudic, who before, during, and after my visit to Brittany was extremely gracious with his assistance—in recommending contacts, providing access to valuable material, reading, and commenting on chapter 3 of this book, and answering patiently and thoroughly my innumerable questions. I would also like to thank Mélanie Jouitteau for her friendliness and enormous help in introducing me to the younger generation of *néo-Bretonnants*, and for her feedback on my write-up on Brittany. Claude Gaugain, an acquaintance of mine from his stint as a Visiting Professor of French at my home institution, introduced me to Mélanie and to the wonderful "derrière la table" hospitality that only the French can provide. I also benefited enormously from my conversations with Henri Gourmelen, Ronan Le Coadic, Michel Nicolas, Philippe Blanchet, Christian Guyonvarc'h, Olier ar Mogn, Jean Le Dû, Yves Le Berre, and many others who were willing to meet with me on a moment's notice.

In South Africa as well, I was very fortunate to encounter a tremendous willingness on the part of many to share their knowledge and time with me. In particular, I would like to thank Neville Alexander, Kathleen Heugh, Peter Titlestad, Elizabeth de Kadt, Russell Kaschula, Anne-Marie Beukes, Chris Louw, Fritz Kok, Raj Mesthrie, Kay McCormick, Vic Webb, Bernard Louw, Frans van Niekirk, Hermann Giliomee, and Dr. Mkhulisi, Director of the National Language Services, Department of Arts, Culture, Science and Technology. Often one interview would lead to suggestions for others. I am grateful to Nkonko Kamwangamalu and Sibs Moodley-Moore, colleagues of mine from the past, for helping me secure my initial interviews. Sibs' sister, Devi Rajab, provided a memorable moment when she took my husband and me along with her to her polling place in Durban for the local December 2000 elections. With the outcome of the American presidential election still undetermined, we all had a good laugh when the multiracial crowd of polling officials and voters suggested that perhaps we Americans could learn from our observations! I left South Africa feeling that there was much I could learn from the graciousness and openness of the many South Africans I met. Anne-Marie Beukes and Chris Louw extended further generosity after my return home by reading and commenting on my South African chapter.

Most of the field research material I used in the Indian and Nepalese case studies was gathered much earlier, in 1993-94. My indebtedness to the many South Asians who assisted me at that time has probably not been adequately acknowledged in my earlier publications. I would like to thank Dr. Nil Ratan at the A.N. Sinha Institute in Patna and Dr. Abdus Salam Siddiqui in Lucknow among many others. In Nepal, Til Bikram Nembangh was an inspiration, not only to me but also to other minority language advocates who so generously shared their knowledge and views with me, such as Padma Ratna Tuladhar, Parshuram Tamang, Suresh Ale Magar, Gopal Gurung, and Bal Gopal Shrestha. I realize my thanks should include many more, including the Fulbright officers in both New Delhi and Kathmandu.

My field research at various times and in various places was funded through various sources. In 1993-94 in South Asia, I had a Fulbright research grant. In South Africa, my research was funded by a study grant through the Joint Berkeley-Stanford Center for African Studies, in conjunction with the Ford Foundation. The Humboldt State University Foundation generously helped out several times with travel grants and manuscript preparation.

This book is entirely my own, inclusive of all faults and shortcomings. I am nonetheless extremely grateful to my colleagues and friends who took the time and had the patience to help me improve the product. Fred Riggs and Hank Sims read the entire manuscript and gave immensely helpful feedback. John Meyer gave critical input at the beginning of the project and at the end—with much appreciated support and empathy in between. Jim Tollefson and Bill Safran also helped me "gel" the project by reading and reviewing my initial proposal. The quick appraisal of my manuscript and continuing positive support that Serena Leigh Krombach at Lexington Books gave was very greatly appreciated.

There are two people above and beyond all others that I would like to acknowledge: my husband, Robert White, and our daughter, Yasmine. Bob is a partner and a colleague—he has read everything I have written and always claims, no matter what he is subjected to reading, that it is my best writing so far. At the beginning of this undertaking, Yasmine quickly learned to ask if I was in the middle of a thought when she wanted to initiate conversation with me while I was at my desk. At the end of the project, she was giving me critical feedback on what I was writing. Although both Bob and Yasmine had to put up with my extended work hours and writer's anxieties, they accompanied me on every field research trip, and we always had a great time!

Introduction

What is Global English?

English is a global language. Its reach into nearly every corner of the earth has been widely commented upon. Particularly noteworthy has been the rapid increase in the number of people worldwide learning English as a foreign language: There may now be more learners of English in China today than there are native speakers of the language.[1]

Numbers and geographical spread alone do not define global English. Global English carries cultural and political implications associated with globalization. Globalization connotes for many a loss of diversity and creeping homogenization. Similarly, one of the main concerns regarding global English is cultural loss: UNESCO now estimates that roughly three thousand languages, or approximately half of the world's total, are likely to become extinct in the not-so-distant future. There is equal concern about cultural saturation as global English permeates youth culture, entertainment, and other popular cultural venues throughout the globe.

The sheer ubiquity of global English also entails its linguistic and cultural adaptation and transformation. I am reminded of my participation at an academic conference on the topic of language and national development in India in the late 1980s—or rather my non-participation while everyone else was enjoying the humor and common sense of a venerable Gandhian who was speaking in English. As a native North American English speaker, I couldn't understand more than a word or two at a time! Global English includes, then, a whole host of linguistic varieties.

The political dimension of global English is as significant as its linguistic and cultural definition, although often subtler and less extensively commented upon. Consider the following smattering of anecdotes:

- A *New York Times* article in August of 2002 carries the headline "China Issues New Warning To Taiwan, Just in English." Why is mainland China using

English to communicate with its "aberrant" province? Because the language of global politics is English: The warning is clearly meant for the international community not to interfere in Chinese internal affairs and is not meant for Taiwan.[2]

- An article from the 13 May 2000 issue of the *Economist* notes that the Aceh rebels on the island of Sumatra and the Indonesian government compromised on English as the language of a cease-fire agreement, given that neither Aceh-nese or Bahasa Indonesia was acceptable to both parties.[3]
- The Islamic resistance in Algeria favors replacing French with English as the country's preferred international language to distinguish itself from the Francophile tendencies of the current regime; Laurent Kabila in the Congo (Zaire), during the ouster of the corrupt dictator, Mobutu Sese Seko, promised the same.[4]
- A sign in front of the Wall Street Institute-School of English in Quito, Ecuador uses a political simile to advertise its product. It reads "Vota por una futura próspera," with a big check mark next to "Inglés."[5]
- The rags-to-politician story of the Black female governor of Rio de Janiero in Brazil highlights her comment that she is now addressed in English in the five-star hotels around town.[6]
- Protesters around the globe invariably carry placards in English, as the cameras of the international media roll.

These anecdotes reveal the degree to which local political battles often embroil global English. English is a global card played in local contestations for power.

We can define global English as part of globalization. It is part of the cause, the process, and the product of globalization. This book tries to make sense of this linguistic globalization by inquiring into the local politics of global English in specific cases: in the United States, France, India, South Africa, and Nepal. Why have we seen the emergence of a local movement to protect English in the United States, the presumable haven of global English? Is France exhibiting reactionary paranoia or progressive solidarity when defending French against English, while language loss continues unabated within France? Is the "Banish English" campaign in India a political agenda of the left or the right? Is English a language of liberation or hegemony in South Africa? Can it be a vehicle of democratization for Nepal? These are the questions looming over local political battles concerning global English.

These real-world political conflicts about language matter to parents making choices about their children's education, to voters casting their ballots, to people struggling to make a living while maintaining a meaningful and dignified life, and to political officials making policy in democratic polities. Their analysis can contribute to our understanding of politics, culture, and globalization. In the following pages, we will analyze how politicians, activists, scholars, policymakers, and others engage in local political battles over global English.

Notes

1. June Thomas, "Chinese Whispers," *Slate* [slate.msn.com/?id=2073150], posted 24 Oct. 2002.

2. Craig S. Smith with Keith Bradsher, "China Issues New Warning To Taiwan, Just in English," *New York Times*, 8 Aug. 2002, A5.

3. "Pausing for Peace in Aceh," *Economist*, 13 May 2000, 42.

4. For the Algerian case, see Mohamed Souaiaia, "Language, Education and Politics in the Maghreb," *Language, Culture and Curriculum* 3, no. 2 (1990): 115. For the Congolese case, see Madelaine Drohan and Alan Freeman, "English Rules," in *Globalization and the Challenges of a New Century*, ed. Patrick O'Meara, Howard D. Mehlinger, and Matthew Krain (Bloomington: Indiana University Press, 2000), 429.

5. Seen by author on main road from airport into town in December of 2002.

6. Larry Rohter, "From Maid to Rio Governor, and Still Fighting" [The Saturday Profile], *New York Times,* 17 Aug. 2002, A4.

Chapter 1

Globalization and the Politics of Language

English [is] *the* language of globalization . . .

—Joshua A. Fishman[1]

English has power . . .

—Braj B. Kachru[2]

In recent years, the political dimension of the global spread of English has become a pronounced topic of discussion among language scholars.[3] In tandem, political scientists have started taking into account cultural factors affecting global politics.[4] Nevertheless, the language factor remains underdeveloped in the study of global politics, and language is at best tangentially referenced in globalization studies.[5] Yet the linguistic dimension of globalization is the ideal focus for an attempt to understand the relation between politics and culture at the turn of the millennium. For language, as is widely acknowledged, is both a cultural marker and a means of communication. Embedded in language use is information about status and identity, as well as cold economic calculations based on efficiency and opportunity. The politics of global English are the politics of globalization, both economic and cultural.

How do we go about studying the politics of global English? In celebrating the global spread of English, David Crystal, one of the leading experts on global English and author of the *Cambridge Encyclopedia of the English Language*, inductively concludes that English was fortuitously "in the right place at the right time."[6] While we do not necessarily need to join in Crystal's celebration, we can agree that focusing on specifics of place and time can be productive in the study of the politics of global English. Scholars of globalization have also noted the importance of specific locales and instances in the study of the global.[7] The popular slogan "Think Globally, Act Locally" captures this importance. To study linguistic globalization, then, we want to focus on the local politics of global English.

1

In which locales should we study the politics of global English? In subsequent chapters, we will examine the local politics of global English in the United States, France, India, South Africa, and Nepal. The choice of these case studies is based on superimposing concepts and categories deemed important in globalization studies onto a typology of global English widely accepted among language scholars. In brief, these cases vary in degree of global integration and global English usage. For example, France and Nepal differ significantly in terms of global integration, but the two countries are similar in that the use of English, at least until very recently, is not widespread. In comparison, while France and the United States are both highly integrated in the globalization process, they obviously differ drastically in terms of English usage. However, the story of English and globalization involves much more than measurements of integration and language usage. Hegemony and resistance, elites and subalterns, liberalization and democratization—these are political concepts that have been applied to the study of globalization. We will use these concepts in our study of the local politics of global English and they will inform our choice of cases. Hegemony will feature in the conceptual framework for our study of the United States in the next chapter. Resistance will be the theme of chapter 3 on France. We will examine the Indian case through the conceptual lens of elites and subalterns. In our case studies of South Africa and Nepal, we will examine, through language politics, how democratization can be perceived as both at odds with and complementing liberalization.

But, ultimately, the local politics of global English turn on local configurations of power. In each of our case studies, we will analyze the local actors in support of and opposed to global English, their understandings of the nature of linguistic globalization, and the power relations between them. In so doing, we will discover that hegemony and resistance, elites and subalterns, and liberalization and democratization figure in each and every case, at least to some degree.

In the rest of this chapter, the concepts, categories, and typologies drawn from the study of English and globalization studies, and used in choosing and analyzing the case studies in subsequent chapters, will be elaborated. In the process of elaboration, we will partake in current debates in both language studies and globalization studies.

A Global English Typology

The linguist Braj Kachru's well-known typology of concentric circles is a useful starting point for differentiating the cases covered in this book according to degree of global English usage.[8] The members of the "inner circle" in Kachru's typology consist of basically Anglo-Saxon countries where English is the majority population's native language—the United States, Britain, Australia, New Zealand, and (most of) Canada. The next concentric circle, the "outer circle," is of particular importance to Kachru. In the countries included in this circle, English has been indigenized. According to Kachru and others, such as Tom McArthur, English is not monolithic or "monomodal."[9] Rather, as English is appropriated and transformed in non-native usage, it fragments and multiplies. As pluralists, Kachru, McArthur, and other linguists embrace this linguistic diversification. It is more accurate today to talk about English in the plural—"World Englishes" in Kachru's nomenclature or, as McArthur refers to the linguistic phenomenon, "the English languages." Outer-circle countries with their own variety of English include India, Nigeria, Ghana, and Singapore. Finally, the "expanding circle" in Kachru's schema is composed of countries where global English is making inroads but is clearly still a foreign language. Kachru names China, Saudi Arabia, Russia, and Nepal as countries in this category.

As mentioned at the outset of this chapter, language scholars have increasingly pointed to political—as well as historical—factors in typing global English. Crystal, for example, points to global English being associated with the leading industrial power in the nineteenth century (Great Britain) and the leading economic and technological power in the twentieth (the United States).[10] Fishman, Cooper, and Rosenbaum identify contemporary measurements such as levels of education, economic development, and urbanization, in addition to historical factors such as colonial status, to grid countries according to global English usage.[11] Language scholars who are critical of the spread of global English emphasize in particular the role of colonialism and imperialism, including neocolonialism and neo-imperialism variants.

Taking into account these additional factors, we can modify Kachru's typology as follows: (1) An English-speaking core corresponding to Kachru's inner circle that consists of global powers where historically the dominant culture has been Anglo-Saxon but which are increasingly becoming multicultural. The United States and Great Britain are the prime examples of this category. (2) A group of countries that are historically linked, in dependent relations, to the English-speaking core, but which have attempted to sunder that dependency. In these countries, English is usually an official language and may be a lingua franca used for purposes of communication between the multilingual components of the nation but, unlike the core countries, has no pretensions of being the cultural bonding glue of the nation.[12] (3) Countries in which the use of English has historically been marginal. In these countries, English is increasingly learned by more and more people, but it remains a foreign language without any recognized official status. The marginality of English in these countries may be due to a host of factors, ranging from level of development, education, and urbanization in Nepal, to historical and contemporary global rivalry with the English-speaking core, as would be the case for France or, let's say, China.

Globalization Concepts

As mentioned previously, Kachru is most interested in his outer-circle category of Englishes. These cases of rapidly changing and mutating English fascinate linguists and provide rich data for linguistic analysis. From this perspective, while other non-linguistic processes may help explain the original spread of English, the linguistic process of creating and changing variants of English remains relatively autonomous.[13] Implicit in many linguists' analyses is a diffusion model of the spread of English, whereby once a language reaches a take-off or tipping point, its spread generates its own momentum.[14] This perspective is too restrictive for our purposes. As Johannes Fabian notes: "Notions such as spread, expansion, and other synonyms of diffusion often encourage a 'natural,' i.e. an ahistorical and apolitical, approach to language change."[15] According to this diffusion model of change, languages themselves are imputed to have the capacity to act.[16] Hence agency is separated from actors. Even radical or critical linguists unintentionally negate human agency from their analyses; in their case, the problem stems from their over-emphasis of structural variables, such as capitalism and imperialism.[17]

Globalization scholars who focus on the cultural dimension of globalization have attempted to reinsert agency into their analysis. Their focus on culture allegedly facilitates this reinsertion. According to cultural globalization scholars, the problem with structural theories of the past, such as dependency theory, is that, while critical, they treated global economic processes as inevitable, leaving Third World peoples as hapless victims. This was not only disempowering, precluding any potential for radical change, but also seemed theoretically problematic. As Alastair Pennycook, one of a few linguists who has ventured over to cultural studies, has noted, "adherence to a version of structural imperialism leaves us at a problematic impasse . . . [The] theory has tended to reduce human relations to a reflection of the political economy, assuming that culture, language or knowledge can be handled like any other commodity."[18]

Despite these important theoretical advances of the cultural studies approach to globalization, there is concern that by de-emphasizing structure in order to emphasize agency, the baby has been thrown out with the bath water. Such eminent scholars as Edward Said and Partha Chatterjee have worried that the pendulum has swung too far the other way, that the cultural emphasis in globalization studies has become apologetic for capitalism.[19] So how are we to maintain the necessary balance, a perspective that includes both structure and agency?[20] Above, I suggested that language usage has important cultural and economic connotations. It is both a medium of culture and of economic transactions between individuals, whether those individuals are in local communities or global institutions. By superimposing concepts drawn from globalization studies on to our global English typology developed above, we can account for both structure and agency in our analysis of the local politics of global English. The concepts also help us in our case selection, for we want to select cases where the interface between structure and agency is particularly apparent. Let us investigate three pairs of concepts, hegemony and resistance, elite and subaltern, and liberalization and democratization, both to aid in our case selection and to furnish a balance between structure and agency in our case analyses. For the most part, each pair represents a juxtaposition. "Hegemony," "elite," and "liberalization" are all terms closely associated with globalization-from-above—a structural imposition of the dominant global paradigm. "Resistance," "subaltern," and "democratization" are concepts seized upon by those attempting globalization-from-below—that is, an imputation of agency to what Michael Hardt and Antonio Negri call "the multitude."[21]

Hegemony

The notion of hegemony has been widely used for some time now to describe the hierarchy of power among states. The United States, since World War II, is considered to be the hegemonic power, because of its military and economic prowess. Many international relations scholars contend that American hegemony declined and American power began dissipating in the mid-1970s, when Western Europe and Japan began catching up economically and the United States was militarily challenged in Vietnam. This period of change in the mid-1970s is frequently dated by globalization scholars as the emergence of the current phase of globalization.[22]

The predominant theory of international relations after World War II was realism. According to realism, each independent country pursues its own national interest in the international sphere, resulting in a non-hierarchical, somewhat anarchic system of international relations. The prevailing metaphor was a billiard ball game, where a ball may indeed strike another, but there was no predictable pattern of relations that governed the ball's action or its ricochets.[23] There were many critics of this realism school of international relations. Neo-Marxists in particular argued that, contrary to the realists' view, the international system was one of domination and hierarchy. World-systems theorists used the terms "core" and "periphery" to depict the unequal structure of international relations. Hegemony was a widely used concept by world systems analysts and their companion dependency theorists to rectify realism's interpretation of international relations. Despite their critique of the mainstream realist paradigm, these alternative theoretical perspectives remained structural.[24] The problem of lack of agency remained—and carried over to analyses by language scholars, such as Robert Phillipson, who adopted a world system analysis.[25] Phillipson's problem, Thomas Clayton has argued, is that he "gives no attention to the responses of subordinate actors to hegemony."[26] Or, as Pennycook put it, people were perceived to be "passive consumers of hegemonic cultural forms" by criticial linguists who adopted the structural models of dependency theory and world-systems analysis.[27]

In attempts to move away from purely structural analyses, the term "hegemony" is again in vogue, not in the international relations sense of power relations among countries, but in the Gramscian sense.[28] Antonio Gramsci, the Italian Marxist writing from prison in the 1930s, argued that hegemony was a means of socio-cultural, and not just structural, control. The masses bought into their subordinate roles by being convinced that the existing social hierarchy was natural, desirable, and inevitable. That convincing took place in the social and cultural realms as much as, if not more than, it did in the economic realm (where, for example, concessions to labor unions are often considered to be a form of cooptation). However, social and cultural control is not totalitarian or complete, because society and culture are products of human interactions and hence subject to constant and daily change. But it is hegemonic. That is, people will interact in such a way to produce little social or cultural change because of both habit and a worldview that the status quo is natural, inevitable, and desirable.

Because hegemony is not totalitarian, there is always a possibility of counter-hegemonic social and cultural construction. In Gramsci's terms, there is always the possibility of a "war of position," where counter-hegemonic rhetoric and debate are produced, and a "war of movement," where real social transformation is achieved through counter-hegemonic activity. In adopting Gramsci's concepts, globalization theorists have attempted to reinsert the possibility of agency into the structural analyses of the past.

As suggested above, it is particularly in the realm of language use that the full implications of hegemony for structure and agency are most apparent. This is because language is used constantly in human interactions and is coded for social hierarchy and cultural identity.[29] Linguists tell us how language is constantly changing as it is used. Noam Chomsky, the best known linguist of our times, popularized the truism that every spontaneous sentence uttered is a unique creation. Despite the spontaneity and creativity of language use, there have to be accepted norms of linguistic interaction—otherwise communication would be impossible.[30] Sociolinguists study how those norms are negotiated every time we interact through language. Most of the time, established norms are reconfirmed in our speech interactions. Deborah Tannen's work on how men and women reestablish gendered power relations in their verbal interactions made sense to many non-linguists precisely because it is in language use that the interplay between structure and agency is so readily visible.[31] Women can, and do, lash out at their male partners in trying to transform relations. A war of position and a war of movement are possible in every argument!

The usefulness of the concept of hegemony is perhaps even greater for language scholars who are interested in global English than for sociolinguists who focus on social interactions between individuals, because in global English hegemony the international relations meaning of the term is conjoined with the Gramscian sense. We want to explore hegemony in both its international relations sense and its Gramscian sense in this book. In chapter 2, we will analyze the politics of language in the United States, the hegemonic global power par excellence. As the United States exerts its hegemony globally, how has that global projection affected and been affected by the local politics of global English in the United States? Why is there an active political English-Only movement in the United States when, both structurally and in the Gramscian sense, English language hegemony is well secured in American society? We will use the concept of hegemony in our analysis of the local politics of global English in the United States, as well as in our other case studies, such as France and South Africa.

Resistance

Our interest in superimposing the concept of hegemony onto our global English typology is to insure that agency as well as structure is accounted for in our analysis. Thinking about hegemony provokes us into considering structure constraining agency as well as agency countering structure. Henry Widdowson, a leading expert on teaching English, invokes Shakespeare's *The Tempest* to illustrate the linguistic dimension of counter-hegemonic agency. He first describes the hegemony Prospero seeks through English: "Caliban is enslaved and Prospero seeks to exercise greater control over him by teaching him English." In Widdowson's rendition, we see Caliban's agency through language usage: "It would appear that although Caliban may be controlled by his master's voice, he is not controlled by his master's language. Instead he masters it himself, makes it his own, and exploits it to express his resistance."[32] Language, more specifically global English, is used as a tool of both hegemony and resistance to hegemony in Widdowson's interpretation of Shakespeare's play.

It is clear that Caliban is not a hapless victim of Prospero, but, as Shakespeare so vividly concocts, a somewhat frightening counterpoint to Prospero. At times, Caliban's actions seem random, haphazard, a desperate lashing out—a chaotic, emotional reaction to Prospero. If Prospero and Caliban's interactions are a metaphor for global politics, then interpreting Caliban's reactions as irrational and destabilizing fits in with what Yahya Sadowski calls global chaos theory.[33] The most popular rendition of global chaos theory, and clearly the most alarmist, is the journalist Robert Kaplan's "The Coming Anarchy."[34] Benjamin Barber's Jihad, in reaction to McWorld, is a more scholarly rendition.[35] According to global chaos theory, globalization provokes an emotional, and often irrational, parochial reaction that threatens world order and stability.

But, as Widdowson evocatively points out, Caliban's language usage is not random and haphazard; there is a structure behind the action. Caliban does not react to Prospero in the "proper" English that Prospero has taught him. Caliban curses at Prospero. Linguists will tell us that the rules and structure of cursing are as complex and as creative, perhaps even more creative, than those governing the standard language.[36] It is through cursing that Caliban resists Prospero.

Caliban does not abandon the imposed linguistic structure of Prospero, but rather creatively transforms it in the act of resistance. As Alastair Pennycook has rightfully noted, counter-discourses to hegemonic global English discourse can be in English.[37] Pennycook argues for "a critical paradigm that acknowledges human agency and looks not only at how people's lives are regulated by language, culture, and discourse but also at how people both resist those forms and produce their own forms."[38]

We can use the concept of resistance to refer to the combination of structure and agency in confronting hegemony. In terms of the topic of this book, we want to investigate resistance to global English. We need to select cases that will allow for such an investigation. In chapter 3, we will look at language politics in France in the context of resistance to global English. France is a particularly appropriate case, not only because it has taken a leading role in resisting global English, but also because the interplay between linguistic hegemony and resistance is so apparent within France. In our case analysis in chapter 3, we will examine how resistance to French linguistic hegemony in the Brittany region of France affects and is affected by French resistance to global English.

Elites and Subalterns

Who are the resisters? Can we make generalizations beyond identifying specific individuals? We can employ the concepts of "elites" and "subalterns" to help direct us toward identifying the Prosperos and Calibans in our case studies of the local politics of global English.

In using the plural of the term "elite," we are signaling that we do not expect to find a monolithic, unified elite in our investigations. Indeed, because we are interested in the interface between politics, language, culture, and global economics, we might expect to find overlapping clusters of elites. We might identify a political elite, an economic elite, a cultural elite, and a linguistic elite. These elites overlap, although not perfectly. The different elites draw on different capital to acquire and retain their elite status. Language can act as capital in this regard. In many countries, mastery of global English generates a significant amount of linguistic capital.[39] The value of this global English capital can increase or decrease, depending on whether English acquisition is restricted and controlled or easily attainable. If restricted, then global English capital is more precious, hence of greater value than if anyone and everyone can easily acquire English. In the core countries identified in our typology developed above, English language capital is fairly widely dispersed, hence normally not the basis of inequality. In countries where English has been historically, and still is, marginal, the linguistic capital derived from global English is also marginal. However, in countries in our second category, global English capital becomes critical for attaining elite status. Of course, other types of capital, e.g., political and economic, are equally important for defining the elites. And often capital of one sort reinforces elite status gained from capital of another sort, or makes capital of another sort easier to attain. In our case studies, we should look for the overlap of elites and the relation between different sorts of elite capital. Case studies that fall into the second category of our typology should be particularly appropriate for this type of analysis. Both India and South Africa belong to this second type.

The use of the term "subaltern" originated with Gramsci. It referred to the lower ranks of commissioned soldiers in European armies. Its utility as an analytical concept has been so fruitfully developed in recent decades by Indian historians that it has been elevated to a school of thought: subaltern studies.[40] Subaltern studies historians have attempted to recover the history of the "other," the subjugated, subordinated, "subaltern" subject who had no voice in the history written by the elite. Elite history is hegemonic: It is assumed to be the "truth." And it normally portrays the subjugated, the subalterns as passive subjects. But subaltern studies historians challenge this hegemonic history. They argue that the subjugated may indeed have been victims, but they were far from passive. They attempt to recover the voice of the subaltern through various non-traditional disciplinary techniques of history, such as extrapolating from official documents, relying on oral histories, and examining innocuous public records. In dispelling the myth of the passive victim, subaltern studies have thus resurrected subaltern agency.

There is some dispute over whom or what social categories should be designated as subaltern. But, once again, language usage provides perhaps a clearer vantage point on this dispute than other subaltern markers. For if the only language you use is not written and not comprehended outside your immediate community, then it is easy to comprehend your status as subaltern. If your story is told in an unwritten language or a language of limited spread, then it will not appear in the history books. In India, for example, subaltern historians point to the role of educated Brahmins and Kayasthas (scribe) castes, who had control over the written word, in "interpreting" India for the British colonial masters, and how distorted and self-promoting that interpretation was. The complex relation between colonial master and subject and, more contemporarily, between elites and subalterns is reflected in the local politics of global English in India. Our analysis of India in chapter 4 will therefore rely heavily on the concepts of elites and subalterns, although we should note that these concepts, like the others we are using, will be referenced in virtually all our case studies.

Liberalization and Democratization

The relation between liberalization and democratization is hotly debated among globalization scholars. While some scholars argue that there is a natural affinity between liberalization and democratization, others suggest that any positive relation must be carefully cultivated. Still others maintain that there are inherent contradictions between the two. We can examine this debate and its implications for the study of the local politics of global English.

Part of the controversy over the relation between liberalization and democratization stems from the broad range of meaning inhering in the concepts. Liberalization most often refers to the process of adopting and implementing a market economy. In the past, a market economy would be adopted and implemented on the national scale. Today, liberalization means adopting and implementing economic policies that promote integration into a global market economy. Hence the term "neoliberalism" to refer to the pro-market bases of economic policies which result in global integration.

The root concept of these terms, "liberalization" and "neoliberalism," also has strong political connotations. "Liberalism," whether of the classical variety of Adam Smith and John Stuart Mill, or of the contemporary European and American varieties, is founded on political values such as individual rights and the rule of law. In talking about liberalization, many scholars are making at least implicit references to both the economic and political connotations of the term.

Those who stress the political connotations often argue that liberalization facilitates or promotes democratization. For example, Francis Fukuyama, in his "end of history" thesis, argued that with the ideological triumph of liberalism at the end of the Cold War, history would no longer unfold as a struggle between competing sets of values.[41] Instead, with the universal adoption of liberal values, rationality rather than ideology would underpin politics and govern individual lives. As more and more countries liberalize, they would implement economic and political procedures by which individuals can attempt to reach their potential. The economic procedures would be market-driven, ensuring that individuals pursuing their economic self-interests would generate wealth for all. The political procedures would be those of liberal democracy: majority rule with minority right protections, regular and fair elections, and rule of law. These would ensure the political participation of individual citizens in rational decision-making for the public good of the whole society.

The underlying premise of Fukuyama's thesis is that, with the fall of the Berlin Wall, the liberal democratic and economic system is now becoming truly global. The influential journalist Thomas Friedman takes this one step further and argues that economic globalization causes democratization. Friedman, in his book *The Lexus and the Olive Tree*, points to three "democratizations" that result from global economic integration: the democratization of technology, of finance, and of information.[42] Because of technological advances, such as the Internet, communication and information are more widespread and hence more democratic. More people are able to take individual control over their economic and political well-being. This is, according to Friedman, the essence of democratization.

The problem with Friedman's conception of democracy, many would argue, is that it is excessively restricted to global elites. Most of the global poor, the subalterns, do not have access to technology, to credit let alone stock-ownership

(Friedman's example of financial democratization), nor to information which is controlled by the elite through hegemonic means. The danger, Friedman's critics would argue, is that economic globalization—the forcing of neoliberal policies on peripheral countries—diminishes democratic participation by the have-nots much more than it enhances Friedman's "three democratizations" for the haves. According to Barry Gills, there exists "the possibility of a serious contradiction or even open antagonism between popular democracy and neoliberal economic globalization." Gills worries that globalization increases "exclusiveness and a narrowing of political power to a small elite." This would be the "antithesis of the globalization of democracy."[43]

Friedman's vision of democracy for the elites accompanying globalization can be termed "globalization-from-above." An alternative democracy would emerge from globalization-from-below.[44] The challenge that many political scientists and political theorists take seriously is creating a new global democratic order that ensures and fosters participation by all. While some, such as Benjamin Barber, envision this order emanating from an emergent global civil society, others emphasize the need to build global governing structures and institutions.[45]

Barber in particular has argued very effectively that "McWorld," a catchy slogan for global economic neoliberalism, is antithetical to democracy. But Barber worries equally about an undemocratic reaction to McWorld, what he coins as "Jihad." Both McWorld and Jihad represent assaults on democracy in Barber's thesis. In terms of the concepts developed above, Barber is in essence warning us that reactions to economic globalization are not by definition instances of democratic resistance.

What do these complex relations between, and mixed interpretations of, liberalization and democratization mean for the study of the local politics of global English? By including case studies of countries that have recently undergone democratization in a global climate of neoliberalism, we can examine the impact of these debates on the local politics of global English. In chapter 5, both South Africa and Nepal are prime case studies in this regard. But we also want to know how the tension between liberalism and democracy plays out in globalization-from-above. How do liberalism and democracy figure in language politics emanating from the global hegemon, the United States? Hence we will also discuss liberal and democratic conceptions of language politics in American thought in our next chapter.

Global Integration

Globalization scholars agree that countries and economies are becoming more globally integrated. The debate is over the normative assessment of this process of global integration. Is globalization fundamentally good or bad? For whom? Are certain dimensions of globalization, let's say the economic, better or worse than others—for example, the political or the cultural? Assessments of global English are part of the same debate. Is global English the linguistic feature of an insidious global hegemony or a medium for transmitting democratic values? Are local linguistic demands fervid parochial reactions to global English or democratic reflections of cultural and linguistic subaltern resistance? Is global English a tool for accessing economic and technological resources or a weapon in the arsenal of a hegemonic elite? Does global English represent globalization-from-above or could it facilitate globalization-from-below?

These are the types of questions that animate the local politics of global English. We have selected a variety of cases in which to examine these local politics. We will use the conceptual tools developed in this chapter in our examinations. Although we will look at hegemony and resistance, elites and subalterns, and liberalization and democratization in all of our cases, each of our case studies will emphasize certain of these concepts in relation to the local politics of global English. Our first case study will be of the global hegemonic power, the United States. How does that global status, as well as political debates and thought about American values such as democracy, liberalism, and individual rights, affect the local politics of global English in the United States? Our argument will be that language politics in the United States provide a context for the projection of a global vision, which has both hegemonic and democratic aspects. France, our next case study, is viewed by many as the birthplace of liberal democracy, as enshrined in French revolutionary values. The French Revolution also produced a linguistically hegemonic definition of the French nation. Hegemony and resistance will be the focus of our analysis of the local politics of global English in France. In the case study of India, our emphasis will be on the elite-subaltern debate, well developed in India. And in both South Africa and Nepal, we will concentrate on the local politics of global English during the democratic transitions that occurred in each of these two countries in the early 1990s. Toward the end of each case study, we will make brief mention of other, comparable cases.

We will try to extract generalizations about linguistic globalization, from above and from below, from our case studies. Our cases vary according to the extent of global English usage and global integration. The United States falls in the category of "core English" country and is well integrated globally. France is a "marginal English" country but also well integrated globally. Since the early 1990s, India has become increasingly globally integrated, although the process is far from complete in comparison to the United States or France. In terms of global English usage, India is a prime example of Kachru's "outer circle," where the historical imposition of colonial English has since been indigenized. We mentioned above that English language usage in this type of country is particularly complex and, for Kachru and other linguists, particularly fascinating. For our purposes, we will label these countries as "official English," which signals that English is an official language but not a native core language of the country. South Africa also falls into this category of "official English" countries. In terms of global integration, South Africa probably is on par if not slightly above India. Finally, Nepal is our case of a "marginal English" country that is poorly integrated globally. It however shares with South Africa recent experience with democratization. To re-iterate in the simplest of terms, according to our global English typology, we have one case study of a "core English" country (the United States), two case studies of "official English" countries (India and South Africa), and two case studies of "marginal English" countries (France and Nepal).[46] Along the axis of global economic integration, we have two highly integrated case studies (the United States and France), two case studies of countries that are fairly well integrated (India and South Africa), and one case study representing a low level of integration (Nepal).

These variations in our case studies are far from constituting control variables or providing control groups for a scientific analysis.[47] Nevertheless, the variations do provide some basis for making tentative generalizations and conclusions about linguistic globalization. These generalizations and conclusions will be presented in the final chapter, along with comparisons across the cases. Also in the final chapter, we will attempt to extrapolate from our case studies and offer some insights about linguistic globalization in contexts and circumstances that transcend the borders of particular countries. What can the local politics of global English teach us about the global politics of local languages?

Notes

1. Joshua A. Fishman, "The New Linguistic Order," *Foreign Policy*, no. 113 (Winter 1998-1999): 36.

2. Braj B. Kachru, "Teaching World Englishes," in *The Other Tongue,* ed. Braj B. Katchru (Urbana: University of Illinois Press, 1992), 355.

3. Fishman's discussion in "The New Linguistic Order" is the most prominent and has received widespread attention from nonlinguists. For a critical perspective on the spread of English, see Robert Phillipson, *Linguistic Imperialism* (Oxford: Oxford University Press, 1992), and Marnie Holborow, *The Politics of English* (London: Sage, 1999). For more mainstream, partial treatments of the political dimension of global English by linguists, see David Crystal, *English as a Global Language* (Cambridge, U.K.: Cambridge University Press, 1997), and David Graddol, *The Future of English?* (London: British Council, 1997). For a particularly insightful treatment, see Alastair Pennycook, *The Cultural Politics of English as an International Language* (New York: Longman, 1992). For collections of articles, many of which touch on the politics of global English, see Thomas Ricento, ed., *Ideology, Politics and Language Policies: Focus on English* (Amsterdam: John Benjamins, 2000). The journal *World Englishes* (Oxford: Blackwell), edited by Braj B. Kachru and Larry E. Smith, frequently publishes contributions discussing political aspects of global English.

4. The subfields of international relations and comparative politics in political science have both undergone a "cultural turn" in the last decade or so. Probably the most well-known, mainstream political scientist who has explicitly addressed culture recently is Samuel Huntington. See Samuel P. Huntington, *The Clash of Civilizations and the Remaking of World Order* (New York: Simon & Schuster, 1996). For a good overview of the concept of culture in political science, see Lisa Wedeen, "Conceptualizing Culture: Possibilities for Political Science," *American Political Science Review* 96, no. 4 (Dec. 2002): 713-28.

5. Brief comments on language are made by Mike Featherstone, *Undoing Culture* (London: Sage, 1995), 8; Cesare Poppi, "Wider Horizons with Larger Details: Subjectivity, Ethnicity and Globalization," in *The Limits of Globalization*, ed. Alan Scott (New York: Routledge, 1997), 291; Anthony Smith, *Nations and Nationalism in a Global Era* (Cambridge, U.K.: Polity Press, 1995), 18, 22; John Tomlinson, *Globalization and Culture* (Chicago: University of Chicago Press, 1999), 79; and Sol Yurick, "The Emerging Metastate Versus the Politics of Ethno-Nationalist Identity," in *The Decolonization of Imagination*, ed. Jan Nederveen Pieterse and Bhikhu Parekh (London: Zed, 1995), 208.

6. Crystal, *English as a Global Language*, 110.

7. For examples of theoretical analyses of "glocalization" (the significance of the particular/the local for the universal/the global, and vice versa), see Roland Robertson, *Globalization* (London: Sage, 1992). Also see Featherstone, *Undoing Culture*.

8. Kachru, "Teaching World Englishes," 356. Kachru's cricles "represent the types of spread, the patterns of acquisition and the functional allocation of English." For our purposes, we will shorthand this to "English usage."

9. Braj B. Kachru, *The Alchemy of English* (New York: Pergamon, 1986), 13. See also Tom McArthur, *The English Languages* (Cambridge, U.K.: Cambridge University Press, 1998).

10. Crystal, *English as a Global Language*, 53.

11. Joshua A. Fishman, Robert Cooper, and Y. Rosenbaum, "English Around the World," in *The Spread of English*, ed. Joshua A. Fishman, Robert Cooper, and Andrew Conrad (Rowley, Mass.: Newbury House, 1977), chapter 2.

12. An official language is one designated by government for use in official government business (which may include, but not be restricted to, use in administrative matters, in schools, in government publications, in courts, etc.). In contrast, "national language" usually refers to the language associated with the dominant culture of the country; it is normally also designated as official, but not necessarily so (English in the United States being the prime example of a national, but not official, language of the country). "Lingua franca" usually refers to a common medium used for communication between different linguistic groups, none of which speak the lingua franca as their native language.

13. As de Swaan has claimed, "it appears that processes of language competition have a limited but distinct autonomy vis-à-vis other social processes in the sphere of politics, culture and the economy." Abram de Swaan, "The Emergent World Language System: An Introduction," *International Political Science Review* 14, no. 3 (1993): 222.

14. Jonathan Pool, "The World Language Problem," *Rationality and Society* 3, no. 1 (Jan. 1991): 78-105; de Swaan, "Emergent World."

15. Johannes Fabian, *Language and Colonial Power* (Berkeley: University of California Press, 1986), 8.

16. Florian Coulmas, for example, avows that "a formulation which makes languages appear as agents with the capacity to act" can be useful for purposes of analysis. Florian Coulmas, *Language and Economy* (Oxford: Blackwell, 1992), 184.

17. Phillipson, *Linguistic Imperialism*; Holborow, *Politics of English*. For an elaboration of "critical linguistics," see James W. Tollefson, "Introduction: Critical Issues in Educational Language Policy," in *Language Policies in Education: Critical Issues*, ed. James W. Tollefson (Mahwah, New Jersey: Lawrence Erlbaum Associates, 2002), 3-15.

18. Pennycook, *Cultural Politics of English*, 56.

19. Edward Said, *Orientalism* (New York: Vintage Books, 1994), 349; Partha Chatterjee, *The Nation and Its Fragments* (Princeton, N.J.: Princeton University Press, 1993), Preface. See also David Harvey, "Capitalism: The Factory of Fragmentation," *New Perspectives Quarterly* 9, no. 2 (Spring 1992): 42-44; Michael Hardt and Antonio Negri, *Empire* (Cambridge, Mass.: Harvard University Press, 2000), 138, 142; Poppi, "Wider Horizons," 286-89.

20. The relation between structure and agency is a long-standing and on-going debate in the social sciences. One of the foremost authorities on this debate is Anthony Giddens, *Central Problems in Social Theory* (London: Macmillan, 1979).

21. Hardt and Negri, *Empire*, 209-18, 357-63.

22. James H. Mittelmann, *The Globalization Syndrome* (Princeton: Princeton University Press, 2000), Chapter 9; Henry Teune, "Global Democracy," *The Annals of the American Academy of Political and Social Science* 581 (May 2002): 23.

23. One of the most prominent renditions of realism can be found in Hans J. Morgenthau, *Politics Among Nations* (New York: Alfred A. Knopf, 1960).

24. Immanuel Wallerstein, perhaps the best known of world-systems theorists, defines hegemony as "a short moment in time when a given core power can manifest simultaneously productive, commercial, and financial superiority over all other core powers." Immanuel Wallerstein, *The Modern World-System II* (New York: Academic Press, 1980), 39. This is a structural definition.

25. Phillipson is explicit about this structuralism: "linguistic imperialism . . . is a theoretical construct forming part of imperialism as a global theory which is concerned with the *structural* relations between rich and poor countries and the *mechanisms* by which the inequality between them is maintained." Phillipson, *Linguistic Imperialism*, 65 (emphasis added).

26. Thomas Clayton, "Decentering Language in World-System Inquiry," *Language Problems & Language Planning* 23, no. 2 (1999): 145.

27. Alastair Pennycook, "English in the World/The World in English," in *Power and Inequality in Language Education*, ed. James W. Tollefson (Cambridge, U.K.: Cambridge University Press, 1995), 48.

28. For a distinction between the two senses of "hegemony," see Roger Simon, *Gramsci's Political Thought* (London: Lawrence and Wishart, 1982), 21.

29. See Basil B. Bernstein, *Class, Codes and Control, Volumes 1-4* (London: Routledge and K. Paul, 1971-1975). Bernstein's ideological inferences from his linguistic analysis have been questioned by other linguists, such as the well-respected William Labov. Of Labov's many works, see *Language in the Inner City* (Philadelphia: University of Pennsylvania Press, 1972) as one of his most celebrated.

30. There are, of course, many famous philosophical implications of this, as epitomized by Wittgenstein's treatment of the private language problem. See Ludwig Wittgenstein, *Philosophical Investigations* (Malden, Mass.: Blackwell, 2001).

31. Deborah Tannen, *You Just Don't Understand* (New York: William Morrow and Company, Inc., 1990).

32. Henry G. Widdowson, "EIL, ESL, EFL: global issues and local interests," *World Englishes* 16, no. 3 (1997): 136-37.

33. Yahya M. Sadowski, *The Myth of Global Chaos* (Washington, D.C.: Brookings Institution Press, 1998), 4-5.

34. Robert Kaplan, "The Coming Anarchy: How Scarcity, Crime, Overpopulation, and Disease Are Rapidly Destroying the Social Fabric of Our Planet," *The Atlantic Monthly,* Feb. 1994, 44-76.

35. Benjamin R. Barber, *Jihad Vs. McWorld* (New York: Ballantine Books, 1996).

36. For a linguistic perspective on non-standard challenges to Standard English hegemony, see Arjuna Parakrama, *De-hegemonizing Language Standards* (New York: St. Martin's Press, 1995).

37. Pennycook, "English in the World," 50. See also A. Suresh Canagarajah, "Negotiation Ideologies through English: Strategies from the Periphery," in *Ideology, Politics and Language Policies*, ed. Thomas Ricento (Amsterdam: John Benjamins, 2000), 121-32.

38. Pennycook, "English in the World," 48.

39. For a discussion of linguistic capital in this regard, see Hans Dua, *Hegemony of English* (Mysore, India: Yashoda Publications, 1994), 238-41. See also François Grin, "English as Economic Value: Facts and Fallacies," *World Englishes* 20, no. 3 (Mar. 2001): 65-78.

40. For an overview of subaltern studies scholarly work, see Ranajit Guha, ed., *Subaltern Studies, Volumes 1-6* (Delhi: Oxford University Press, 1982-1990).

41. Francis Fukuyama, *The End of History and the Last Man* (New York: Penguin, 1992). For an analysis of Fukuyama's thesis, see Manfred B. Steger, *Globalism: The New Market Ideology* (Lanham, Md.: Rowman & Littlefield, 2002), 3-4. Steger offers a thorough analysis of the many-faceted academic debate on globalization.

42. Thomas L. Friedman, *The Lexus and the Olive Tree* (New York: Anchor Books, 2000), chapter 4.

43. Barry Gills, "Democratizing Globalization and Globalizing Democracy," *The Annals of the American Academy of Political and Social Science* 581 (May 2002): 165.

44. For a general argument of this sort, see, for example, John S. Dryzek, *Democracy in Capitalist Times* (New York: Oxford University Press, 1996), especially chapter 7.

45. For the former, see Benjamin R. Barber, "Globalizing Democracy," *The American Prospect* 11, no. 20 (11 Sept. 2000); for the latter, see David Held, *Democracy and the Global Order* (Stanford: Stanford University Press, 1995), 270-83.

46. The modification and development of my typology of global English benefited from the suggestions of Professor Emeritus Fred Riggs of the University of Hawaii, who offered extensive feedback on an earlier version of this chapter.

47. For a rigorous quantitative analysis, see Grin, "English as Economic Value." Grin, in ascertaining the economic value of global English, uses essentially the same broad dimensions that I do. His analysis is based on a case study of Switzerland, where English is marginal (that is, it is not an official or core language) and global economic integration (measured in terms of foreign trade per capita) is high. Grin concludes that global English does indeed have a relatively high, albeit possibly short-term, market value.

Chapter 2

Language Politics in the United States: Projecting a Global Vision?

Globalization in the current era is associated, for better or for worse, with Americanization. This is particularly true of its cultural dimension. For it is the United States, as the world's "hyper-power," that has the economic, military, and political power to project its culture and values globally.[1] Yet, as many commentators have noted, Americans appear parochial and unworldly, hardly the cosmopolitan sophisticates needed to proffer a truly global vision.

The ambiguity of the United States representing globality is perhaps no more apparent than in the projection of its language globally. On the one hand, Americans are particularly notorious for their linguistic insularity, rarely exhibiting the foreign language proficiency so common elsewhere in the world. Yet, as we all know, the American language, English, is a global import, inherited from an earlier global power, England. Hence American ownership of global English is more tenuous than its ownership of other global cultural icons, such as McDonald's or Disney. Global English is also a global export of both the United States and Great Britain, as critics such as Robert Phillipson point out in their depiction of a seamless imperialist continuum between the two hegemonic powers.[2] Despite the success of this shared export, most of the scholarly, as well as popular, debate on language politics in the United States has not dealt with its global or imperial dimension, but remains limited to its domestic context. Only recently have American scholars come to recognize that, in analyzing language politics in the United States, "[p]erhaps the most salient background condition of all is the global dominance of the English language."[3]

Political scientists in particular have been slow to focus on American language politics, even in the domestic context, despite the fact that local language politics in the United States is in many ways a case study of the workings of the American political system. Bilingual education, one of the more enduring and controversial language issues, can be tracked through the countless checks and balances characteristic of American government. The Bilingual Education Act was passed by the U.S. Congress in 1968, as part of President Lyndon Johnson's vision of the "Great Society." The courts then legally fine-tuned it (e.g., *Lau v. Nichols* in 1974) and the federal bureaucracy administered it (e.g., through the Office of Civil Rights).[4] In the 1980s, during the Reagan administration, nearly the same political institutions were employed to reverse the direction of support for bilingual education.[5] A similar trajectory characterized the adoption, implementation, and attempted reversal of bilingual balloting in the 1970s and 1980s. Also gaining considerable momentum in the 1980s was the movement to officialize English, often referred to (primarily by its detractors) as the "English-Only" movement. The tactics of this movement are a prime case not only for the study of the interest group politics, but also for federalism: The movement's successes have primarily been in making English the official language in constitutions of the states of the federal union.[6] All the ingredients of the American political process are clearly revealed in language politics and policy in recent decades.

One reason for the scholarly neglect despite the richness of the case is that language issues have not been particularly politically salient in the United States.[7] The de facto dominance of English marked by a strong assimilationist push to which immigrants seemingly willingly submit, along with the dominant society's parochial and insular cultural and linguistic mentality, has meant that only rarely has language become a topic of national debate. More recently, however, language politics have grabbed the headlines—in the 1996 presidential election, for example, when Republican candidates Bob Dole and Pat Buchanan both vocally supported the English-Only cause (while Democrat Bill Clinton expressed his opposition). In California, the supposed bellwether state for the rest of the country, there has been open controversy over issues of official English, bilingual education, and bilingual electoral ballots in the last decade or so. Edward Cohen argues that the reason for this increased saliency is globalization: "Globalization has pushed language onto the political agenda as a central symbolic and practical aspect of the struggle over how American society will adapt to its growing engagement with the larger world."[8]

What is the relation between globalization and American language politics? How has the domestic context of language politics in the United States informed the American global project? That is, what are the local politics of global English in the case of the global hyperpower or hegemon, the United States? The local politics of global English in the United States reveal both the consistencies and contradictions between American hegemony and the American self-understanding. Debates over democracy and diversity, individual rights, and the public versus private distinction that have animated local American politics have also informed and defined the American projection of global English. In examining these debates, we will find that that projection has strong hegemonic tendencies, mediated however by an American democratic tradition that at least rhetorically extols "politics from below."

Hegemony, Democracy, and Diversity

The United States understands itself to be a democracy. The American democratic tradition is a long-standing one. The tension between a hegemonic projection of power and values from above and democratic politics from below is also long-standing and is particularly apparent in debates on language issues. Indeed, we can go back to the founding document of American democracy, the Constitution, as one of the earliest instances of this debate. Shirley Brice Heath has described how the American founding fathers debated and, in the end, rejected the inclusion of English as the official language in the U.S. Constitution.[9] According to Heath, a primary factor in this decision was the realization of the need to enlist support of non-English-speakers for the controversial new Constitution. In other words, the reality of the new nation was multilingual, and the new Constitution's silence on an official language reflected this reality. It also reflected an abhorrence of hegemony by imposition. If non-English-speakers, such as the Germans in Pennsylvania, were to be won over, it would not be through constitutional fiat.

Much of the controversy over the new Constitution revolved around the question of democracy. How democratic would the new republic set forth in the Constitution be? Opposition to the new Constitution took several forms, most of which are rather confusingly lumped together under the "Anti-Federalist" rubric. The Anti-Federalists, despite their diversity, were clearly concerned about what were perceived to be anti-democratic elements in the Constitution. They argued that a large republic, as envisioned in the new Constitution, would not afford the same degree or kind of self-government that small republics could. In small republics, such as provided for by the Articles of Confederation, the civic virtue needed for self-government could be inculcated through education and participation. Sectarian and class differences would be eliminated, making genuine democracy through self-government achievable—so reasoned at least some of the Anti-Federalists. Yet other kinds of difference would also be eliminated. These small republics would not only be leveled in terms of class, but would also be culturally and religiously homogeneous.[10] The social order would be stifling in its conformity: a type of cultural hegemony but without class distinctions.

The political preference among many Anti-Federalists was for small, participatory—albeit conformist—democracies, as opposed to the large, procedural liberal democracy proposed in the new Constitution. Even supporters of the new Constitution had concerns about the size and extent of the new republic they were creating.[11] The implicit assumption, apparently on both sides of the debate, was that more democracy, at least more participatory democracy, required more homogeneity and conformity. Procedural liberal democracy, based on the assumption that humans act out of self-interest and not civic virtue, was less restrictive in terms of diversity, but also less conducive to direct, participatory democracy.

Nearly the same debate over democracy and diversity can be heard today. The contemporary communitarian argument, whose lineage is often traced back to the

Anti-Federalists' "civic republicanism,"[12] extols democracy while acknowledging the possible pitfalls of exclusion and coercion.[13] Indeed, in its more conservative variant—what Michael Sandel refers to as "communal conservatism," inculcated by such groups as the Moral Majority—exclusion and coercion seem prioritized over any kind of democratic values. There are clear affinities between this communal conservatism and the English-Only movement, leading many critics of the movement to charge its linguistic exclusion, or English Only, as thinly veiled racism.[14] While many contemporary communitarians certainly abhor the communal conservatism variety, their "civic republican school of thought . . . closely approximates the English Only movement's call for common Americanness."[15] Communitarians seem willing to forsake diversity in order to pursue a greater good. For conservative communitarians, including English-Only advocates, that greater good is national unity defined in linguistic and cultural terms, i.e., a "common Americanness." For many contemporary communitarians, the commonality binding the community should be political, i.e., participatory democracy.[16]

Because of their intense concern for democracy, contemporary communitarians are disparaging of the democratic limitations of procedural liberalism. Liberalism based on self-interest rather than civic virtue begets a capitalist society based on class hierarchy—an anathema to participatory democracy. Benjamin Barber, one of the foremost political theorists in America today, suggests, for example, "[r]ecommended reading for democrats of the twenty-first century is not the U.S. Constitution or the French Declaration of Rights of Man and Citizen but the Articles of Confederation."[17] By making this suggestion, Barber is appealing to the Anti-Federalist side of the early American debate over democracy. In his analysis of the contemporary debate on democracy and globalization, Barber has been critical of global commercial and cultural homogeneity, which he has cleverly coined "McWorld." He contends that McWorld undermines democracy. In this regard, then, he deviates from the earlier civic republicans he admires, who, as we saw above, assumed a need for homogeneity and conformity in participatory democracy. But Barber is equally critical of "Jihad," that is, cultural fragmentation and parochial reactions to McWorld—this, too, can undermine participatory democracy. Barber, in his original "Jihad vs. McWorld" article in *The Atlantic Monthly*, includes linguistic diversity as a likely indicator of Jihad. "[L]inguistic multiculturalism," he argues, "could mean the cultural break-up . . . into hundreds of tribal fragments," and the undermining of democracy by linguistic tribalism.[18]

This projection of the communitarian vision onto the globalization debate clearly contains contradictions. On the one hand, it is a critique of American hegemony and globalization-from-above. On the other hand, it does not resolve the tension between democracy and diversity in that it still implies a wariness of diversity, a fear that diversity means tribalism and an ensuing global chaos.[19] Perhaps it cannot resolve this tension because, just as its predecessor, the *Anti-Federalists*, it remains first and foremost a *critique* of the dominant political mode, liberal democracy. Because of its critical stance, communitarianism is appealing to "critical linguists" such as Thomas Donahue, in their efforts to break down the de facto assimilation reinforced by liberal democracy.[20] Liberal democracy in its promotion of de facto assimilation is no more successful at resolving the democracy-diversity tension than communitarianism, albeit for different reasons.

The liberal democratic tradition has dominated domestic politics in the United States since the adoption of the American Constitution in 1787—the liberal democrats or Federalists in effect "won" the debate with the Anti-Federalists. The liberal democratic tradition also dominates the projection of the American vision onto the global scale. The liberal vision of English is not as an identity marker for building community, but as a neutral procedure necessary for democracy. Given their emphasis on the means to the end, procedural liberals see language as a neutral *tool* for attaining democracy. That is, liberal democrats often impute efficacy as well as neutrality to language. For many procedural liberals, "linguistic rationalization" (one language, one community) "facilitate[s] democratic deliberation."[21] A common language enables all to participate in democratic debate and deliberation—none are excluded because of an inability to use the medium or linguistic tool of deliberation.

The association of English with both democracy and rationality is an old and persistent American liberal tradition.[22] It is this ideological association that underlies the dominant American vision of linguistic globalization—a vision of global English as an efficient tool to facilitate the spread of democracy. Perhaps the clearest expression of this vision was crafted by Franklin D. Roosevelt, the American president at the initiation of the United States' hegemonic global power. Roosevelt was an advocate of Basic English, a honed-down artificial version of English that was meant to serve as an international medium of communication, particularly in technology and commerce (indeed, BASIC English stands for "British American Scientific International Commercial English").[23] Not only was English technologically efficient, in Roosevelt's view, but it was also capable of imparting democratic values. This is apparent in Roosevelt's analysis of the role of English in Puerto Rico: "Only through the acquisition of this language [English] will Puerto Rican Americans secure a better understanding of American ideals and principles."[24] Roosevelt was undoubtedly echoing an earlier Brookings Institution report which claimed that "English is the chief source, practically the only source of democratic ideas in Puerto Rico."[25]

Because of its inherent association with democracy, English was to be the privileged language in the American projection of a global vision. The hegemonic tendency in this projection of global English is characteristic of a recurrent problem with the procedural neutrality of liberalism: Despite liberal claims of neutrality, de facto hegemony persists.[26] This problem is most familiar to Americans in the context of an allegedly color-blind legal system coinciding simultaneously with the reality of a societal racial hierarchy: a liberal profession of (racial) equality infused with de facto (racial) hegemony. The problem with neutrality is even more apparent in language matters. Whereas liberal democratic institutions can feign benign neglect or a veil of ignorance in regard to race—that is, in principle race should not be a factor under consideration in any circumstances—these same institutions *must* use language as a medium of communication. This entails de facto recognition and privileging of the language(s) used in the institutions over others. In the United States, this language is English. As the United States projects its liberal democratic procedures outside its borders, the default, privileged language remains English.

Roosevelt's vision of global English persists today, although perhaps not enunciated so starkly: The spread of global English is still perceived by many to be concomitant with the spread of democracy globally. This is certainly the view of liberal democrats who see globalization as essentially unproblematic because of its attendant diffusion of democracy.[27] It is also implicitly the vision of those who see globalization-from-above as a problem. Language issues remain non-salient for advocates of an alternative globalization-from-below. In their view, global English is merely a neutral tool to be used in forging a global democracy. As we shall explore further in chapter 6, globalization-from-below does not necessarily entail a rejection of global English.

As outlined above, the American debate over democracy and its relation to hegemony and diversity has helped shape and has been shaped by the politics of language. The same anxieties and faiths that are manifested in local language politics are reproduced in the American projection of a global vision: (linguistic) fragmentation undermines democracy (the Anti-Federalist/communitarian/Barber thesis) and (linguistic) hegemony is a benign by-product of the globalization of democracy (the procedural liberal democracy thesis).

Language Rights

We saw above how, at the time of America's political founding, the reality of multilingualism and a rejection of de jure hegemony explained the constitutional silence on an official language. An additional factor was respect for individual rights, held by both Federalists and Anti-Federalists.[28] This respect forms the basis for the de facto assimilation espoused by liberalism. Respect for individual rights in language matters means treating "competence in the dominant language as a tool for access to resources, not as a step in molding minorities to the dominant culture."[29] Procedural liberalism as a school of political thought does not prescribe culture or community for the individual—it merely prescribes institutions that facilitate the autonomy of the individual to determine for herself "the good life" and the acquisition of the necessary tools to achieve it. On the global level, this translates into an advocacy for universal human rights to be upheld by democratic institutions.

This American global vision of democracy based on human rights contains contradictions, particularly when applied to linguistic matters. As Will Kymlicka has pointed out, individual choice and autonomy cannot be divorced from their cultural context, as procedural liberalism seems to imply.[30] Human and individual rights are culturally determined, or at least interpreted through cultural lens. For example, as noted previously, the liberal rights argument treats competence in the dominant language as a tool for access to resources—but what constitutes a "tool," "access," and "resources" is at least partially determined by cultural values and, of course, political power. Thus the procedural liberal approach of individual choice in linguistic and cultural matters is often a thin veil for linguistic and cultural hegemony. The minority individual allegedly "chooses" assimilation. And indeed the minority individual may "prefer" assimilation, seeing it as natural and inevitable—a classic case of Gramscian hegemony (see chapter 1).

Critics of cultural and linguistic hegemony also often rely on a rights discourse to make their argument. Theorists such as Kymlicka, as well as practitioners, invoke minority rights in attempts to reverse the loss of cultural and linguistic diversity, whether that loss results from the de facto assimilation inherent in procedural liberalism or from more prescriptive assaults such as those of the English-Only movement. These attempts to reverse linguistic hegemony and language loss are usually pursued through the courts. For example, there have been numerous legal challenges to the English-Only movement's successes in enacting statutory and constitutional official English provisions at the state level.[31] Yet this rights-based approach has not fundamentally altered the American projection of its vision of global English. This is because a rights-based approach to promoting linguistic diversity reinforces the dominant liberal democratic project rather than dismantling it. It is interesting to note in this regard that Kymlicka advocates a *liberal* theory of minority rights. As Martha Minow explains:

> [R]ights claims deployed to ensure respect for ethnic, racial, or cultural differences (couched in individual or group terms) do not jeopardize unity because they channel dissent and opposition into a communal language and secure participation and respect for the dominant structures of law. The willingness of a minority group to use the language of rights thus constitutes in a profound sense a willingness to join the dominant community. Linguistically, conceptually, and politically, rights claims draw the claimants into the community that prescribes the terms for claiming and obtaining rights. Framing their assertions in rights terms, the claimants at least gesture toward obedience to the dominant legal system and the state that maintains it.[32]

In the same sense, the willingness to use the language of human rights on the global level to frame local linguistic demands vis-à-vis global English may merely be affirming the global vision projected by American liberal democracy. That is, resisting global English hegemony by appealing to a rights discourse may actually be reinforcing the ideological premises underlying that hegemony.

Of course, the legitimacy of local linguistic demands will depend on the body of law to which the appeal is made. Although language rights are established in international covenants and in the laws of many countries, they are not in American law. This impairs the ability of Americans to envision language demands as legitimate and helps foster the notion that local linguistic demands are parochial and illiberal reactions to global English rather than democratic reflections of cultural and linguistic global diversity.

In the United States, while race, religion, sex, and national origin have been legally protected categories from discrimination, language has not. Speakers of languages other than English do not constitute a "suspect category" in the eyes of American law, suspect in the sense that they may be the subject of discrimination prohibited by law. There may be several reasons why language discrimination does not raise the suspicion of U.S. courts. One important reason is that language is seen in the American liberal democratic tradition as a neutral tool for communication and not as an identity marker. After all, people can and do learn and adopt new languages. Language in this sense is not ascriptive like race, sex or national origin and seems, at least in the American context, to be more mutable than religion.[33] Only when language is linked in a specific case with national origin, or less frequently with race, do U.S. courts occasionally acknowledge the legitimacy of language demands.[34] Thus, for example, in the well-known *Lau v. Nichols* case in 1974, where the U.S. Supreme Court ruled that Chinese-speaking children in San Francisco were being denied equal educational access and opportunity because of the language barrier, the legal basis of the court's decision was national origin discrimination. Hence, when language demands are entertained by the U.S. courts, the tendency is to perceive them as essentially ethnic, rather than purely linguistic, demands. Projected onto the global level, this translates into demands for linguistic diversity in the face of global English being understood as, basically, ethnic, racial or religious demands. They are then easily conceived as part of a reactionary, tribal Jihad against the inevitability of globalization and global English.

When the U.S. Congress has enacted language legislation, such as the Bilingual Education Act of 1968, or the Voting Rights Act Amendments of 1975 which provide for ballots and voter information in languages other than English, the justification has not been in terms of language rights, but in terms of overcoming educational and economic disadvantages. A "poverty criterion" was incorporated in the Bilingual Education Act, ensuring that the target population was poor children by stipulating that only schools with a high concentration of students from low-income families could apply for grants.[35] Bilingual balloting is only triggered in electoral districts where the illiteracy rate is higher than the national average.[36]

In perceiving minority language usage as an economic obstacle to be overcome, not only is the notion that language is a neutral tool reinforced, but also to view one's mother tongue in any other way than an impediment is discouraged. Hence, the infamous admonition given by a Texas judge in the mid-1990s to a mother who spoke Spanish to her daughter: "You're abusing that child and you're relegating her to the position of housemaid."[37] From the judge's perspective, viewing a minority language as an identity marker worth maintaining and preserving, rather than an economic barrier to be overcome, is a violent (or at least abusive) and irrational reaction. In projecting this vision to the global level, ethnolinguistic demands are deemed reactionary, irrational, and characteristic of Jihad.[38] At times, an added explanation of the triggering of irrational reactions is that self-interested and self-promoting ethnic leaders are manipulating the minority population.[39] Once again, the projection from the local to the global context is fairly easy: Jihad spreads through manipulative leaders.

Language rights have thus been a double-edged sword in the promotion of linguistic diversity and the challenge to linguistic hegemony. While minority rights appear to be one of the only avenues to address linguistic discrimination and English language hegemony, their invocation reinforces the American projection of global English as an unproblematic accompaniment to globalization and any negative reactions to that process as characteristic of Jihad.

Public and Private Spheres of Language Use

It is arguably in the marketplace that the American liberal democratic vision of linguistic globalization is most robust. The liberal democratic laissez-faire attitude toward English, based on the presumption of assimilation to English domestically and the inevitable spread of English globally, is compatible with the neoliberal paradigm of economic globalization. The free market, not government, should determine demand, including linguistic demand. Although there have been occasional calls for increasing Americans' foreign language competence in order to provide a competitive edge for American business overseas, U.S.-based multinational corporations have seldom adopted or perceived a business need for explicit language policies.[40] And the U.S. government has been reluctant to regulate the private sector in regard to global language issues even when national security imperatives are at stake.[41]

Multinational corporations' expectations and behavior are usually based on their initial experience in their home country.[42] Domestically U.S. companies have not experienced regulation in linguistic matters. For example, U.S. courts have tended to absolve businesses of accusations of linguistic (or rather, national origin) discrimination, especially if the company can justify the intolerant practices as a business necessity.[43] This experience is coupled with the very strong domestic labor market pull toward English-language assimilation and reinforces a business outlook that English is the natural and inevitable language of business—a view that is easily projected globally.[44]

The unambiguous reality of English language hegemony both locally and globally leaves scholars puzzling over the emergence of an English-Only movement in the United States. As the renowned sociolinguist, Joshua Fishman has pondered:

> [A]t a time when English is the world's most prestigious, most effective and
> most sought-after vehicle of communication the world over . . . , when political
> careers in non-English mother tongue countries are made and ruined partially
> on the basis of whether candidates for national office there can handle English
> effectively..., when English is still spreading and gaining uses and users in the
> entire non-English mother tongue world, why should a concern for its functional
> protection arouse so much interest in the wealthiest, most prestigious and most
> powerful core-English-mother-tongue country in the world . . .?[45]

Why does the call for officializing English in the United States strike such a
resonance among the American population if there is no real threat to English?
Recently, several authors have pointed to globalization as the culprit.[46] Immigration is identified as an important characteristic of globalization in this regard. But
immigration *per se* is not a causal explanation for the appeal of the English-Only
cause—after all, assimilation to English happens remarkably rapidly for immigrants, including recent ones.[47] Rather, it seems that immigration as a facet of globalization has exposed insular Americans to globalization's cultural and linguistic
dimensions, causing a xenophobic reaction manifested in the English-Only movement. More generous explanations point to the general insecurity fostered by globalization and by the decline in American hegemony in the classical international
relations sense since the mid-1970s, as discussed in chapter 1.[48] Some scholars
speculate that there is a perceived need to assert an American national identity in
cultural and linguistic terms at a time when economic and territorial boundaries
have become more porous.[49] At the very least, globalization clearly has politicized
the language issue in the United States.[50]

The irony of the current local politics of global English in the United States is
that it is the proponents of English who are reacting to globalization by embarking on an illiberal language crusade rather than marginalized subalterns touting
Jihad-inspired fragmentation. The English-Only movement calls for government
regulation in areas where traditionally and ideologically the U.S. government has
been hesitant to intervene. A liberal government should be reluctant to regulate
the private sphere, be it in regard to social and cultural issues or to economic
ones. But the U.S. government does intervene, particularly under pressure from
conservative causes, in a whole range of social and cultural issues where no true
liberal would dare tread.[51] At the same time, conservative causes, including the
English-Only movement, refrain from advocating any retreat from economic
liberalism; that is, they remain committed to unfettered and unregulated activity
in the economic sphere. Hence the willingness of the English-Only movement to
push for mandating English-Only in schools and voting booths, while treading
much lighter in the workplace.[52]

In contrast, many subalterns in the American case, e.g., Spanish-speaking
immigrants, have emphatically embraced the liberal democratic model of language politics with its public-private distinction. They accept and understand,

even advocate, the necessity of English as *the* public language. Indeed, many of them voice support for English as the official public language, with the hope that this officialization will lead to the provision of more formal opportunities to learn English. Hence their disillusion when it becomes apparent that increasing English-learning opportunities is not a priority of the English-Only movement.[53] Rather the movement's priority is regulating linguistic behavior through impos- ing English-Only in everyday life—an illiberal position generally not supported by linguistic minorities.[54] Although linguistic minorities are desperate to attain English-language capital, many of them also want to retain their mother tongue, at home, in the private sphere.

Some scholars argue that the liberal public-private distinction is a false dichot- omy. The perception of its validity merely masks discrimination and oppression. As Bikhu Parekh has put it:

> [T]he attempt to combine a monocultural public realm with a multicultural pri-
> vate realm has a tendency to work against the latter. The public realm in every
> society generally enjoys far greater dignity and prestige than the private realm.
> The culture it institutionalizes enjoys state patronage, power, access to valuable
> resources, and political respectability, and sets the tone of the rest of society.
> Although other cultures are free to flourish in the private realm, they exist in its
> overpowering shadow, and are largely seen as marginal and worth practising only
> in the relative privacy of the family and communal associations. Subjected to the
> relentless assimilationist pressure of the dominant culture, their members, espe-
> cially youth, internalize their inferior status and opt for uncritical assimilation,
> lead confused lives or retreat into their communal ghettos.[55]

Richard Rodriguez, a controversial Latino journalist and author, makes basi- cally the same point. His argument is compelling yet discomforting. On the one hand, Rodriguez agrees with the premises of multiculturalists such as Parekh regarding the myth of the public versus private distinction: he admonishes his fel- low Latinos for unrealistically wanting "to believe that there is an easy way for the child to balance private and public."[56] On the other hand, the prescription he de- rives from these premises is disquieting: in order to not be marginalized, in order to participate fully in the American democratic experience, linguistic minorities should assimilate to English, in both private and public life. Indeed, for Rodri- guez, the civic pull (i.e., of participating fully in the public sphere) is stronger than the economic pull to assimilate to English.[57] However, Rodriguez is not proposing an uncritical assimilation. Putting it in terms perhaps only accomplished writers can fully appreciate, the end goal for Rodriguez of assimilation in both his public and private life is "the conviction [that] English [is] my language to use."[58] With that appropriation comes the possibility of participation and deliberation, critique and resistance.[59]

Despite this possibility, Rodriguez's prescription does not differ significantly from that of the English-Only movement, at least on the surface. This is what makes so many uncomfortable with his argument. Rodriguez is advocating assimilation to English in both the public and private spheres. But he is advocating assimilation as an individual choice, not as a hegemonic imposition. For Rodriguez and liberals in general, the autonomy and integrity of the linguistic minority are enhanced when using English to participate in democratic deliberations in an open and free civil society.

How does Rodriguez's position carry over to the global level? Can global English be a counter-hegemonic medium facilitating democratic deliberation in an emerging transnational civil society or will it remain the linguistic feature of a global marketplace, where youth worldwide uncritically adopt the insidious commercial values that it embodies? This is indeed the paradox of a liberal democratic vision: liberal principles that seem to foster individual choice, autonomy, and integrity in politics also seem to foster economic inequality and class distinctions. This is, and has been, the dilemma of the language politics in the United States.

Conclusion

What can we learn from the local politics of global English in the United States? We learn that the underlying issues and debates that have characterized language politics in the United States have remained fairly constant over time. Debates about the trade-off between democracy and diversity, about liberal democratic understandings of individual rights, and about public and private spheres of political and economic activity and behavior continue to inform American language politics.

We also learn that there are clearly contending views among Americans on language politics. Some Americans perceive the role of English to be the cultural glue of unity and community, while others see the ubiquity of English as a rational accompaniment to American democracy. Some argue that individual language choice and use should be upheld by the rule of law, while others see individual rights as a façade for linguistic hegemony. Some see language issues as intensely political and public, while others see language choice and use as a private, individual matter.

Globalization brings a new dimension to American language politics. Globalization not only impacts local language politics in the form of anti-immigrant and English-Only sentiment, as noted by Edward Cohen and others, but it also brings the projection of American views of language politics onto a global scale. Contending views reproduce themselves in this projection of a global linguistic vision. Hence, as we have seen, global English is viewed as both assimilating and democratic. It facilitates both participation and hegemony. And opposition to global English is deemed both democratic and reactionary.

In this global projection of American language politics, the tendencies toward hegemony have become pronounced, but the possibilities of counter-hegemony, or "wars of position" remain (see chapter 1). For the most part, these "wars of position" are contained within the liberal democratic paradigm. It has been the procedural liberal view of benevolent and inevitable linguistic (i.e., English) assimilation that has predominated in the American global vision and to which linguistic counter-hegemony addresses itself. As we discussed in the first chapter, "wars of position" are rhetorical acts of resistance to hegemony. They are linguistic acts that are not yet performative or transformative.[60] Because they are not yet "wars of movement" that fundamentally challenge hegemony, they find resonance with the global hyper-power, particularly given America's ambivalence of being both hegemonic and democratic, of pushing globalization-from-above while empathizing with those advocating globalization-from-below. Perhaps one of the starkest image of this ambivalence was President Bill Clinton addressing the World Trade Organization meeting in Seattle in 1999 and professing his understanding of the protesters outside who had effectively shut down further progress on economic global integration. America exudes both hegemony and democracy in economic as well as linguistic globalization.

American hegemony can be challenged. Challenges may very well be in global English, as we will explore in subsequent chapters. The United States is not the only hegemonic power to be challenged in its own language.[61] The global powers of the past were also challenged by their colonial subjects in the colonial language, invoking the same values and ideas, such as democracy, liberalism, and self-determination, that animated local politics in the colonial cores. As we now know with hindsight, these "wars of position" in British English and in French turned into "wars of movement" and liberation that transformed the global map. What will the new global map look like in the wake of globalization, including linguistic globalization? We will examine this question more fully in the final chapter.

Notes

1. The term "hyper-power" was coined by France's foreign minister, Hubert Védrine. See his book, *Les cartes de la France à l'heure de la mondialisation* (Paris: Fayard, 2000), 9, which has been translated into English under the title *France in an Age of Globalization* (Washington, D.C.: Brookings Institution Press, 2001).

2. Robert Phillipson, *Linguistic Imperialism* (Oxford: Oxford University Press, 1992).

3. Cristina M. Rodriguez, "Accommodating Linguistic Difference: Toward a Comprehensive Theory of Language Rights in the United States," *36 Harvard Civil Rights-Civil Liberties Law Review* 36, no. 1 (Winter 2001): 133-223. [On-line; available from Lexis-Nexis, Academic Universe; accessed 19 Feb. 2002.]

4. For fuller details, see Colman Brez Stein, Jr., *Sink or Swim: The Politics of Bilingual Education* (New York: Praeger, 1986); and Rosa Castro Feinberg, "Bilingual Education in the United States: A Summary of Lau Compliance Requirements," *Language, Culture and Curriculum* 3, no. 2 (1990): 141-52.

5. See James J. Lyons, "The Past and Future Directions of Federal Bilingual-Education Policy," *Annals of the American Academy of Political and Social Science* 508 (1990): 66-80.

6. For analyses of the English-Only movement by language scholars, see Joshua A. Fishman, "Bias and Anti-Intellectualism: The Frenzied Fiction of 'English Only'," in Joshua A. Fishman, *Language and Ethnicity in Minority Sociolinguistic Perspective* (Clevedon, U.K.: Multilingual Matters, 1989), 638-54; and Geoffrey Nunberg, "Linguists and the Official Language Movement," *Language* 65, no. 3 (1989): 579-587. Although there have been a few political science articles on the English-Only movement, these have tended to focus on the ideological and symbolic appeals of the movement rather than on political tactics and interest group politics. See, e.g., Heidi Tarver, "Language and Politics in the 1980s: The Story of U.S. English," *Politics and Society* 17 (June 1989): 225-45; and Jack Citrin, Beth Reinhold, Evelyn Walters and Donald P. Green, "The 'Official English' Movement and the Symbolic Politics of Language in the United States," *Western Political Quarterly* 43, No. 3 (1990): 535-59. For federalism, see Raymond Tatalovich, *Nativism Reborn? The Official Language Movement and the American States* (Lexington: University of Kentucky Press, 1995).

7. I make this argument, supported by survey data, in Selma K. Sonntag, "Language Contact in the United States: Symbolism and Saliency," in *Recent Studies in Contact Linguistics* (Plurilingua XVIII), ed. Wolfgang Wölck and Annick De Houwer (Bonn: Dümmler, 1997), 356-64.

8. Edward S. Cohen, *The Politics of Globalization in the United States* (Washington, D.C.: Georgetown University Press, 2001), 161.

9. Shirley Brice Heath, "A National Language Academy? Debate in the New Nation," *International Journal of the Sociology of Language* 11 (1976): 9-43.

10. See Herbert J. Storing, *What the Anti-Federalists Were For* (Chicago: University of Chicago Press, 1981), 15-23; Gordon S. Wood, *The Creation of the American Republic, 1776-1787* (New York: W.W. Norton & Co., 1969), 427.

11. Storing, *What the Anti-Federalists*, 83.

12. William M. Sullivan, *Reconstructing Public Philosophy* (Berkeley: University of California Press, 1982), 18.

13. Michael J. Sandel, *Democracy's Discontent* (Cambridge, Mass.: Belknap Press of Harvard University Press, 1996), 319.

14. See, e.g., James Crawford, "What's Behind Official English?," in *Language Loyalties*, ed. James Crawford (Chicago: University of Chicago Press, 1992), 171-77; Thomas S. Donahue, "'U.S. English': Its Life and Works," *International Journal of the Sociology of Language* 56 (1985): 99-112; and Roseann Dueñas González, "Introduction," in *Language Ideologies: Critical Perspectives on the Official English Movement*, Volume 1, ed. Roseann Dueñas González with Ildikó Melis (Mahwah, N.J.: Lawrence Erlbaum, 2000), xxvii-xx.

15. C. Rodriguez, "Accommodating Linguistic Difference."

16. Geoffrey Nunberg makes that argument that the English-Only movement is a manifestation of the shift from a political to a cultural definition of nationhood in the United States. See Geoffrey Nunberg, "Afterword: The Official Language Movement: Reimagining America," in *Language Loyalties*, ed. James Crawford (Chicago: University of Chicago Press, 1992), 479-94.

17. Benjamin R. Barber, "Jihad Vs. McWorld," *The Atlantic Monthly*, Mar. 1992, 63.

18. Barber, "Jihad Vs. McWorld," 61.

19. See the discussion in chapter 1 of global chaos theorists.

20. Thomas S. Donahue, "Language Planning and the Perils of Ideological Solipsism," in *Language Policies and Education: Critical Issues*, ed. James W. Tollefson (Mahwah, N.J.: Lawrence Erlbaum, 2002), 137-62.

21. Alan Patten, "Political Theory and Language Policy," paper presented at the American Political Science Association Annual Meetings (Washington, D.C., Aug. 2000), 18. This liberal tradition is Weberian rather than Rousseauian—the appropriate verbiage is "linguistic rationalization" rather than "one language, one community."

22. Dennis E. Baron, *The English-Only Question* (New Haven, Conn.: Yale University Press, 1990), 38.

23. C. K. Ogden, *Basic English: International Second Language* (New York: Harcourt, Brace and World, Inc., 1968); I. A. Richards, *Basic English and Its Uses* (New York: W.W. Norton & Co., 1943).

24. Quoted in Arnold H. Leibowitz, *Educational Policy and Political Acceptance: The Imposition of English as the Language in American Schools* (Washington, D.C.: ERIC, Clearinghouse for Linguistics, Mar. 1971), 96-97.

25. Quoted in Leibowitz, *Educational Policy*, 90. See also Nunberg, "Afterword," 486-87.

26. See Will Kymlicka, *Multicultural Citizenship* (Oxford: Clarendon Press, 1995), 108; Bikhu Parekh, *Rethinking Multiculturalism* (Cambridge, Mass.: Harvard University Press, 2000), 201-202.

27. E.g., Francis Fukuyama and Thomas Friedman; see chapter 1 for a discussion of their perspectives of globalization.

28. Storing, *What the Anti-Federalists*; Heath, "A National Language Academy?"

29. Selma K. Sonntag and Jonathan Pool, "Linguistic Denial and Linguistic Self-Denial: American Ideologies of Language," *Language Problems and Language Planning* 11, no. 1 (Spring 1987): 48.

30. Kymlicka, *Multicultural Citizenship*.

31. Note, "'Official English': Federal Limits on Efforts to Curtail Bilingual Services in the States," *Harvard Law Review* 100, no. 6 (1987): 1345-62.

32. Martha Minow, "Rights and Cultural Difference," in *Identities, Politics, and Rights*, ed. Austin Sarat and Thomas R. Kearns (Ann Arbor: University of Michigan Press, 1995), 355.

33. See C. Rodriguez, "Accommodating Linguistic Difference" for the religion analogy.

34. See Herbert Teitelbaum and Richard Hiller, "The Legal Perspective," *Bilingual Education: Current Perspectives, Vol. 1* (Arlington, Va.: Center for Applied Linguistics, 1977), 1-64; and C. Rodriguez "Accommodating Linguistic Difference."

35. See Susan Gilbert Schneider, *Revolution, Reaction, or Reform: The 1974 Bilingual Education Act* (New York: Las Americas, 1976); Walter G. Secada, "Research, Politics, and Bilingual Education," *Annals of the American Academy of Political and Social Science* 508 (1990): 81-106; Lyons, "Past and Future," 89.

36. U.S. Code, P.L. 94-73, "Voting Rights Act of 1965-Extension," *Congressional and Administrative News* 1 (94th Congress, 1st session, 6 Aug. 1975): 403.

37. Quoted in R. González, "Introduction," xxvii.

38. See note 19.

39. This explanation is described and critiqued in Kathryn A. Woolard, "Sentences in the Language Prison: the Rhetorical Structuring of An American Language Policy Debate," *American Ethnologist* 16, no. 2 (1989): 268-78.

40. See Carol S. Fixman, "The Foreign Language Needs of U.S.-Based Corporations," *The Annals of the American Academy of Political and Social Science* 511 (Sept. 1990): 25-46; Marianne Inman, "Foreign Languages and the U.S. Multinational Corporation," in *President's Commission on Foreign Language and International Studies: Background Papers and Studies* (Washington, D.C.: U.S. Government Printing Office, 1979), 247-310; and Sue E. Berryman, *et al.*, *Foreign Language and International Studies Specialists: The Market-Place and National Policy* (Santa Monica, Calif.: RAND [R-2501-NEH], 1979). One of the most explicit solicitations for increasing American foreign language competence was made by President Carter's Commission on Foreign Language and International Studies in the late 1970s.

41. See Selma K. Sonntag, "The US National Defense Education Act: Failure of Supply-Side Language Legislation," *Language, Culture and Curriculum* 3, no. 2 (1990): 153-71.

42. Raymond Vernon, *Sovereignty at Bay: The Multinational Spread of U.S. Enterprises* (New York: Basic Books, 1971).

43. Douglas A. Kibbee, "Legal and Linguistic Perspectives on Language Legislation," in *Language Legislation and Linguistic Rights*, ed. Douglas A. Kibbee (Philadelphia: John Benjamins, 1996), 1-23.

44. For an empirical analysis of the labor market pull, see Arturo Gonzalez, "Which English Skills Matter to Immigrants? The Acquisition and Value of Four English Skills," in Roseann Dueñas González with Ildikó Melis (eds.), *Language Ideologies: Critical Perspectives on the Official English Movement*, Vol. 1 (Mahwah, N.J.: Lawrence Erlbaum, 2000), 205-26.

45. Fishman, "Bias," 642-44.

46. See, e.g., Cohen, *Politics of Globalization*; R. González, "Introduction."

47. Calvin Veltman, "The Status of the Spanish Language in the United States at the Beginning of the 21st Century," *International Migration Review* 24, no. 1 (1990): 108-23; A. Gonzalez, "Which English Skills."

48. Fishman, among others, proposes this explanation. See Fishman, "Bias."

49. See Nunberg, "Afterword"; Cohen, *Politics of Globalization.*

50. This is the main argument made by Cohen, *Politics of Globalization*, chapter 6.

51. Raymond Tatalovich and Byron W. Daynes, *Social Regulatory Policy* (Boulder, Colo.: Westview Press, 1988), 1-4.

52. Sonntag, "Language Contact," 362. Ronald Schmidt, Sr., *Language Policy and Identity Politics in the United States* (Philadelphia: Temple University Press, 2000), 82-83, provides further evidence of my contention that there is more Anglo support for English-Only in schools and the voting booth than in the workplace. Whereas, according to Schmidt's reporting of surveys and studies, nearly 80 percent of Anglos support officializing English and around 70 percent of Anglos support English-Only schooling and balloting, only barely over half support English-Only in the workplace.

53. Surveys and studies clearly indicate that recent immigrants to the United States want to learn English, fully expect to learn English and actively seek the few opportunities provided them to formally learn English. See Bill Ong Hing, *To Be An American* (New York: New York University Press, 1997): 153; Schmidt, *Language Policy*, 78. James Crawford has pointed out how the English-Only group, US English, in lobbying for English-Only governmental regulations, does not advocate increasing the availability of English language classes for immigrants, claiming that "the job of English instruction should be handled by the private sector." James Crawford, *At War with Diversity* (Clevedon, U.K.: Multilingual Matters, 2000), 34.

54. See Ana Celia Zentella, "Who Supports Official English, and Why?: The Influence of Social Variables and Questionnaire Methodology," in *Perspectives on Official English,* ed. Karen L. Adams and Daniel T. Brink (Berlin: Mouton de Gruyter, 1990), 160-77.

55. Parekh, *Rethinking Multiculturalism*, 204.

56. Richard Rodriguez, "The Romantic Trap of Bilingual Education," in *Language Loyalties,* ed. James Crawford (Chicago: University of Chicago Press, 1992), 354.

57. Terrence Wiley makes a noteworthy argument that the American prescription of linguistic assimilation intentionally affects different language minorities differently. For some, the expectation is that assimilation will lead to structural incorporation (i.e., Richard Rodriguez's civic participation). But for others (e.g., indigenous and racialized minorities), the intent is subordination and subjugated incorporation in the economic sphere. See Terrence G. Wiley, "Continuity and Change in the Function of Language Ideologies in the United States," in *Ideology, Politics and Language Policies: Focus on English,* ed. Thomas Ricento (Philadelphia: John Benjamins, 2000), 67-85.

58. R. Rodriguez, "Romantic Trap," 353. This echoes the Nigerian writer, Chinue Achebe's assessment of English.; see Chinue Achebe, "English and the African Writer," in *The Political Sociology of the English Language*, ed. Ali Mazrui (Paris: Mouton, 1975), 216-23.

59. Indeed, Richard Rodriguez begins his autobiography with the sentence, "I have taken Caliban's advice." Richard Rodriguez, *Hunger of Memory* (Boston: David R. Godine, 1981). See chapter 1 for discussion of the Caliban metaphor for re-appropriating English as a counter-hegemonic language of resistance.

60. See John R. Searle, *Speech Acts: An Essay in the Philosophy of Language* (London, Cambridge University Press, 1969), for a theory of speech acts, including performative ones.

61. See Alastair Pennycook, *The Cultural Politics of English as an International Language* (New York: Longman, 1994), chapter 8, for an insightful discussion of "writing back" in colonial and neo-colonial languages.

Chapter 3

Language Politics in France, or How Do You Say "Junk Food" in Breton?

Mid-morning on 19 April 2000, a bomb exploded at the backdoor of a McDonald's restaurant in Quévert, in the Brittany region of France. A young female employee was killed, her body hurled into nearby bushes by the force of the explosion.[1] No person or organization claimed responsibility. But suspicions and accusations were readily forthcoming.

Was this is a case of anti-Americanism taken to the extreme? The previous summer, a McDonald's in south central France had been a target of farmers' retaliation against the United States. The U.S. had angered the farmers by slapping stiff tariffs on Roquefort cheese, a product of the region, after France and the European Union refused to allow the import of hormone-treated American beef. The farmers, however, had been careful to limit their action to a peaceful and festive "dismantling" of a Golden Arches outlet that was under construction.[2] Their leader, José Bové, had repeatedly stressed that the farmers' cause was not anti-American but rather anti-globalization, with McDonald's being a "symbol of industrial food and agriculture" that was being foisted upon small farmers worldwide by an increasingly globalized world economy.[3] McDonald's—or McDo, as the French call it—was the epitome of junk food, or *malbouffe*, the French term coined by Bové.

Bové readily condemned the bombing of McDonald's in Quévert.[4] Although the McDonald's head office in France seemed to implicitly blame Bové in a message of condolence it placed in major newspapers, most cast their suspicions elsewhere for the tragedy.[5] Suspicions came to rest on militant Breton separatist organizations, in particular the ARB (*Armée Révolutionnaire Bretonne*).

The police claimed that they had evidence that would confirm these suspicions. The same day as the McDo explosion in Quévert, a bomb had been apprehended and diffused before it exploded in front of the main post office in Rennes, the administrative seat of the Brittany region. The explosives used were traced to a cache of dynamite stolen the previous September from an explosives depot in Plévin, Brittany. Already, members of the Basque separatist organization, ETA, as well as members of ARB, had been indicted in this theft. The police claimed they could link remnant traces of powder from the Quévert explosion to this same stolen cache.

Several people were arrested during the police investigation of the Quévert bombing, but indictments of those arrested have been slow in coming. There is speculation that the police and prosecutors are dragging their feet because they lack incontrovertible evidence. The absence of filed dockets (*dossiers*) is particularly sensitive because some of those who had been in provisional detention (*détention provisoire*) for over two years by late 2002 were not ARB members, but belong instead to a legitimate political group, Emgann. The police claim, and the media have repeated, that Emgann is the political wing of the ARB, drawing on analogies of ETA and Herri Batasuna in the Basque region and the IRA and Sinn Fein in Ireland. However, there has been no evidence, or claims by the organizations themselves, that this is indeed the case.[6]

Despite their pronouncements and arrests, the police remained puzzled. As one of the investigators noted, "The choice of targets [in the Quévert case] is bizarre. Normally, it is an attack on a post office, or mayor's office, or tax building—that is, symbols of the [French] state, that is the classic [target] for separatist movements. But hitting a McDonald's makes one think primarily of anti-American [campaigns]."[7] What was the possible connection between a separatist movement within France and bombing the Golden Arches, that ubiquitous symbol of American-led globalization?

Although the ARB denied any role in Quévert, it did claim to have attempted, a couple of days earlier, a McDo bombing in Pornic. Pornic is a small town near Nantes, a city of historical significance for Bretons, which is no longer administratively situated in the Brittany region. This earlier bombing attempt initially went unreported in the news, as the damage was miniscule and apparently the Pornic McDo manager preferred to cover up the resulting hole in the pavement with a garbage can rather than inform the police. At first, the ARB thought the bomb had failed to go off, but then, in a communiqué, blamed the government's secret service of stealing the Pornic bomb before it detonated and planting it at Quévert.[8] It was on the basis of possessing a computer disk copy of the ARB communiqué denying responsibility that the police arrested the Emgann spokesperson, Gaël Roblin.[9]

The Quévert incident illustrates what William Safran calls infranational and supranational challenges in France and, more importantly, the relation between them.[10] The relation between the two challenges is based on a commonality of resistance to hegemony. Both resistance and hegemony in this case take on a linguistic dimension. Although prominent Breton citizens clearly stated that what happened at Quévert had absolutely nothing to do with years of struggle to defend the Breton language,[11] Quévert can be seen as a symbol of the conflation in French language politics of local and global linguistic hegemony and resistance. Breton resistance to French linguistic hegemony and French resistance to global English are fused and confused in the choice of McDonald's as the target in Quévert. The targeting of McDonald's—allegedly by an organization (the ARB) whose political objective is to resist French domination, including French linguistic hegemony—can tell us a lot about how and why France is at the forefront in battling global English. When the French State puts forth the same arguments and logic for its battle against global English that the Breton nationalists use against French linguistic hegemony, there is inevitably a confusion of hegemon and subaltern. This transference between local and global of oppressor and oppressed is characteristic of the local politics of global English in France. As will be illustrated below, local language politics in France are intertwined with French political perspectives on global English.

Resisting French Hegemony

In its post-WWII evolution, *Emsav* (the Breton movement) illustrates the shifting nature of resistance to French linguistic hegemony. Brittany is the western peninsula on the periphery of the French territorial hexagon. Buffeted by conflict and conquest, Brittany officially acceded to the French monarchy through royal matrimony in the 1500s. However, Brittany retained its distinct culture, based on autochthonous Celtic heritage, more or less until the mid-twentieth century. At the end of WWII, there was still a significant number of Breton speakers in Brittany: up to 75 percent of the population in lower Brittany, the traditional Breton-speaking area of the Armorican peninsula, knew Breton.[12]

In the aftermath of WWII, when *les trentes glorieuses* (thirty glorious years) of economic modernization and urbanization took off in France, the Breton language completed its precipitous decline. Breton-speaking parents switched to speaking French to their children. The death of the Breton language *au sein de la famille* (at the family hearth) was climactic: As linguists have noted, intergenerational transmission of a language is vital for its survival.[13] Breton also suffered from the legacy of segments of *Emsav* joining up with Nazism during the war in hopes of gaining autonomy for Brittany.[14] Today, only about 20 percent of the population in lower Brittany knows Breton, with many fewer actually using it on an everyday basis, and those who do are almost exclusively over 60 years old.[15]

"Modernization" clearly is implicated in the near-death of Breton. Parents were anxious for their children to succeed in the new, modernizing economy and saw French as one of the necessary tickets to economic participation.[16] French was embraced for economic reasons. Sentimental attachment to the Breton language now seemed outdated. Resistance to assimilation dissipated.[17] The Breton movement at the time was identified with CELIB (*Comité d'Études et de Liaison des Interêts Bretons*). CELIB actively promoted modernization, albeit in a regional context. It acted as a disseminator of, rather than resister to, the French State's economic modernization.[18]

By the late 1950s, Charles de Gaulle, as President of the new Fifth Republic, epitomized the modern French State. His party (RPR or Rally for the Republic) and regime were closely associated with the economic and political modernization France experienced in the late 1950s and 1960s. For many, de Gaulle also personified renewed pride in French language and culture. They believed de Gaulle would restore the glory and grandeur of France.

By the late 1960s, however, alienation from economic modernization and disillusionment with de Gaulle's political domination had set in, particularly among youth. The youth vividly demonstrated their dissatisfaction in May 1968. Given the extent of resistance displayed in May 1968, many inferred that France seemed poised to repeat its revolutionary history. Instead, de Gaulle resigned and the revolutionary fervor faded. Nevertheless, a host of groups and organizations inspired by May 1968 flourished, in what initially looked like French leadership in the new social movement phenomenon in Europe. However, most of these organizations had virtually faded by the early 1980s in France.[19]

Regional ethnolinguistic movements took a similar trajectory.[20] In the 1970s, many of the regional movements, like their social movement counterparts, were Marxist- or at least socialist-inspired.[21] Thus their target was capitalism as promoted by the French State. By adopting the popular "political economy" analysis and abandoning a more traditional cultural embedding, these movements, in the 1970s, "move[d] away from linguistic grievances."[22] Notably, this was about the same time that the decline in native Breton speakers, triggered by parental linguistic behavior in the late 1940s and 1950s, was becoming pronounced. *Emsav* grievances took an intensely political turn: "By the mid-1970s, the level of ethnic conflict in France had reached a scale unequalled . . . in modern French history . . . [T]he conflict had escalated to the use of clandestine political violence against the French state and its symbols. The best known of these incidents occurred in 1978 with the bombing of the Palace of Versailles by Breton nationalists."[23] The Breton movement was at the forefront of resistance to the French State.

By the early 1980s, social and regional movements and their activities had tapered off. Some scholars point to French "exceptionalism" and/or a weak civil society to explain the decline in movement activity. Others attribute it to the Socialists finally taking the reins of power in 1981. François Mitterrand won the presidency, and the Socialists, along with their Communist allies, formed the majority in the National Assembly. In advocating a more radical social agenda, the new government in essence co-opted the regional movements' demands as well as those of other social movements.[24] The French State, now governed by the Left, shifted its position on social and cultural issues. Most significantly, the Socialists implemented a degree of decentralization by gingerly empowering the twenty-two regions of France and localizing departmental politics.[25] With these changes, the French State became a moving target, no longer the center focus of resistance.

The shift was distinctly visible in linguistic matters. There had been a few cosmetic concessions to linguistic diversity in France prior to the Socialists. For example, the Deixonne law, passed in 1951 but not implemented until 1969, provided for a modicum of voluntary regional language instruction in the school curriculum.[26] However, more substantial concessions were not forthcoming until the governing parties felt electoral pressure from the Socialists. In the late 1970s, President Valéry Giscard d'Estaing of the center-right UDF (*Union pour la Démocrâtie Française*) party agreed to and signed a "Breton Cultural Charter." The Charter would have dramatically increased the fortunes of the *Diwan* (the Breton-language school movement), but was seriously watered down and generally neglected by the time it went into effect.[27] The Left's assumption of power in 1981 ushered in both tangible and rhetorical changes in language policy vis-à-vis the peripheral regions of the French territorial hexagon.

The Socialists had found support in Brittany for their electoral platform and were expected to deliver. But once again, despite the Socialists' new rhetoric of *droit à la différence* ("right to be different," i.e., an explicit acknowledgement of cultural pluralism), significant language policy changes remained somewhat superficial. The Socialist government made some ostensible advances, such as issuing the Giordan report, which recognized regional languages and called for reparations for historical injustices. They implemented the Savary Circular, which strengthened the teaching of regional languages, and established a *Conseil National des Langues et Cultures Régionales* (National Council of Regional Languages and Cultures). However, these did not dent the hegemonic position of French in the periphery of the hexagon. Overall, "the decade from 1981 to 1991 [was] one of lost hopes" in terms of the aspirations and expectations of ethnolinguistic minorities.[28]

In the disillusionment with the Socialists' progress and the return of conservative governments (and the emergence of the far-right as electorally significant), both regional and social movements in France seem to have recently found a new vigor. Although not all may agree with the "exceptionalism" label applied to movements in France, there does appear to be a consensus that the recent spate of activity in French civil society is different from the post-1968 activity. The new "wave" of movements seems to be less concerned with the grandiose "what is to be done" questions of the past and more focused on specific issues.[29] The issues may themselves be global (AIDS, Third World poverty, racism) and linked, but the paradigmatic analysis (mostly Marxist) of the past seems to have been abandoned. José Bové's movement, which is focused on alternatives to industrial agriculture and genetically modified food, is a prime example. As the movements are less politically ideological, the target of resistance remains less clearly defined, shifting from one issue to the next. On some issues, such as industrial agriculture, the policies of the French State and the European Union are the target. On other issues, such as hormone-treated meat or the Tobin tax (the pet issue of Attac, a very prominent French new social movement), the French State appears to side with the activists.[30]

In this new wave of civil society activity, language and culture have reappeared on the regionalists' agendas. In Brittany, activists have shifted their attention "towards concrete cultural initiatives" at the local level that would save the Breton language from extinction.[31] One of the most active and significant initiatives has been the *Diwan* movement. Originally founded in 1977, with the purpose of establishing Breton-medium schools at the primary and secondary levels, it has recently conducted contentious negotiations with the French State to secure public funding. Through the *Diwan* schools, a new Breton identity is emerging. *Néo-Bretonnants* are those who did not learn Breton as their mother-tongue but have consciously tried to learn the language through schools, often as adults, or have consciously made the choice for their children. Learning Breton can become, in and of itself, a form of resistance to French linguistic hegemony. For some, it is an important step in active resistance.[32] For others, the revival of the Breton language may represent a more passive type of resistance, a "re-appropriation" of Breton by different social groups.[33] Some have even questioned whether the *Diwan* movement represents anything more than self-interest, suggesting that parents may be more attracted to the small class size and parental involvement of *Diwan* schools than having their children learn Breton.[34] Whether presenting active or passive resistance, the revival of the Breton language is described, by both promoters and detractors, as a new and different language, a hybrid between French and "real" Breton, between the new and the old, the modern and the authentic.[35]

In addition to being issue-specific, the *Diwan* and other recent manifestations of *Emsav* have other affinities with their social movement counterparts. Recent movements, whether regional or social, attempt to transcend old barriers to solidarity. As one of the *néo-Bretonnants* has put it, the new strategies of language movements in Europe include "the adoption of transnational cultural models."[36] A transnational model undoubtedly underlies the European Council's 1992 Charter for Regional or Minority Languages, which France, under pressure from regional groups including Brittany's, belatedly and somewhat reluctantly signed in 1999.[37]

This new scope of solidarity is not confined to Europe, however. Although young *néo-Bretonnants* today may give their children Breton names, they may just as well give them Berber names, as was the case with the Emgann spokesperson arrested after the Quévert bombing.[38] This name-giving appears to be an explicit demonstration of commitment to subaltern solidarity. A similar transnational cultural solidarity is often expressed at *Emsav* demonstrations. For example, a Berber musical group was featured at a June 2001 rally and demonstration for the reunification of Nantes with the Brittany region. Although CUAB (*Comité pour l'Unité Administrative de la Bretagne*), the demonstration organizer, is an issue-specific group with no clear political ideology, it nonetheless invited groups as varied as the Breton Bikers (motorcyclists), Emgann, and traditional Breton groups, as well as nation-wide groups such as SCALP (an anti-racism group), to participate. However, this inclusive solidarity does not extend to the far right. The one group that was not welcomed at the CUAB demonstration and in the end asked to leave was Adsav, a right-wing Breton group that had spray-painted "*La Bretagne pour les Bretons*" (Brittany for Bretons) on side-boards during the demonstration and had heckled the Berber singers.

The CUAB demonstration was capped with a *fest-noz*, the enormously popular large-group, late-night Breton folk dance. The Breton cultural revival in music and dance is the most effervescent, yet all-inclusive, component of the renewed Breton movement in recent years.[39] As the *fest-noz* phenomenon now spreads to other parts of France, it is not clear however that the attraction is anything other than *loisir*, i.e., the fun of sampling the culturally exotic. It seems that enlarging the scope of solidarity weakens the extent of resistance. Other components of the movement seem equally superficial, at least in terms of resistance. For example, regional media—Breton publishing houses, radio, and television—are increasingly popular. But, as Jean Bothorel cynically notes, when Rupert Murdoch and Silvio Berlusconi are the invited guests, as well as the investors, for the launching of *TV Breizh*, the first satellite "identity TV" station in France, one wonders to what extent, if any, resistance figures in the calculation.[40] Similar questions can be raised about the "Made in Brittany" business association: Is it merely tapping a superficial consumer desire for the "authentic" for profit?[41]

Is resistance to French linguistic hegemony anything more, then, than new age individualism with an ethnic flair?[42] Is the extent of transnational cultural models the late-night partying of *fest-noz*? Where are the politics of recent resistance? The Breton movement is very diverse and nuanced today, perhaps more so than in the past. Indeed, there is disagreement within Brittany on whether there is "a" movement or several movements. The lack of definitiveness may at least partially be due to the heterogeneity of the components of the movement. It is more of a "network" than a movement, characterized by tendencies (in the plural), diversity and polemics, particularly in its linguistic rendition as disputes over who speaks "real" Breton rage. But whether one perceives one or many movements, there is a general agreement that the political expression of the Breton movement has been weak in recent decades.[43]

The movement's diversity is undoubtedly one of the sources of its political weakness. But the movement also has some bases of political commonality. As noted previously, since the 1960s the movement has been mainly leftist in its leanings. The "established" Breton political party is the UDB (*Union Démocratique Bretonne*). It was created in 1963 when a group of younger members walked out of the MOB (*Mouvement pour l'Organisation de la Bretagne*), a fairly conservative remnant of the Breton political movement that had been devastated because of its collaboration during WWII.[44] The walk-out was provoked by MOB's refusal to condemn the French State's activity in Algeria. The "young radicals" who staged the walk-out propagated the controversial slogan "Brittany = Colony," an affront to France traumatized by decolonization. This "founding" of the UDB is repeatedly invoked with pride today. Indeed, the allure of an anti-colonial legacy is so strong that the new "young radicals" of today have a hard time believing that it originated with such an "established" party as the UDB.[45]

There is, then, a common basis of leftist ideology and anti-imperialism in the political movement. Although this allows for a degree of solidarity across generations and classes at a time when the traditional working class no longer encompasses the majority, it provides a rather tenuous basis for common actions and goals.[46] So while there are still struggles by workers against the State that are intensely political as well as regional, such as the 1994 struggle of Breton fishermen evocatively described by Ronan Le Coadic,[47] many instances of resistance are more amorphous and ephemeral in terms of actors and targets.

One explanation of the McDo targeting in Quévert would point to the strong anti-imperialism tradition within the movement; the more radical within the movement, those who "play with bombs," targeted McDo as a symbol of American imperialism.[48] The ARB, the accused perpetrator of the McDo bombing, is an "old wave" organization, a continuation of the 1960s FLB (*Front de Libération de la Bretagne*).[49] It has the ideological grounding characteristic of the militant, and often violent, left-wing movements of the 1960s and 1970s. For an obsolescing old-wave movement, what better way to gasp a last breath and grab headlines than attacking McDos? Bombing the local tax collector's office garners virtually no media attention.

Bombs are not the *modus operandi* of the new movements of the 1990s, which are generally explicitly non-violent. Instead, it is the creativity and festivity of the direct actions of social movements today that often make McDonald's a likely symbolic target. As argued above, these direct actions are often fairly inclusive of different movement components. When the scope of solidarity is enlarged and leadership and decision-making decentralized, as is characteristic of social movements in France today,[50] the possibility for error, fatal in the Quévert case, undoubtedly increases.

There are, then, numerous strands that may have coalesced in, or at least tangentially impacted, the Quévert bombing. The inclusive solidarity of recent resistance, where political ideology is downplayed, may make experimentation with bold tactics more appealing than endless debates on "what is to be done." The decentralization emphasized and prized by recent movements may make inter-movement connections and communications tenuous and faulty. Just as the center of resistance activity is no longer fixed, neither are the targets of resistance. Why is McDonald's a target rather than the many more French-owned hamburger outlets in France?[51] Who is the target—the French State or globalization, or both? How can we decipher the target if the State both represses resistance and colludes with it in targeting American-led globalization? What is the relation between resistance to French linguistic hegemony by Bretons and French resistance to global English?

Resisting Global English

In France, resistance to global English hegemony has been primarily undertaken by the French State and not by civil society. For, in France, "language is an affair of State."[52] This attention by the State to language is historically ingrained and not dependent on the political persuasion of those in office.[53] The focus of attention, dating back to the French Revolution and before, is to preserve and promote the French language at the expense of all others. Fernand Braudel, the renowned French historian, acknowledged this focus when stating, in hyperbole, that "France *is* the French language."[54] Today, global English threatens the French language, and hence France.

Defensive activity by the State on behalf of the French language has coincided with the assertion of France's role as a global power. Under de Gaulle, France "stood up" to the "big bullies" of the international community, kicking NATO out of Paris and creating the "empty chair" crisis within the European Community in the mid-1960s. De Gaulle also decreed the establishment of a "High Committee for the Defense and Expansion of the French Language." Soon after, Jean-Jacques Servan-Schreiber, a leftist journalist and politician, published *Le défi américain*, decrying economic and cultural penetration of American multinational corporations. In the echelons of power, both the left and the right defined American hegemony as the target against which to defend French power and glory. The French parliament gave a linguistic turn to the defense and in 1975 passed the Bas-Lauriol law, which mandated French and prohibited English in various economic sectors.[55] This was the predecessor to the better-known and more controversial 1994 Toubon law, but without the teeth of the latter.

François Mitterrand, in assuming the presidency of France in 1981, symbolically eased up on internal French linguistic hegemony, as we saw above, but continued to vigorously guard the status of French in the international arena. Forced, in essence, to back off of his reflationary policies in 1983 by the counteractivity of the other major economic powers, Mitterrand surely felt the "assault" of economic globalization. The bemoaning of the global English assault, already well established, became increasingly vitriolic.[56] Acrimony was directed against American culture, which was assumed to be embedded in global English. American culture was portrayed as crass consumerism, based on corporate values and creating the insipid "homo coca-colens."[57]

More recently, Jack Lang, the Minister of Culture under Mitterrand, has accused American English of projecting a global "linguistic McDonaldization."[58] He and many of his fellow politicians explicitly ascribe to the theory that globalization, driven by American capitalism, is creating a global monoculture against which France must defend itself.[59] From this perspective, McDonald's is the symbol not only of globalization, but more importantly of American hegemony. So, for example, while Bové repeatedly stressed that his actions against McDonald's in 1999 should not be construed as anti-American, French politicians, in contrast,

> tried to talk up the anti-American element: some by playing the 'typically' Gallic card, others by invoking 'sovereignty' in a way that fuelled nationalism. This was the populist side of things: it's easy enough to rubbish America, to discard a problem as not being of direct concern to us, rather than confront it. From this point of view, it was very easy [for the politicians] to support our actions.[60]

McDonald's as a target has been co-opted by the French State in its ongoing battle against American hegemony and imperialism. And it is "to the State that the majority of the French look for protection against American imperialism."[61] Despite any complicity by the French State in globalization, the State is projected as resisting American hegemony.

In the past decade, the French State's linguistic resistance to American hegemony has taken several concrete forms. Best known perhaps is the 1994 Toubon law. The law attempts to halt the creep of English into various spheres of activity.[62] As Leila Wexler notes, "the principles underlying the law's adoption are clear: (i) to protect the French language by mandating its use in French territory and (ii) to ensure its 'linguistic purity' by outlawing the introduction of foreign (read English) elements into its lexicon."[63] According to the French government, the law was needed primarily, as Wexler puts it, "to protect France's identity and the identity of the French people; to maintain French participation in the sciences and the economy; and to eliminate 'contamination' of French culture by the English language and American ideas."[64] The law followed on the heels of France's successful negotiations for a "cultural exemption" in the 1993 GATT negotiations. Jean-Michel Eloy thus places it in the general political context of French politicians enunciating a "discourse of resistance to neoliberal economics . . . in the name of national interest."[65] The general target of resistance is American-led globalization; the specific target is global English. Resistance is undertaken by the French State, specifically by politicians and elected officials acting in the name of the French nation. And the French language is the French nation in this case.

The Toubon law was, in many ways, an elaboration of a 1992 constitutional amendment designating French as the official language of France.[66] Ostensibly this latter measure had more obvious implications for France's regional languages than did the Toubon law. Nevertheless, parliamentary debates

> on the Toubon Bill were dominated by the regionalists, all of whom were concerned about the dangers insistence on the use of French held for the identity and character of their region. They were worried, among other things, by the strange

defence of French which claimed it was in danger of suppression by greater political and economic forces when it had itself been responsible for ferociously suppressing regional languages on exactly the same grounds.[67]

The hypocrisy in the French vitriol against global English hegemony, given the propagation of French linguistic hegemony *within* France, is not lost on Breton regionalists. As Noël Lainé sarcastically remarks, at least French children today who are enthralled with English "are not subjected to the brutal requirement to abandon French as were numerous generations of young Bretons [to abandon Breton] who, as a result, are living with psychological trauma in regard to their mother tongue."[68] Some Breton language supporters see a silver lining: The hypocrisy of the State is so blatant that it has forced the State to begin rethinking its internal language policy. Other Breton activists, however, do not see contradictions but rather compatibility between resistance causes. Breton resistance to French linguistic hegemony and French resistance to global English are deemed analogous.[69]

The State's defense to charges of hypocrisy couples global cultural pluralism with the Jacobin portrayal of French as *the* universal and humanist language par excellence.[70] French, it is argued, offers the best defense against global linguistic monoculture inherent in the spread of English. Hence, the purpose of the Toubon law, according to Jacques Toubon, the Minister of Culture and Francophonie responsible for the law named after him, was to foster multiculturalism.[71] As Sharon Shelly has put it, "As a strategy against English hegemony, France has now cast itself in the role of champion of diversity, as the defender of minority languages and cultures against monolithic English."[72]

Furthermore, it is argued, French is best placed to challenge global English hegemony, given its historical legacy of being an international language, indeed *the* language of diplomacy. It is currently a working language in numerous international organizations. And it has the institutions and resources, established and provided by the French State, for this momentous challenge.[73] It also has the ideological associations with "liberty, equality, and fraternity" that appeal to those seeking to confront American imperialism.[74] Thus it has the "cultural baggage" of universal humanism, translated today as a democratic human rights agenda; it is, after all, the language of the Declaration of the Rights of Man and Citizen. As stated by the lawyer who actually wrote the Toubon law as counsel to Minister Toubon, "the defenders of the Republic and of human rights are on the [same] side."[75]

The logic of this argumentation places the French State at the center of the "good fight" against global English hegemony. The presumption is that "all of humanity has a need for us [the French] to preserve our identity"—a somewhat arrogant stand, as Eloy notes.[76] There is a degree of irony in this arrogance. During the Senate debates on his bill, Minister Toubon pontificated: "The French language is a language of liberty, of democracy. It is the language of dreams for many persons imprisoned, who, for years have dreamed of democracy, of liberty, of independence."[77] The Breton prisoners sitting in French jails who dream of liberty and independence do indeed do so in French, not because French is inspirational, but because Breton is no longer their mother-tongue.

A Post-Modern Language Politics?

So how do we reconcile Breton resistance to linguistic hegemony perpetrated by the State with the French State's resistance to linguistic globalization? How do we make sense of the local politics of global English in this case? Language politics in France contains a heavy dose of continuity. It remains, in many ways, a confrontation between regional languages and French linguistic hegemony. But in other ways, there is discontinuity. The confrontation has been globalized. French linguistic hegemony has been compromised, not only globally as English makes in-roads into Francophone countries and becomes the sole working language of international organizations, but also internally in France. As France mounts a global defense of the French language, the local dynamics between resistance and hegemony are altered. The French State becomes both defender of linguistic pluralism and propagator of linguistic homogenization. It becomes a shifting and moving target. Eloy, in discussing the Toubon law, notes that "one has the impression that such a debate [on language] is only possible in France."[78] That is, France's historical and ideological legacy of universalism and grandeur is the context in which its current appeal to cultural pluralism in its fight against global English hegemony must be understood. Breton language politics must be similarly contextualized: It is in the archetype of the modern, centralized State, where *la langue* is equated with *l'État*, where vestiges of pre-state, pre-modern identities barely exist, that a "post-modern" resistance, based on the particular but clearly grounded in a globalized world, manifests itself.

The post-modernism of the local politics of global English in France and in Brittany is captured in neologisms. Bové had come up with the French neologism *malbouffe* for the food served under the Golden Arches of McDonald's. I wondered if there was a Breton equivalent. I asked a young, leftist, Breton language teacher the Breton word for "junk food." After a few minutes of reflection, my informant came up with what she considered would be the perfect Breton word: *boued-lastez*. It would, she claimed, evoke the image of McDo in the Breton imagination. Later, I tried the word on some Breton linguists who dismiss the relevancy and significance of the Breton movement and its attempts to revive the Breton language. They immediately claimed, jokingly, that it meant McDo. But then they were equally quick to note that to a *true* Breton speaker, i.e., not a *néo-Bretonnant*, it would mean something like food for pigs. It seems that the word invokes both images of traditional, rural Breton life and of global Golden

Arches, of the local and the global, of the past and the present, of continuity and discontinuity.

This Breton word for junk food is not publicly known; it is indeed a new word invented by my informant. But it appears to be intuitively understood. The juxtaposition of images it invokes is a reflection of French language politics. Language politics today in France are at a conjuncture, appealing to diversity in the face of global English while simultaneously claiming the universality of French. The democratic expression of the French nation, as it contends with its own internal diversity and its global significance, is now confronting and challenging the historical conception of the French State as the representative of the French language and culture. In certain ways, this is the same democratic challenge expressed by José Bové. Bové's desire for preserving local culture yet engaging in "cultural exchange and solidarity"—globalization-from-below—is similar to a post-modern *Emsav*; both are "combat[ing] the standardization of the world."[79] But the French State is also combating global homogenization in its battle against English. Will the real hegemons and subalterns in post-modern France please stand up?

This simultaneity of local and global, hegemon and subaltern, continuity and rupture is represented in Emgann, the organization accused of allying with the ARB in targeting McDonald's in Brittany. Emgann attracts today's young radicals. Established in 1983, it is seen, and sees itself, as a grouping of the young, educated, and unemployed. With anywhere from twenty to two hundred members, it doesn't have the resources, organizational structure, leadership or, for that matter, the desire to function in the more traditional manner of a political party.[80] It contains a variety of tendencies, a diversity of views that, for the most part, can be considered as far left (*extrême gauche*). Uniting these tendencies is a commitment to independence for Brittany.[81] While not fully defined, Breton independence is more concrete and localized, with roots in *Emsav* tradition, than the amorphous autonomy normally sought by post-modern movements.[82] Although independence is the only recognized common platform for the various Emgann tendencies, an anti-globalization discourse has been discernible in recent years in Emgann's publication, *Combat Breton*. Emgann's demonstrations of solidarity with other new social movements in France (such as SCALP, the anti-racist movement) also suggest a broader, non-local orientation. However, Emgann clearly presents something more than a post-modern, anti-globalization theme. Emgann is, after all, a group committed to a particular locale, Brittany, and a particularistic identity, Breton-ness.[83]

The nuances of Emgann's ideology are articulated by Eric Bainvel, a member of Emgann who, although not involved nor accused of involvement in the McDo incidents in Brittany, was nevertheless close to those accused, arrested, and still in prison.[84] Bainvel claims that there is a *conscience bretonne*, a Breton identity, although he is reluctant to acknowledge anything more substantial than an indeterminate common history as its base. There is not, he claims, a linguistic basis to Breton identity—at least not currently. Emgann is, in fact, made up of mostly *néo-Bretonnants*, as well as young radicals who know no Breton at all. There is no claim of primordialism in Bainvel's ascription to Breton-ness as a foundation for his political action. Yet he also rejects the fad of celebrating cultural hybridization (*métissage*).

Bainvel defines Emgann's politics as left in orientation. For him, this means respecting difference and striving for equality. A moment of opportunity was lost, he suggests, at the time of the French Revolution, when the centrist Jacobins won the battle against the federalists. A true left for Bainvel would be a type of decentralized communism, something not practiced or advocated, he claims, by any of the established left parties in France today. The "recovery" of the cultural in Brittany today is a first indication of the potential for decentralized autonomy. But being Breton means something more than the cultural; it means fighting for socioeconomic change. By prioritizing the larger political-economic picture over specific cultural issues, Bainvel's discourse potentially signals a new phase of movement activity emerging in Brittany today—harking back to the political-economy analysis of the past in some ways, but also projecting a globally embedded analysis. In this analysis, the "problem" is both the French State, with its drive for centralization and uniformity, and the capitalist economy. However, Bainvel does not necessarily equate capitalism with the United States or American hegemony. The French State, he says, is as much a progenitor of global capitalism as is the United States. Elf, the giant French oil company, is just as much implicated in globalization as McDonald's. In resisting capitalism, the target could be French or American or transnational.

The target of resistance to cultural and linguistic hegemony is equally ephemeral and shifting. McDonald's does not bother Bainvel ("*ça me gêne pas*"). McDo serves a function, he says. People now live in big cities and are pressed for time. McDo is convenient; in principle, it is nothing more. It is not going to change French or Breton culture.[85] The French and the Bretons will get *derrière la table* in the evening and on weekends—the cult(ure) of food will not disappear. Furthermore, at its restaurants in Brittany, Bainvel notes, McDo flies the Breton flag and provides bilingual menus. Bainvel acknowledges that targeting McDo was popularized by José Bové. Bové did not target McDonald's because it was American or because it represented cultural globalization—it was targeted because it represented capitalist industrial agriculture.[86] The struggle against ubiquitous capitalism, Bainvel argues, and Bové would probably agree, needs to be grounded in the local, and the local cannot exist without decentralization and autonomy, both political and cultural.

Bainvel's analysis indicates an apprehension of post-modern jargon and glib anti-globalization rhetoric. He adheres neither to a reactionary parochialism nor to a transcendent rupture with contemporary politics. In this sense, he differs from the New Age, back-to-nature, teepee-dwelling young Bretons trying to recover their peasant roots in the hills and mountains of Brittany that Maryon McDonald described a little over a decade ago.[87] At least in terms of life-style, Bainvel and his Emgann companions are probably similar to those elected on a Breton list in

Carhaix in March 2001. The list won with a whopping third of the vote (compared to, for example, the UDB's garnering of usually around 7 percent). The Carhaix list was not a party list. It was headed by a young left but independent (in terms of political parties) Breton entrepreneur, who has made his fortune in producing the most popular Breton beer and the most popular rock concert in Europe. Some are now suggesting that this is the new face of *Emsav.*

Conclusion and Comparisons

The French frequently claim a certain "exceptionalism" in their domestic politics as well as in their global role.[88] How exceptional are the local politics of global English in France? France has exhibited the most resistance to global English among "marginal English" or "expanding circle" countries that are well integrated globally (see chapter 1). Nevertheless, recent accounts in newsmagazines such as the *Economist* have noted that France's neighbors, Germany and Switzerland, are also increasingly concerned about the impact of global English.[89] However, neither of these neighbors have the Jacobin predisposition of centralization and assimilation that France acquired as long ago as the French Revolution.[90] Switzerland, of course, has a well-established tradition of linguistic pluralism and decentralization. In the post-WWII period, at least, Germany has been wary about pushing an exclusionary German identity for the nation, in its attempts to atone for its history. In comparison, France's Jacobin tradition has led to the suppression of regional and minority identities while presenting the "glory" of France, in terms of its cultural and political unity, as a strength in global affairs. It is the interplay of local language politics and France's (and the French language's) global role that defines the local politics of global English in France.

Given France's international linguistic presence historically and its continuing efforts today to promote *"la Francophonie"* (a grouping of countries where French has official status), a more suitable comparison may be Spanish. Spain, like France, has a language academy. Like French (and English), Spanish spread globally as a result of colonial activity. But today Spain's oversight of Spanish worldwide is minimal, quite unlike the French State's control and financing of *la Francophonie.* The local appropriation or indigenization of Spanish in, for example, Latin America is probably as great as that of English (see chapter 1). Moreover, Spain's internal linguistic diversity (e.g., Catalan, Basque) is no longer suppressed as it was during Franco's regime. Indeed, there is a robust revival or "normalization" of previously repressed minority languages accompanying Spain's post-Franco democratization and decentralization.[91] As a result, it is unlikely that the local politics of global English in Spain are as entrenched in an ongoing drama of linguistic hegemony and linguistic resistance as they are in France.

France is well known for its *dirigiste* language policy, in which the State takes commanding control and action. Harold Schiffman argues that despite revisionist historians questioning the success of the Jacobin strategy of linguistic assimilation in France, there is nevertheless a strong *belief* in France that linguistic central planning works and is the responsibility of the State.[92] In effect, the State's agency in language matters politicizes the everyday behavior of communication between individuals and within and between communities. The politics of language takes center stage in France. The starring roles of hegemon and resister are constantly shifting, however, particularly when the stage is global.

Notes

1. Donald G. McNeil, "French McDonald's Bombed; Breton Terrorists Suspected," *New York Times*, 26 Apr. 2000, A8.

2. The farmers' side of the story is told in José Bové and François Dufour, *The World is Not for Sale: Farmers Against Junk Food* (London: Verso, 2001).

3. Bové and Dufour, *World is Not*, 5.

4. "Les McDonald's en France: une cible symbolique," *Agence France Presse*, 19 Apr. 2000.

5. Pierre Marcelle, "Provoc' Burger," *Libération* (Section: Rébonds), no. 5890, 24 Apr. 2000, 4. See also Pierre Georges, "Le communiqué," *Le Monde*, 25 Apr. 2000, final page.

6. Much of the information for this chapter comes from interviews conducted with academicians, language planners, elected politicians, journalists, and activists in Brittany in June 2001, as well as numerous newspaper accounts of the events surrounding Quévert.

7. Pierre-Henri Allain, David Dufresne and Patricia Tourancheau, "Un premier colis piège avait été neutralisé dans la matinée dans une poste du centre de Rennes," *Libération* (Section: Événement), no. 5887, 20 Apr. 2000, 2. This and all subsequent translations from French sources are the author's own. The two previous explosions in Brittany attributed to the ARB were indeed tax offices: in Argentré-du-Plessis on 11 March 2000 and in Callac on 10 Dec. 1999.

8. This information is culled from various interviews conducted in Brittany in June 2001 and newspaper accounts. See, for example, David Dufresne, "ARB: le communiqué qui brouille les pistes," *Libération* (Section: Société), no. 5896, 2 May 2000, 18; David Dufresne and Patricia Tourancheau, "L'attentat du McDo en cachait un autre," *Libération* (Section: Société), no. 5897, 3 May 2000, 20. The government agency accused by the ARB is the DST (Direction de la surveillance du territoire), responsible for counterespionage. See Pascal Ceux, "L'ARB nie toute responsabilité dans l'attentat de Quévert," *Le Monde* (Section: Société), 3 May 2000. While in Brittany, I attained a fictional account from the ARB perspective of how the secret police could have infiltrated their organization and relocated the Pornic bomb: see Lena Diraison, "Une bergère et trois commis," in *Crachins, Nouvelles fraiches de bretagne*, ed. Gerard Allé (Paris: Baleine-Le Seuil, 2001), 33-66. Although all the information and most of the specific details I am reporting have

been confirmed by more than one source, I should note that I am not claiming journalistic standards.

9. See Dufresne, "ARB: le communiqué." Dufresne questions the police logic of assuming that possession of a computer disk is somehow more incriminating than receiving and transmitting an illegal organization's communiqué by fax or phone, an activity regularly undertaken by numerous news organizations.

10. See William Safran, "Politics and language in contemporary France: Facing supranational and infranational challenges," *International Journal of the Sociology of Language*, no. 137 (1999), 39-66.

11. These statements were featured in a documentary by Fañch Broudic on the social history and evolution of the Breton language that I previewed at the France 3 television station in Rennes in June 2001 and that aired on television throughout Brittany and France in October 2001. The documentary is now available in DVD: Pierrick Guinard, *Brezhoneg, un siècle de breton*, (Paris: Doriane Films, 2002), videorecording.

12. Fañch Broudic, *Qui parle breton aujourd'hui?* (Brest, France: Brud Nevez, 1999).

13. See, for example, Daniel Nettle and Suzanne Romaine, *Vanishing Voices* (Oxford: Oxford University Press, 2000), 177-78.

14. Jack E. Reece, *The Bretons against France* (Chapel Hill: University of North Carolina Press, 1977), chapter 7.

15. Broudic, *Qui parle breton.*

16. See Broudic, *Qui parle breton*; Ronan Le Coadic, *L'identité bretonne* (Rennes, France: Terre de Brume, 1998); Pierre-Jakez Hélias, *The Horse of Pride: Life in a Breton Village* (New Haven, Conn.: Yale University Press, 1975).

17. The story is well told in Hélias, *Horse of Pride.*

18. See Jill Lovecy, "Protest in Brittany from the Fourth to the Fifth Republics: From a Regionalist to a Regional Social Movement?," in *Social Movements and Protest in France*, ed. Philip G. Cerny (New York: St. Martin's Press, 1982), 172-201.

19. This disappearance was puzzling to many scholars. See Sarah Waters, "New Social Movement Politics in France: the Rise of Civic Forms of Mobilisation," *Western European Politics*, 21, no. 3 (July 1998): 170-86.

20. See Bernard Poche, *Les langues minoritaires en Europe* (Grenoble, France: Presses Universitaires de Grenoble, 2000), 96-97. France, or rather the French State, does not admit to having national minorities. It prefers the term "region" and "regional languages/ groups." Indeed, it insists on this terminology in official documents; hence the new Council of Europe directive on linguistic diversity is titled "European Charter for Regional or Minority Languages."

21. See Suzanne Berger, "Bretons and Jacobins: Reflections on French Regional Ethnicity," in *Ethnic Conflict in the Western World*, ed. Milton J. Esman (Ithaca, N.Y.: Cornell University Press, 1977), 161; Maryon McDonald, *'We are not French!' Language, Culture and Identity in Brittany* (New York: Routledge, 1989), 82; Poche, *Les langues minoritaires*, 95.

22. James E. Jacob and David C. Gordon, "Language Policy in France," in *Language Policy and National Unity*, eds. William R. Beer and James E. Jacob (Totowa, N.J.: Rowman & Allanheld, 1985), 126.

23. Jacob and Gordon, "Language Policy," 122-23.

24. Andrew Appleton, "The New Social Movement Phenomenon: Placing France in Comparative Perspective," in *The Changing French Political System*, ed. Robert Elgie (London: Frank Cass, 2000), 57-75; Jan Willem Duyvendak, *The Power of Politics: New Social Movements in France* (Boulder, Colo.: Westview, 1995), 5-6.

25. *Départements* are the basic administrative unit within France. It was through the departments that Paris controlled the provinces by appointing a *préfet* (prefect) to be in charge. This changed with the Defferre law in 1982. The grouping together of departments into regions dates from the mid-1970s under the UDF government, but the regions remained inconsequential and powerless until the early 1980s (and some would argue this is still the case today).

26. Safran, "Politics and language," 44; Jacob and Gordon, "Language Policy," 120-21; Dennis Ager, *Identity, Insecurity and Image: France and Language* (Clevedon, U.K.: Multilingual Matters, 1999), 31.

27. Vaughan Rogers, "Cultural Pluralism under the One and Incorrigible French Republic: *Diwan* and the Breton Language," *Nationalism & Ethnic Politics*, 2, no. 4 (Winter 1996): 550-81; see also Noël Lainé, *Le droit à la parole* (Rennes: Terre de Brume, 1992).

28. Ager, *Identity, Insecurity*, 33; see also John Loughlin, "A New Deal for France's Regions and Linguistic Minorities," *Western European Politics*, 8, no. 3 (July 1985): 101-13.

29. Waters, "New Social Movement Politics"; Appleton, "New Social Movement Phenomenon."

30. The Tobin tax, originally an idea of James Tobin, a Nobel economist, would be applied to international financial transactions. Attac (Association pour la taxation des transactions financières pour l'aide aux citoyens) argues that the proceeds could then be earmarked for ending international debt, poverty and environmental degradation. Lionel Jospin, the Socialist Prime Minister under the Gaullist President, Jacques Chirac, came out in favor of the Tobin tax in 2001, while jockeying for advantage in the spring 2002 presidential election (which he lost and Chirac won). State support on hormone-treated meat triggered the 1999 trade war with the United States, noted at the outset of this chapter.

31. Rogers, "Cultural Pluralism," 552.

32. This was apparent from the interviews I conducted with young Emgann activists in Nantes in June 2001.

33. This was the goal of a "Yes to the Breton Language" campaign sponsored by the Office of the Breton Language (*Office de la langue bretonne*), which is set up and funded by the regional government. The campaign was described in a pamphlet I collected at the Rennes branch of the Office in June 2001. See also Anna Quéré, *Les Bretons et la langue bretonne* (Brest, France: Brud Nevez, 2000), 96.

34. This was suggested by Jean Le Dû and Yves Le Berre, both linguists at the University in Brest, during an interview in Brest on 29 June 2001.

35. See McDonald, *'We are not French!'*, 279; Mari C. Jones, "Death of a Language, Birth of an Identity: Brittany and the Bretons," *Language Problems and Language Planning*, 22, no. 2 (Summer 1998): 129-42.

36. Lainé, *Le droit à la parole*, 185.

37. Broudic, *Qui parle breton*, 131.

38. Along with Gaël Roblin, Eric Bainvel (see pp. 49-50 of this chapter) has given his children Berber names. The police, in investigating Emgann subsequent to the Quévert bombing, seemed to attach significance to this. (Interviews with Emgann members and supporters, June 2001.) The politics of name-giving in France is a somewhat confusing topic. Up until the early 1990s, the acceptance or rejection of unusual first names for birth registry seemed to depend on the whims of local notaries. See Richard Bernstein, *Fragile Glory* (New York: Alfred A. Knopf, 1990), 99-103. In Brittany, it was not unusual to give Breton first names and for the most part these were officially registered. Hence, the claim by some that Breton names were prohibited up until recently is inaccurate. See, e.g., Charles Hauss, *Comparative Politics* (Belmont, Calif.: Wadsworth/Thomson Learning, 2003), 97.

39. One of the most apolitical academicians I interviewed, who is clearly dismissive of *Emsav* in general because of what he claims is its irrelevancy to the everyday lives of most Bretons, noted that the one thing he could not explain was the revival and popularity of the *fest-noz*. Interview with Jean Le Dû, Brest, 29 June 2001.

40. Jean Bothorel, *Un terroriste breton* (Paris: Calmann-Levy, 2001), 9-10.

41. See Le Coadic, *L'identité bretonne*, 280-90.

42. This seems to be what Maryon McDonald found to be the case in the late 1980s. See McDonald, *'We are not French!'*.

43. Interviews with elected officials, activists, and journalists in Brittany in June 2001.

44. Jean-Jacques Monnier, *Le comportement politique des Bretons* (Rennes, France: Presses Universitaires de Rennes, 1994), 234-35; Reece, *Bretons against France*, 190 ff.

45. This story of the UDB founding was narrated to me by Henri Gourmelen, a UDB elected official and secondary education instructor (in Saint Malo, Brittany, 21 June 2001). The UDB also claims to have originated the "solidarity" with the Berber minority in Algeria that is evident throughout the left of the *Emsav* movement, as discussed earlier. The disbelief in the UDB originating the internal colonialism thesis was expressed to me by Emgann members I interviewed in June 2001 in Brittany.

46. Bové and Dufour also note the cross-generation and cross-class nature of their movement against globalization. See Bové and Dufour, *World is Not*.

47. Le Coadic, *L'identité bretonne*, 13.

48. "Playing with bombs" was an explanation offered by Jean Le Dû and Yves Le Berre, linguists I interviewed in Brest (see notes 34 and 39). They also claimed that a consequence of Quévert was the calling off of an unwritten "truce" between the French State and *Emsav*. The truce was in essence that the French State would allow a certain degree of cultural autonomy (e.g., in the State's financing of *Diwan* schools, in its support for a Cultural Institute of Brittany) as long as movement activities were relatively benign. Now all bets are off, and the consequences could negatively affect *Diwan*, etc. There was no mention of this "truce" in other interviews I conducted.

49. Reece, *Bretons against France*, 201 ff.

50. See Bové and Dufour, *World is Not*.

51. Rick Fantasia, "Fast Food in France," *Theory and Society*, 24 (1995): 206.

52. From the Senate Report of Apr. 1994 on the Toubon law, cited in Leila Sadat Wexler, *Official English, Nationalism and Linguistic Terror: A French Lesson,* Working Paper No. 95-11-1 (St. Louis: Washington University School of Law, 1995), 7. The original in French is "la language est une affaire d'État."

53. See Dennis Ager, "Language and Power," in *Structures of Power in Modern France,* ed. Gino G. Raymond (New York: St. Martin's Press, 2000), 146-80.

54. Quoted in Safran, "Politics and language," 42.

55. Wexler, *Official English, Nationalism,* 20ff.

56. Ager, *Identity, Insecurity and Image,* 98ff.

57. Jeffra Flaitz, *The Ideology of English: French Perceptions of English as a World Language* (Berlin: Mouton de Gruyter, 1988), 109.

58. Jack Lang, "L'amour de Babel," in *Langues: une guerre à mort,* ed. Guy Gauthier (Courbevoie, France: Panoramiques-Corlet, 2000), 128.

59. See Bernard Cassen, "Les langues, ces fils d'or du combat contre la mondialisation libérale," *Le Monde Diplomatique* (Section: Manière de Voir), May-June 2001, 88-91.

60. Bové and Dufour, *World is Not,* 13.

61. Ronan Le Coadic, "Les Bretons au pays des merveilles" (paper presented at the "La Bretagne à l'heure de la mondialisation" colloquium, Institute d'Études Politiques de Rennes, Rennes, Dec. 2000).

62. Claude Truchot, "The spread of English: from France to a more general perspective," *World Englishes,* 16, no. 1 (1997): 65-76.

63. Wexler, *Official English, Nationalism,* 34.

64. Wexler, *Official English, Nationalism,* 35.

65. Jean-Michel Eloy, "Les débats parlementaires français sur la loi linguistique de 1994: actualité politique et permanence d'un modèle de langue à la française," in *Linguistic Identities and Policies in France and the French-Speaking World,* eds. Dawn Marley, Marie-Anne Hintze and Gabrielle Parker (London: Association for French Language Studies in association with the Centre for Information on Language Teaching and Research, 1998), 267.

66. Ager, *Identity, Insecurity,* 207.

67. Ager, "Language and Power," 160.

68. Lainé, *Le droit à la parole,* 88-89.

69. Christian Guyonvarc'h, adjunct to the mayor of Lorient and member of the Union Démocratique Bretonne (UDB), a regional political party, noted the hypocrisy and silver lining in an interview in Lorient on 29 June 2001. It was another UDB member and elected official in Saint Malo, Henri Gourmelen, who thought the French state was completely justified in protecting against global English hegemony through the Toubon law, and that this did not represent a contradiction despite France's internal language policy. In an opinion piece, "Langues régionales," Henri Gourmelen quotes Pierre-Jakez Hélias, the well-known Breton writer, as stating, "as much as the Breton language endures, it constitutes a front for the defense of French, by resisting homogenization by a more powerful language" ("tant que le breton durera, il constitue un post avancé pour la défense du français, en s'opposent à une uniformisation sur la base d'une langue plus puissante"). Henri Gourmelen, "Langues

régionales: fragile avancée," *Ouest France* ("Le courrier des lecteurs" section), 16 May 2001. See also McDonald, *'We are not French!'*, 120.

70. Cassen, "Les langues, ces fils"; see also Eloy, "Les débats parlementaires," 268-72.

71. Wexler, *Official English, Nationalism*, 36.

72. Sharon L. Shelly, "Une certaine idée du français: the dilemma for French language policy in the 21st century," *Language & Communication*, no. 19 (1999): 312.

73. See Robert Chaudenson, *Mondialisation: la langue française a-t-elle encore un avenir?* (Paris: Institut de la Francophonie, Diffusion Didier Eruditon, 2000); Ager, "Language and Power."

74. The French Revolutionary slogan became the chant at a mass gathering in southern France in the summer of 2000, with the emphasis on "fraternity," meaning solidarity. The gathering was both in support of José Bové during his trial and against globalization. See Bové and Dufour, *World is Not*.

75. Yves Marek, "The Philosophy of the French Language Legislation," in *Language Legislation and Linguistic Rights*, ed. Douglas A. Kibbee (Amsterdam: John Benjamins, 1998), 346.

76. Eloy, "Les débats parlementaires," 272.

77. Quoted in Wexler, *Official English, Nationalism*, 37.

78. Eloy, "Les débats parlementaires," 266.

79. Bové and Dufour, *World is Not*, 159, 185.

80. Emgann members I interviewed claim they have 200 card-carrying members. This is the figure mentioned in the mainstream press also. See Par Clarisse Lucas, "Emgann: la jeune garde du mouvement independantiste breton," *Agence France Presse* ("Informations Générales" section), 6 May 2000. The lower estimates come from sceptical academicians in Brittany.

81. Emgann members claimed (in an interview with the author) that the only reason Emgann was targeted by the police after Quévert was because of its stand for independence.

82. See Christine Kelly, *Tangled Up in Red, White, and Blue: New Social Movements in America* (Lanham, Md.: Rowman & Littlefield, 2001) for a brief discussion of autonomy in the post-modern variants of new social movements.

83. This is not an exclusionary identity, however. Emgann members quickly spray-painted inclusive rhetoric over the Adsav (right-wing) slogan "Brittany for Bretons" at the 29 June 2001 rally in Nantes.

84. Interview conducted with Eric Bainvel in Nantes on 27 June 2001.

85. See also Fantasia, "Fast Food," 231.

86. Bové and Dufour, *World is Not*.

87. McDonald, *'We are not French!'*, 256-65.

88. See Dominique Moïsi, "The Trouble with France," *Foreign Affairs* 7, no. 3 (May-June 1998): 94-104.

89. The Japanese government also is apparently joining the anti-global-English club of "marginal English," highly globally integrated countries. See Howard W. French, "Tokyo Journal: To Grandparents, English Word Trend Isn't 'Naisu'," *New York Times*, 23 Oct. 2002, A4.

90. For treatment of the linguistic dimension of France's Jacobinism, see Roland Breton, "Solidité, généralisation et limites du modèle 'jacobin' de politique linguistique face à une nouvelle Europe?" in *The Regional Languages of France: an Inventory on the Eve of the XXIst Century*, eds. Philippe Blanchet, Roland Breton and Harold Schiffman (Louvain-la-Neuve, Belgium: Peeters, 1999), 81-94.

91. See Patricia Petherbridge-Hernández, "The Recatalanisation of Catalonia's Schools," *Language, Culture and Curriculum*, 3, no. 2 (1990): 97-108.

92. Harold Shiffman, "Forward," in *Regional Languages*, 7.

Chapter 4

Subaltern Language Politics in India

In the summer of 1993 in the state of Bihar, India, the chief minister (the elected executive head of the state government) suggested introducing the mandatory study of English into the school curriculum. A few years earlier, next door in Uttar Pradesh, that state's chief minister had launched the implementation of a "Banish English" (*angrezi hatao*) policy in the state administration. Both chief ministers were Yadavs, the cow-herding peasant caste at the lower end of the caste hierarchy. Despite the overt divergence of their policies on the use of English, there is a fundamental convergence underlying them—that of re-appropriating local, vernacular languages as part of an anti-elite project. Both the pro-English policy preferred in Bihar and the anti-English policy in Uttar Pradesh were manifestations of subaltern language politics.

The two chief ministers were part of a contingent of rural, left-leaning, lower-caste politicians that came to power in North India in the late 1980s and early 1990s. The Gramscian term "subaltern," indigenized in India by the renowned subaltern studies circle of Indian historians and intellectuals, is an apt descriptor for these new politicians. They represent the anti-elite, anti-upper caste wave finally washing over North India as it had decades before in South India.[1] They have ushered in political change, which has brought about change in the local politics of global English in India. Their language politics espouse subaltern resistance to the linguistic hegemony of the elite.

The contours of the local politics of global English in India will be outlined below by examining the evolution and relation of elite and subaltern discourses on global English in post-colonial India. We will see that although subaltern resistance to English language hegemony has been articulated in India since the anti-colonial movement in the early twentieth century, this articulation was for the most part co-opted or marginalized, through politically opportunistic alliances. This may also be the case for subaltern language politics in India today; nevertheless the memory of the past instances of resistance inspires this more recent subaltern project.

Anti-Colonial Resistance[2]

As in many British colonies at the turn of the twentieth century, the English language provided access to the discourse on liberalism and political democracy for the Western-educated urban professionals who dominated the Indian nationalist movement. Through the (Indian National) Congress, these nationalists initiated a dialogue, in English, with the British imperial rulers on the illegitimacy of colonial rule. As was the case throughout the colonial world, Western education provided the ideological tools to challenge colonialism within its own paradigm: "[T]he main lines of an urban middle and professional class critique of colonialism was to grow out of English education itself."[3]

The Indians, however, did not let English get "under their skin."[4] According to Partha Chatterjee, Indians maintained an "inner domain" that British cultural hegemony could not penetrate.[5] This inner domain was the fountainhead for the cultural renaissance that provided the spiritual base for anti-colonial resistance. The language of this inner domain was indigenous common speech. In making this case for Bengal, Chatterjee notes: "Where written prose marked a domain already surrendered to the colonizer, common speech thrived within its zealously guarded zone of autonomy and freedom."[6] Chatterjee describes the attraction the vernacular held for the urban, middle-class, English-speaking professionals. Despite the gap between the poverty-stricken masses and these professionals, the latter's desire for affinity, indeed their search for that affinity through the "discovery of India," was as important as the anti-colonial agenda to them.[7] It was Mohandas K. Gandhi, the *Mahatma*, who turned that desire into practice. Mahatma Gandhi blamed the gap between the Indian masses and the elite on English language education: "[B]y reason of English being the medium of instruction . . . we have been isolated from the masses."[8] Furthermore, Gandhi questioned the role of English in challenging British political power: "Of all the superstitions that affect India, none is so great as that a knowledge of the English language is necessary for imbibing ideas of liberty . . ."[9] In the 1920s, Gandhi convinced Congress to organize along regional language lines.[10]

Mahatma Gandhi was enunciating an alternative to British English hegemony. But there was more than one alternative. While the text of spiritual leaders such as Ramakrishna contained a "rustic colloquial idiom,"[11] other spiritual organizations advocated Sanskritized Hindi as the alternative to English.[12] These Hindu organizations in the Hindi heartland (such as the Arya Samaj, Hindu Mahasabha, and the Rashtriya Swayamsevak Sangh, or RSS) provided the increasingly Westernized middle class with a theology that was Hindu yet reformist, furnishing them with their sense of self-hood and nationhood. The Hindi these organizations promoted was "perceived as the symbolic instrument for fighting colonialism and English."[13] But it was not Gandhi's Hindi. It was a formal Hindi that was theologically validated by its proximity to and borrowing from the language (Sanskrit) of Hindu texts. It was class-laden as well, with the Hindi literati arguing that Hindustani, the commonly spoken Hindi advocated by Gandhi, was not appropriate for "serious discourse, as in education and parliament."[14] It also had a strong communal element as its promoters sought to distance it from the influence Urdu, with its Persian and Arabic vocabulary roots, had on colloquial Hindi.[15] As a result, the language debate became politicized. According to Krishna Kumar, "[t]he struggle for Hindi . . . became a means for upper caste groups, some of whom had substantial landed interest, to establish political identity."[16] Many, committed to protecting their caste-privileged traditional elite status, joined the Congress party in an attempt to steer it in a conservative direction. They perceived themselves as a counterweight to the English-speaking Nehruvian wing of Congress.[17]

Language Politics at Independence

On the eve of independence, then, there were at least three positions on the English language: the Nehruvian, the Gandhian, and the Hindu revivalist/traditionalist. All three positions were represented in the Congress party, which assumed power upon independence. There was overlap between the positions. Both the Gandhian and the revivalist positions perceived English as an impediment to Indian cultural identity and as a tool of British hegemony; indigenous language was a symbol of anti-colonialism. The two positions differed however on the nature of the indigenous languages. This difference implied a difference in perception of the symbolism of language for class and communalism. For Mahatma Gandhi, English was a barrier to equality and the mass mobilization necessary for the anti-colonial struggle; it reinforced class privilege and status hierarchy. Gandhi's position was "essentially a revolt against the practices of the [communally] partisan literary elite and the political revivalists."[18] In this he made common cause with Jawaharlal Nehru, as both Gandhi and Nehru advocated Hindustani, that is, spoken Hindi-Urdu, over Sanskritized Hindi. For the traditional elite, Sanskritized Hindi was a bulwark against English and would also reinforce the Hindu status hierarchy.

With the anti-colonial struggle over, the debate on Hindustani versus Sanskritized Hindi, with its symbolism for class and communal issues, intensified at the political center, leading to a close vote in the constituent assembly adopting Hindi over Hindustani.[19] In the end, "Gandhi's pleas for Hindustani proved a straw in the wind."[20] Not only did Gandhi "lose" on the language issue, but his advocacy for political and economic decentralization was also dismissed by his protégé, the new Prime Minister of India, Jawaharlal Nehru. Nehru's advocacy of a modern, industrial society pitted him against Gandhi and the traditional elite. And it had linguistic overtones: "[T]he ideological tie-up between a secularizing modernity and the use of English came to be established during the Nehruvian phase."[21] For Nehru, Hindustani was a tool for combating the backward, communally inspired traditional elite on their own terms (and Nehru and Gandhi had lost that battle), but the larger issue for Nehru was the future of India as a modern, secular polity, and English was the tool to accomplish this. Indeed, Nehru did not seriously join in the Hindi-versus-Hindustani debate until the battle lines were sharply drawn, and then only to have his irrelevance pointed out by the traditional elite when they mocked his dependence on English.[22] Nehru and other "secular-minded political leaders had rather little genuine interest" in Hindi and the Hindu revivalist symbolism it implied.[23] Pointedly, Kumar suggests a "foul contract" was implicitly agreed upon by the Nehruvian and revivalist/traditional elites, marginalizing the Gandhian alternative in the process.

This "contract" resulted in what Granville Austin has called "the half-hearted compromise."[24] Although Hindi (and not Hindustani) would become the official language, it would not become the "national" language, and English would continue to have "associate" official language status for at least fifteen years. Nehru in essence won the battle on English—global English was deemed necessary for modernity, for science and technology in the promotion of industrialization. While indigenous languages were necessary in the mass mobilization phase of anti-colonialism, the assumption of power meant prioritizing English as the language in which to construct a modern state, according to the Nehruvian vision.[25]

For Nehru, English increasingly was needed for national unity as well, to glue together the "fissiparous tendencies" inherent in a multilingual country with reportedly over 1500 different mother tongues.[26] English was also necessary for co-opting South Indians into participating in the new national project, given their animosity to proposals to adopt the North Indian language, Hindi, as the national language in the constituent assembly.[27] In the early 1960s, Nehru reassured the South Indians that English would retain its status as associate official language as long as the South desired. The South's anxiety over the sincerity of this promise after Nehru's death led to language riots in Tamil Nadu as the 15-year transition period for retaining English as associate official language drew to a close.[28] For the youth in Tamil Nadu who led the riots, English was a ticket for coveted central government jobs, jobs geared toward building Nehru's modern, secular, industrialized—and English-speaking—polity. Their apprehensions were finally laid to rest by a parliamentary act in 1967 definitively legislating Nehru's promise.

Nehru's perception of English as "national cement" fortified as he grew increasingly anxious about a re-organization of the Indian states in the federal system along major regional language boundaries, as had been promised by Congress, under Mahatma Gandhi's leadership, since the 1920s.[29] Nehru "suspect[ed] the Indian languages of harbouring populism and sentiment as their natural element"[30]; "[a]nybody who show[ed] greater familiarity or attraction to the vernacular [was] immediately suspected of things that would ultimately slide into secessionist tendencies of various types."[31] Although the States Reorganization

Act of 1956 began the process of redrawing state boundaries along language lines despite Nehru's reservations, these suspicions further signaled the rejection of Mahatma Gandhi's subaltern language politics among the Nehruvian elite.

Rammanohar Lohia's Brand of Resistance

There was one politician who continued to espouse anti-elite language politics in the late 1950s through mid-1960s. This was Rammanohar Lohia, leader of the socialist party in its various incarnations during this period. Lohia wrote extensively on the language issue, calling for the banning of English. He viewed English as a barrier to class equality, to democratization, and to economic development for the poor. He called on socialists to organize committees and conferences on the *angrezi hatao* (Banish English) issue and to deface English signs throughout North India. But he was clear that "the chief aim of our movement should be removal of English and not the establishment of Hindi."[32] He complained that "[o]rthodox pundits with their high-flown Sanskritised Hindi and Bengali are doing a great harm to the cause of their languages. The Hindi of our newspapers is becoming more and more unintelligible."[33] According to his biographers, Lohia himself "had his own style of writing and speaking Hindi, which was very simple and direct."[34]

Although Lohia was clearly for the use of spoken Hindi, i.e., Hindustani, in government and schools in North India and against the communal tendency of those advocating Sanskritized Hindi, he was obsessed with opposing Congress (Nehru in particular) and hence prioritized banishing English over elevating the language(s) of the have-nots. Lohia "had dedicated himself, with an amazing singleness of purpose, to the task of destroying Congress rule."[35] In the 1960s, this led him to seek electoral alliances and coalition partners with other non-Congress parties, including the Jana Sangh, a Hindu nationalist party with strong communal overtones that had formed in the early 1950s as the traditionalists lost out to the Nehruvians within Congress.[36] The Jana Sangh espoused Sanskritized Hindi as the national language. Just as the traditionalists and the Nehruvians had a "foul contract" that marginalized a subaltern discourse on language, Lohia contracted with the Jana Sanghis against the Nehruvian Congress, muting his own language politics in the process.

The Lohia-Jana Sangh contract was temporary and for purely electoral purposes. By comparison, the Nehruvian-revivalist "foul contract" had deeper cultural implications, which, according to Kumar, remain today. Nevertheless, even an ephemeral electoral alliance between Lohia-ites and Jana Sanghis aided in the marginalization of Lohia's subaltern language politics. Exemplary of this was the language policy of the state government of Bihar in the late 1960s. This government, resulting from the 1967 election, the first to chip away at the dominance of the Congress party, was a broad-based coalition, with socialists predominating but including Jana Sanghis. The education minister and deputy chief minister of the government, Karpoori Thakur, a disciple of Lohia, banished compulsory English from the school curriculum. But when the government moved to recognize Urdu as a second official language in the state, second to (Sanskritized) Hindi, and thus implicitly to re-appropriate Hindi by legitimizing Hindustani, communal riots, allegedly fomented by the Jana Sangh, erupted, resulting in the death of close to 200 people.[37] The policy regarding Urdu was abandoned. By the end of the decade, Lohia had died, the non-Congress governments in the North Indian states had fallen, and Indira Gandhi was beginning to consolidate her power in the Congress party and the country.

The Indira-Rajiv Dynasty

By the early 1970s, Indira Gandhi had adopted populist rhetoric and a centralizing, authoritarian style of rule pointedly different from that of her father, Jawaharlal Nehru. The epitome of her ruling style was her assumption of near dictatorial control in June 1975 under the pretext of a national emergency. The Emergency lasted until 1977 when, politically isolated and surrounded by sycophants, she sought legitimation of her authority through the electoral process—and lost horribly. Her return to power in 1980 and the prime ministership of her son, Rajiv, from 1984 to 1989, continued the pattern of strong central control with the chief ministers of states of the Union having no independent base for power or policy-making (including language policy).[38] Rajiv Gandhi didn't quite have the touch of his mother and his attempt to copycat her strong centralization resulted in floundering on policy initiatives. To compensate, he increasingly invoked the "foul contract" of his grandfather and played the communal card, hoping to shore up Hindu support.[39] In urban areas, his communal rhetoric struck a chord with aspiring entrants into the burgeoning middle class. He changed his mother's populist rhetoric to yuppie rhetoric, appealing to young technocrats (as he was himself). And of course English was and is the symbol and language of this class.[40] It was also the language of the "Centre" (the political center of the Indian federal system or Union, physically located in New Delhi, the nation's capital) and centralization; Rajiv "condemned linguistic states [set up by the 1956 States Reorganization Act] as the greatest blunder of free India."[41]

Despite Indira Gandhi's authoritarian policies, resistance politics didn't disappear, but indeed flourished in a blooming of new social movements in the early 1970s.[42] With experimentation and alternatives cut off in the political sphere, civil society picked up the slack. The epitome of this efflorescence was the JP (Jayaprakash) movement against Indira Gandhi's increasingly amoral and corrupt politics. The movement started in Gujarat and then was transported to Bihar by Jayaprakash Narayan himself, an old socialist and former colleague of Lohia. However, the movement gained its organizational strength from the involvement of the RSS, the right-wing Hindu nationalist paramilitary organization. The RSS agonized over whether this anti-Indira alliance with the left would dilute its rightist ideology.[43]

This left-right alliance carried over into the formation of the Janata party, which came to power at the Centre (i.e., at the national level) upon the defeat of Congress (Indira) in the elections at the end of the Emergency. The Janata party was made up of virtually the same coalition that Lohia had helped forge in the North Indian states in the late 1960s—i.e., socialists, Jana Sanghis, dissident Congress party members, and representatives of the backward-caste middle peasantry. The Prime Minister was Morarji Desai, a former Congress party man in the mold of the traditionalists. Largely because of its Jana Sangh component (the Jana Sangh being the party wing of the RSS), the Janata government advocated Sanskritized Hindi.[44] However, it had to contend with a powerful reaction from the South, something the coalition governments of the northern states in the late 1960s didn't have to confront. Because of this and the intense in-fighting within the coalition, the Janata government's rhetoric on language was never implemented.[45] Indeed, once in power, the Janata ministers slipped into using the language of power, English.[46] The one exception to this slippage that is frequently recounted is the address in Hindi the foreign minister at the time, Atal Behari Vajpayee, gave to the U.N. General Assembly.

The Yadavs as Subalterns

By the end of the 1980s and Rajiv Gandhi's tenure as Prime Minister, the political dominance of Congress had deeply eroded, particularly in North India. In late 1989, Rajiv's Congress party lost in the general elections. His former finance and defense minister, V. P. Singh became the new Prime Minister, as leader of a new party, the Janata Dal. Although V. P. Singh himself was an upper-caste Hindu royal scion and had been politically dependent on Indira Gandhi in the early 1980s,[47] he now appealed to the lower-caste, middle peasantry who had benefited from land reform and Green Revolution technology in 1950s and 1960s. These were the same constituents to whom Lohia had appealed, but by the 1980s their economic gains had translated into increasing political sophistication and a desire for political power. The largest among these "backward castes" in Bihar and Uttar Pradesh (UP) is the Yadav caste. In 1989, Mulayam Singh Yadav became Chief Minister of Uttar Pradesh; in the spring of 1990 Laloo Prasad Yadav became Chief Minister of Bihar.[48] Upon taking office, Mulayam Singh Yadav launched his "Banish English" (*angrezi hatao*) policy. In Bihar, not too long thereafter, Laloo Prasad Yadav went in the opposite direction, promoting the re-introduction of mandatory English in schools. Both chief ministers were allied with the V. P. Singh government in New Delhi.

The V. P. Singh government lasted less than a year. There were two primary causes for the fall of his minority government, both of which clearly illustrate the changing nature of politics and indicate a maturing of the constituency that Lohia had nurtured in North India in the 1960s. The first was V. P. Singh's attempt in the summer of 1990 to dust off the Mandal Commission report. This report, written a decade earlier and then shelved, recommended extending the central government's reservations (affirmative action) policy beyond Scheduled Castes (untouchables) and Scheduled Tribes (tribal indigenous groups) to include backward castes, such as Yadavs and other rural "bullock capitalists."[49] Upper-caste youths reacted violently and tragically to what they perceived as a policy allocating fewer university seats and government jobs for open competition in which they were advantaged. Several dozen of them engaged in self-immolation in protest. V. P. Singh backed off of implementing the Mandal Commission report.

The final straw that led to the fall of the V. P. Singh government was the withdrawal of support by the BJP (Bharatiya Janata Party, the successor to the Jana Sangh), support that was necessary for Singh's minority government. The BJP withdrew its support because V. P. Singh, through Laloo Prasad Yadav, had the leader of the BJP arrested. At the time of his arrest, the BJP leader, L. K. Advani, was in Bihar in his motorized van decorated to look like Lord Ram's mythical chariot, on his way to the Babri Masjid (a sixteenth-century mosque) in Ayodhya, Uttar Pradesh, the alleged birthplace of Lord Ram. This *rath yatra* or chariot ride was infamously successful at rousing up anti-Muslim fanaticism. V. P. Singh and Laloo Prasad Yadav decided to put a stop to it (although they only succeeded in doing so temporarily).

Although the V. P. Singh government at the Centre was short-lived, the Yadav chief ministers endured uninterruptedly in Bihar and intermittently in Uttar Pradesh (UP). Like his counterpart in Bihar, the Chief Minister in UP, Mulayam Singh Yadav, enacted policies and conducted politics strongly indicating his anti-BJP, pro-backward caste sympathies. "Yadav politics" were anti-communal and anti-upper caste. They also had a linguistic component, according to Badri Raina:

> Social groups and formations that began to register a political and economic presence in the sixties (and emerged into leaderships—with the franchise of 1989) seem to retain in potent measure critical and conceptual links with [Mahatma] Gandhi and Lohia. Such leaderships which speak for a new resurgent rural elite are beginning to critique, from all accounts along a secular politics, the linkages between a dominant English-knowing urban middle class and developmental hypotheses which have, over the last four decades, fattened the metropolitan sectors at the expense of the vast countryside. In that critique, once again, the English language and English education are perceived to be key determinants of a comprehensive historical oppression. Thus, in the strategic states of Uttar Pradesh

and Bihar, Hindi protagonism seems to re-emerge not as a communal or entirely provincial phenomenon, but essentially as a second anti-colonial movement.[50]

Raina is equating the Yadav resistance to linguistic hegemony with the anti-colonial resistance to British English hegemony. Hence his suggestion of a "second anti-colonial movement." Writing in 1991, he did not foresee Laloo Prasad Yadav's 1993 pro-English policy recommendation. Can we explain the differences in English-language policy advocated by the two chief ministers in North India and still retain the gist of Raina's analysis? Why was Lohia's Banish English turned into policy by Mulayam Singh Yadav in Uttar Pradesh, while in Bihar Laloo Prasad Yadav pushed for the re-introduction of compulsory English in the school curriculum? A simple explanation is a political one: Although both Mulayam Singh Yadav and Laloo Prasad Yadav appealed to the same constituencies, i.e., backward castes (particularly Yadavs), Muslims, and Dalits (untouchables/Scheduled Castes), Laloo Prasad Yadav's consolidation of this support base, and hence of political power, was much further along than Mulayam Singh Yadav's.[51] In other words, political competition in Uttar Pradesh had been much fiercer in the 1990s than it had been in Bihar. Laloo Prasad Yadav could afford risking what many would interpret as an elitist language policy, the re-introduction of English for school matriculation.

However, this political explanation suggests that Laloo Prasad Yadav did not represent subaltern politics but instead was co-opted into the dominant English-speaking elite.[52] It suggests that in the quotation above, Raina is mistaken to lump the new leadership in Uttar Pradesh and Bihar together. How can Laloo Prasad Yadav's pro-English stand possibly be a "second anti-colonial movement"? Although Mulayam Singh Yadav's "Banish English" policy could easily be construed as a component of the politics of subaltern resistance-from-below that predominated in UP in the 1990s,[53] it seems far-fetched to characterize the near-opposite language policy promoted in Bihar as reflecting the same subaltern politics. Yet there is an underlying ideological commonality in the linguistic political agenda of Mulayam Singh Yadav and Laloo Prasad Yadav, a commonality that defines both as instances of subaltern politics. This commonality is easy to miss if one perceives the local battle as solely pro-English versus anti-English. There are more than two sides to the battle, a point on which Lohia failed to follow through. The anti-Sanskritized Hindi battle, which is a strategic component of the war against communal forces, is just as important to subaltern politics as an anti-English agenda. The language policies of Mulayam Singh Yadav and Laloo Prasad Yadav must be policies validating vernacular common speech, rather than being just anti-English, to be part of an anti-elite project. For the elite is not monolithic linguistically; there is an English-speaking elite and a (Sanskritized) Hindi-speaking elite that, as we saw above, have been entrenched in the political establishment since independence. As Francesca Orsini has stated, "post-1947

Hindi cannot be considered a 'popular national language' versus the 'elite national language' English. Rather they represent two different elites."[54]

Vernacular Language Politics

What, then, are the vernacular language politics of the subaltern Yadavs? Mulayam Singh Yadav, in pushing for *angrezi hatao* (Banish English), also established a vernacular language center where both the Dravidian languages of southern India and the Indo-Aryan languages of northern India, other than Hindi, were taught.[55] When he began his second stint as Chief Minister in late 1993, his rhetoric regarding Urdu, the language nearly identical to Hindi but associated with Muslims, suggested a state re-appropriation of Hindi as the language of the masses and a vocal rejection of the Sanskritized Hindi elevated and appropriated by the upper castes.[56]

In Bihar, Laloo Prasad Yadav has cultivated the image of the common man—indeed, some see him as a rustic buffoon. He projects this image globally, showing up at IMF headquarters in Washington, D.C. in country garb looking for a spittoon for his mouthful of betel nut juice—exemplary perhaps of a "personal resistance" to global elitism. He speaks colloquially, lacing his Hindustani with Bhojpuri (his mother tongue, officially designated as a dialect of Hindi). This makes him popular, and demonstrates his political astuteness: a journalist reporting on his pro-English policy recommendation claimed Laloo Prasad Yadav "gave impetus to the backward [caste] movement by his perfect use of the language of the poor, dalits and slum-dwellers in his speeches."[57]

If Laloo Prasad Yadav represents the subaltern masses, why, then, would he embrace English, the symbol of the upper-class urban elite? He's not embracing English, he's hijacking it, suggests a young Indian sociolinguist:

> Like gunboat diplomacy, in the hands of a few English helps maintain a kind of balance that will be destroyed if the instrument passes over to those who have been kept beyond its reach so far.
>
> By wanting to hand over the instrument to the backward castes or the local people, Laloo Prasad Yadav has in fact attempted piracy. [58]

By attempting to dispense English capital to the Indian masses, Laloo Prasad Yadav is undermining one of the most important struts of the elite establishment: command of global English.[59] As we noted in chapter 1, use of English in and of itself is not a hegemonic act; resistance to global English can be in English.[60]

Laloo Prasad Yadav has definitely shifted the parameters of the discourse on global English in India. For Laloo and supporters of his English language policy, the debate on global English needs to be indigenized, just as the English language itself has been indigenized in India according to Kachru and others.[61] India is exemplary of Kachru's "outer circle," or what in chapter 1 we termed "official English" countries. As we noted in chapter 1, the status of global English in countries of this category is often a legacy of colonialism. But global English is now being de-colonized in India. By claiming to appropriate English for the masses, the "Other" for Laloo Prasad Yadav is not the British colonialists but rather his political opponents, the right-wing Hindu nationalist elite represented in the BJP (Bharatiya Janata Party, successor to the Jana Sangh). Indeed, the Bihar chapter of the BJP opposed Laloo Prasad Yadav's pro-English proposal (although the Bihar Congress party supported it). In Laloo's subaltern language politics, those who oppose English for the masses are the elites because they are wary of any policy that might encourage the emergence of lower castes as a political force. Hence the elite fear of the dispersion of English language capital, as well as educational and economic capital in the form of reserved seats for backward castes and others in universities and government jobs. As one of Laloo's supporters noted, "those who are opposed to English would naturally be treated as persons opposed to the very concept of reservation [i.e., quota affirmative action]."[62] Laloo Prasad Yadav is assuming that the same forces that oppose the mass appropriation of English will also fight against reservations policy for the lower castes. And he is for the most part correct, especially when it comes to his fiercest opponents, the right-wing Hindu nationalists. The BJP has consistently opposed reservations policies. In Bihar, just as the BJP opposed Laloo Prasad Yadav's English language policy, its predecessor, the Jana Sangh, vehemently opposed the reservations policy of Laloo's mentor, Karpoori Thakur, when he was the Bihari Chief Minister in the late 1970s, causing his government to fall. And, as discussed previously, a decade earlier the Jana Sangh had opposed the Bihar government's recognition of Urdu, the vernacular of the Muslims, as proposed by Karpoori Thakur, who was then education minister, leading to communal riots. The local context of caste and communalism is never very far from the surface of the politics of global English in India.

In the end, Laloo Prasad Yadav was forced to back down from his proposal to mandate English for the Bihari school curriculum by members of his own administration and party. Opponents to his proposal within his party invoked past imaginings of colonial English and acknowledged the seductive qualities of global English, proclaiming that "Hindi is our mother while English is a beautiful prostitute."[63] Local imaginings were invoked by other of his party colleagues, who reminded Laloo of his indebtedness not only to Mahatma Gandhi, Rammanohar Lohia, Jayaprakash Narayan, and Karpoori Thakur, all opponents of English from the left, but also to Purushottam Das Tandon and Madan Mohan Malviya. The latter two were the epitome of revivalist/traditionalist elites in favor of Sanskritized Hindi.[64] Still other party colleagues steered clear of traditional right-wing communalist discourse in opposing Laloo's proposal, implicating instead Rajiv Gandhi's renewal of the "foul contract" between the English-speaking elite and the right-wing communalist elite. It was the elites' adoption of "English culture," they claimed, that "was responsible for the demolition of the Babri Masjid as well as continuation of casteism in society."[65]

Democratic Language Politics

In using the categories of subalterns and elites in our analysis of the local politics of global English in India, we need to be cognizant that these are analytical tools, not moral and political judgments. In India in particular, the world's largest democracy, where the voter turnout of Dalits (untouchables) is often greater than that of Brahmins (the highest caste), any means of winning and keeping political power is often par for the course. Political opportunism impacts language politics just as much as it does other issue-based politics. In India, politics, including language politics, are not necessarily moral, but they are democratic. As D.L. Sheth has claimed, "the language debate is an outgrowth of the democratic process of politics."[66]

We suggested above that subaltern language politics entail more than an anti-English, pro-Hindi language policy. They also entail anti-elitism and anti-communalism. Our analysis does not suggest, however, that subaltern politics are more righteous than elite politics. Thus, as Laloo Prasad Yadav's political career became increasingly precarious in the late 1990s because of incompetence and scandal, Laloo himself would occasionally revert to revivalist/traditionalist imagery. He suggested, for example, replacing "Bihar" and "Patna" (the state capital of Bihar) with their Mauryan empire names, invoking a re-imagining of the state's (and by implication, his) past glory.[67] And while illiteracy and infant mortality decreased under his administration, corruption and sycophancy were widespread.[68] Walter Hauser has suggested that the Bihar Chief Minister lacked the ability to even conceive of structural change, let alone implement it.[69]

The opportunistic nature of democratic politics was also apparent in Uttar Pradesh. By the mid-1990s, Mulayam Singh Yadav was back in power in UP after a brief interlude of a BJP state government.[70] One of the more prominent campaign promises of Mulayam Singh Yadav's Samajwadi party in its successful attempt to regain power in December 1993 was to repeal the "anti-copying" law enacted by the previous BJP state government. This law, Mulayam Singh Yadav argued, gave an unfair competitive advantage to upper-caste university students, who didn't need to cheat (i.e., copy exams) because they had the educational background that lower-caste students lacked. It was only fair to let lower-caste students cheat! Mulayam also promised to, and did, pardon Phoolan Devi, the infamous "bandit queen" who was in jail for allegedly massacring her upper-caste rapists. Mulayam even gave Phoolan Devi a ticket on the Samajwadi party list.[71]

Mulayam Singh Yadav's second government was a coalition between his Samajwadi party and a relatively new Dalit (untouchable) party. Despite the initial euphoria over the empowerment of lower castes and Dalits, the coalition fell apart after internal bickering. The Dalits then formed a short-lived minority government on their own—with support from the right-wing, predominantly upper-caste BJP! This Dalit-upper-caste ruling combination has since been repeated. Although such coalitions are obviously based on expediency rather than ideological convictions, they also suggest that caste identity is increasingly used as a marker of political voting blocs rather than social taboos. And, of course, blocs and numbers matter in political strategies for democratic politics. Rural-based backward castes, frequently in alliance with Muslims and Dalits, are using democratic politics to challenge both the English-speaking, Nehruvian, urban-based elite and the communally inspired, upper-caste, right-wing conservative elite. In fact, they are becoming masters of democratic politics to such an extent that Sheth refers to them as the new "vernacular elite," in contrast to the English-speaking elite and the Sanskritized Hindi elite.[72]

This emerging vernacular elite came to power at the Centre (national level) in 1996. In the 1996 elections, the Congress party, widely regarded, at least in the past, as the bastion of the English-speaking urban professional elites, lost significantly. The BJP, representing the upper-caste Hindu nationalist elite, emerged as the largest party and attempted to form a government. Atal Behari Vajpayee, the BJP Prime Minister, took his oath in Hindi, rather than in English as had been the tradition among the Nehruvian elite, while other BJP MPs took the oath in Sanskrit. But the BJP could find few coalition partners and lasted less than two weeks in office, with Vajpayee resigning rather than facing a vote of confidence he was sure to lose. The government that followed was a left coalition, which included Laloo Prasad Yadav's Janata Dal, Mulayam Singh Yadav's Samajwadi Party, some small regional parties, and some Communists. Supported in Parliament by the defeated Congress party, it was in essence an anti-BJP alliance. The first Prime Minister of this coalition government, Deve Gowda, from the state of Karnataka in southern India, came from backward-caste peasant background, and spoke very little Hindi. The defense minister was Mulayam Singh Yadav, the "Banish English" warrior from Uttar Pradesh, whose English is limited. Apparently cabinet meetings were difficult linguistically, with Mulayam Singh Yadav not able to communicate with Gowda in English and Gowda unable to communicate in Hindi (although Gowda worked on improving his Hindi).

Even the seamier side of these new, democratic politics ran into linguistic difficulties. One of the coalition supporters of the government was the JMM, Jharkhand Mukti Morcha, a party based in the Jharkhand tribal area of southern Bihar. The JMM and other Jharkhandi parties have been fighting for social justice for the tribals. But they play politics as well. One JMM MP, not long before the 1996 election, went public with the accusation that the Congress Prime Minister in the early 1990s, Narasimha Rao had, through an intermediary, bribed him to vote against a no-confidence vote that the opposition had organized. His public statement regarding this bribe was released by the BJP, to which he had defected. He subsequently rescinded his defection, claiming that the BJP had bribed him to make this false accusation against the Prime Minister. As the plot thickened and the JMM MP looked increasingly sleazy, he mounted his defense: "I didn't sign it [the BJP-released statement alleging the bribe]. It was in English. I do not know what it said."[73] One can bemoan a political system that not only condones but seems to encourage such corruption. Or one can celebrate the fact that it is credible that a non-English-speaking tribal would be bribed—that he is part of the political process, however seamy, and not excluded from it.

The change in power at the national level, from the English-speaking, well-educated, urban politicians to a new vernacular elite, was possible because of changes at the state level in India's federal system, beginning in the late 1980s and represented by the chief ministerships of Laloo Prasad Yadav in Bihar and Mulayam Singh Yadav in Uttar Pradesh. Although their overt language policy preferences regarding English differed, these two chief ministers shared a common anti-elite agenda, in stark contrast to the agenda of either the BJP or Congress party. However, this change did not hold at the national level. By late 1997, the left coalition government was fragmenting into its component parts, setting the stage for new general elections in 1998 and again in 1999.

Hindutva Language Politics

With no party winning a clear majority in the 1998 elections, the BJP formed a weak coalition government, only to be brought down a year later by a seemingly revitalized Congress party—revitalized under the leadership of Sonia Gandhi, the Italian-born widow of Rajiv. However, Sonia's charisma failed to deliver in the ensuing elections in the fall of 1999 and the BJP returned to power as head of a more solidified coalition.

Ideology has been the "BJP's Achilles' heel" in forming alliances and coalitions.[74] The BJP has had to dilute its ideological agenda of *Hindutva*, or Hindu cultural nationalism, to attract friends and allies. This has been difficult to achieve despite the political compulsions to do so, because the agenda is determined not just by the party but also by the RSS, one of the revivalist right-wing Hindu organizations established in the 1920s that advocated Sanskritized Hindi as the national language. Indeed, in recent years, as the BJP has endured in power, the infighting over the political agenda between the moderated-by-power BJP, represented by Prime Minister Atal Behari Vajpayee, and the more militant RSS has increased. As the former RSS leader and the current number-two man in the BJP has characterized this agenda, *Hindutva*, is "not only the substratum of India's unity but also a dynamo for the country's progress and transformation into a modern progressive and prosperous nation."[75]

In focusing on cultural nationalism, the RSS and the BJP have also espoused, at times, economic nationalism, frequently linking the latter with an anti-global English stand. In the late 1990s, the RSS was, for example, "attacking foreign multinational firms" and simultaneously "demanding curbs on the widespread use of English."[76] The anti-corporate globalization tone of these attacks facilitates alliances with components of the left. One of the BJP's staunchest coalition partners in recent years has been George Fernandes' Samata party. Fernandes, the Defense Minister in the BJP coalition government, was responsible for kicking Coca-Cola out of India in the mid-1970s.

One might expect that the anti-global English tone might also win the BJP some allies on the left. This, however, hasn't been the case. Mulayam Singh Yadav, the politician with the best anti-English credentials, remains the fiercest of the BJP's opponents. Furthermore, the BJP has been far from consistent on the global English issue. While the local BJP government in Delhi in the mid-1990s attempted to push through an anti-English (*angrezi hatao*) policy, the influential RSS-BJP leader L. K. Advani, recognizing the BJP's appeal to the urban upper-caste middle class, admonished the "Banish English" advocates within his party.[77] After all, this class has profited from its global English capital in recent years through the outsourcing of contracts in information services to India. The benefits from the globalization of information technology for a particular constituency (urban, upper-caste, middle-class, English-educated youth) have not been lost on Indian politicians.

Both the anti-economic globalization and anti-linguistic globalization stands of the RSS appear to be rhetoric for local consumption as the BJP government plows ahead with economic liberalization and globalization.[78] The BJP political agenda appears to be moving toward increasing integration into the global economy while asserting *Hindutva* at home. One of the most contentious domestic assertions of Hindu cultural nationalism in recent years has been the re-writing of history texts with a decisive *Hindutva* bias for school use throughout India by the BJP-controlled Ministry of Education. This issue allows the BJP to play the communal card at home without risking showing its global hand.

Conclusion and Comparisons

The politics of the English language, even in its global form, is essentially local in India. The messy local politics of Indian democracy are a key determinant of Indian responses to linguistic globalization. English in India, albeit introduced by a global (colonial) power, has become part of the local political (and linguistic, as Kachru would argue) landscape. Global English in India is Indian English, a marker of elite status as well as a vernacular appropriation by subalterns. And in India, subalterns can become the new local elite.

The Indian case also reveals two clear anti-globalization positions that are ideologically differentiated but often similar, policy-wise. There is a right-wing cultural nationalist, anti-globalization, and anti-English strand in Indian politics, most clearly represented by the RSS and less clearly by its political partner, the

BJP, which is now in power at the national level. Indeed, when the BJP first came to power at the national level in the early 1990s, many predicted that India was embarking on a Hindu version of Jihad, a reactionary rejection of McWorld.[79] Reality, or power, is different; it may turn out that free-market globalization never had a better friend in India than the BJP. On the other hand, the left alternative in India, what is frequently referred to as the "third force" (i.e., anti-BJP and anti-Congress), professes a grass-root opposition to globalization-from-above but succumbs to the rituals of courting foreign investment when confronted with dismal state budgets and disastrous development results. Perhaps the only valid conclusion is that there are truly multiple voices in India worth listening to, and occasionally some of those voices are subaltern ones.

The local politics of global English in India can be compared to those in other outer circle or official English countries (see chapter 1). Alastair Pennycook, in his book, *The Cultural Politics of English as an International Language*, details the history and politics of global English in Malaysia and Singapore, both former British colonies. Both countries had made English an official language after independence, but with much more consistency and support in Singapore than in Malaysia. In the latter, assertions of Malay culture and language have fed into the tense post-independence communal relations between *bumiputras* ("sons of the soil," i.e., Malays) and the minority Chinese, who have been quite economically successful. In Singapore, where the Chinese dominate demographically, politically, and economically, global English has been indigenized to such an extent that linguists recognize Singaporean English as an established linguistic variety.

In the past decade, India has embraced economic globalization while asserting Hindu cultural nationalism, particularly under the BJP but also under previous Congress party central governments in the early 1990s. In contrast, Malaysia has tended toward a different mixture. Malaysia has reprioritized English, particularly in tertiary education, in the last decade, while complaining about economic globalization.[80] The most boisterous example of the latter was when Malaysia's Prime Minister, Mahathir Mohamad chewed out the international financier, George Soros, during the Asian financial crisis of the late 1990s, as widely reported in both the Asian and Western press. Each country is attempting a different combination of weighing economic and cultural nationalism vis-à-vis the economic and cultural dimensions of globalization, while both are hoping to maximize benefits accruing from global English capital.

There is an even more significant difference between India and Malaysia for the study of the local politics of global English, given our "globalization-from-below" categories (resistance, subalterns, and democratization) developed in the first chapter. India is much more democratic than Malaysia. It has well-established practices of free speech, a free press, dissent, and debate. Parties and politicians are subject to voter scrutiny and regularly alternate in power at both the national and state levels. The Indian opposition is robust and plays a critical watchdog role. Although Indian politics may be infused with corruption and political opportunism, as we discussed previously, this is readily exposed through an independent press and democratic practices. In contrast, Malaysian politics have been dominated by one party (the UMNO) since the 1960s, and, indeed, one politician, Dr. Mahathir, since the early 1980s. Dissent and criticism, even about language issues, are constitutionally prohibited.[81] Regime opponents often end up in jail for long periods of time. In the Malaysian context, then, subaltern resistance is less visible and inevitably takes different forms than in India. This makes subaltern language politics in Malaysia at least more difficult to study, if not to practice.

Notes

1. See Narendra Subramanian, *Ethnicity and Populist Mobilization: Political Parties, Citizens and Democracy in South India* (New York: Oxford University Press, 1999), especially chapters 4 and 5.

2. Most of the body of this chapter is adapted from Selma K. Sonntag, "Ideology and Policy in the Politics of the English Language in North India," in *Ideology, Politics and Language Policies: Focus on English*, ed. Thomas Ricento (Amsterdam: John Benjamins, 2000), 133-49.

3. Badri Raina, "A Note on Language, and the Politics of English in India," in *Rethinking English*, ed. Svati Joshi (New Delhi: Trianka, 1991), 286.

4. Probal Dasgupta, *The Otherness of English: India's Auntie Tongue Syndrome* (New Delhi: Sage, 1993), 99.

5. Partha Chatterjee, *The Nation and Its Fragments* (Princeton, N.J.: Princeton University Press, 1993), 7.

6. Chatterjee, *Nation*, 55.

7. The most famous example of discovering one's Indian roots was Jaharwalal Nehru's *The Discovery of India* (Garden City, N.Y.: Anchor Books, 1960), written while he was in prison for his anti-colonial activities.

8. Quoted in Raina, "Note on Language," 284.

9. Quoted in Raina, "Note on Language," 279.

10. Granville Austin, *The Indian Constitution: Cornerstone of a Nation* (Bombay: Oxford University Press, 1966), 270-71.

11. Chatterjee, *Nation*, 51.

12. See Jyotirindra Das Gupta, *Language Conflict and National Development* (Berkeley: University of California Press, 1970).

13. Krishna Kumar, "Quest for Self-Identity," *Economic and Political Weekly*, 9 June 1990, 1247.

14. Kumar, "Quest," 1253.

15. In the Indian context, "communalism" refers to the antagonistic relations between the two major religious groups, Hindus and Muslims. At the colloquial level, Hindi and Urdu are basically the same language. At more formal levels, the two languages diverge

as Hindi becomes laden with Sanskrit vocabulary and Urdu relies on Persian and Arabic vocabulary. Written Hindi uses the Devanagri script; written Urdu is in Arabic script. For a treatment of the linguistic dimension of the communal divide in the early twentieth century, albeit from a sympathetic Indian perspective, see Amrit Rai, *A House Divided* (Delhi: Oxford University Press, 1984). For a larger historical sweep, with emphasis on the nineteenth century, see Christopher R. King, *One Language, Two Scripts* (Bombay: Oxford University Press, 1994).

16. Kumar, "Quest," 1254.

17. J. Das Gupta, *Language Conflict*, 118; John R. McLane, "The Early Congress, Hindu Populism, and the Wider Society," in *Congress and Indian Nationalism*, eds. Richard Sisson and Stanley Wolpert (Berkeley: University of California Press, 1988), 54, 56.

18. J. Das Gupta, *Language Conflict*, 111.

19. See Austin, *Indian Constitution*.

20. Kumar, "Quest," 1253.

21. Raina, "Note on Language," 288.

22. J. Das Gupta, *Language Conflict*, 163; Austin, *The Indian Constitution*, 271-74. See also Robert D. King, *Nehru and the Language Politics of India* (Oxford: Oxford University Press, 1998).

23. Krishna Kumar, "Foul Contract," *Seminar* 377 (Jan. 1991): 44.

24. See Austin, *Indian Constitution*.

25. P. Dasgupta, *Otherness of English*, 142; Sudipta Kaviraj, "Capitalism and the Cultural Process," *Journal of Arts & Ideas* 19 (1990): 68; E. Annamalai, "Satan and Saraswati: The Double Face of English in India," *South Asian Language Review* 1 (Jan. 1991): 37.

26. R. King, *Nehru*; Selig S. Harrison, *India: The Most Dangerous Decades* (Princeton, N.J.: Princeton University Press, 1960). The designation "mother tongues" would include dialects as well as languages.

27. See Austin, *Indian Constitution*. Hindi is spoken by approximately 40 percent of the Indian population.

28. Paul R. Brass, *The Politics of India Since Independence* [The New Cambridge History of India IV, 1] (New Delhi: Cambridge University Press, 1990), 143-44.

29. Raina, "Note on Language," 287; R. King, *Nehru*; Clifford Geertz, *The Interpretation of Cultures* (New York: Basic Books, 1973), 255-56.

30. P. Dasgupta, *Otherness of English*, 168.

31. Kaviraj, "Capitalism," 69.

32. Rammanohar Lohia, *Language* (Hyderabad: Navakind, 1966), 6-7.

33. Lohia, *Language*, 16.

34. Girish Mishra and Braj Kumar Pandey, *Rammanohar Lohia: The Man and his Ism* (New Delhi: Eastern Books, 1992), 53.

35. Madhu Limaye, *Birth of Non-Congressism* (Delhi: B.R. Publishing Corp., 1988), 169.

36. See Bruce Graham, *Hindu Nationalism and Indian Politics* (New York: Cambridge University Press, 1993), chapter 4.

37. Paul R. Brass, *Language, Religion and Politics in North India* (London: Cambridge University Press, 1974), 260-69.

38. Selma K. Sonntag, "The Political Saliency of Language in Bihar and Uttar Pradesh," *The Journal of Commonwealth & Comparative Politics* 34, no. 2 (July 1996): 4-5.

39. See Christophe Jaffrelot, *The Hindu Nationalist Movement in India* (New Delhi: Viking, Penguin India, 1996), 333.

40. D. L. Sheth, "No English Please, We're Indian," *The Illustrated Weekly of India*, 19 Aug. 1990, 34-37.

41. Balraj Puri, "Politics of Ethnic and Communal Identities," *Economic and Political Weekly*, 7 Apr. 1990, 705.

42. See Gail Omvedt, *Reinventing Revolution: New Social Movements and the Socialist Tradition in India* (Armonk, N.Y.: M.E. Sharpe, 1993), parts II-III.

43. Jaffrelot, *Hindu Nationalist Movement*.

44. Robert L. Hardgrave, Jr. and Stanley A. Kochanek, *India: Government and Politics in a Developing Nation* (New York: Harcourt Brace Jovanovich, 1986), 132.

45. Selma K. Sonntag, "Elite Competition and Official Language Movements," in *Power and Inequality in Language Education*, ed. James W. Tollefson (New York: Cambridge University Press, 1995), 103-4.

46. Limaye, *Birth of Non-Congressism*, 184.

47. Sonntag, "Political Saliency," 4-5.

48. The identical last name of these two chief ministers indicates that they are from the same caste. They are not blood-related.

49. As they are called in Lloyd I. Rudolph and Susanne Hoeber Rudolph, *In Pursuit of Lakshmi* (Chicago: Chicago University Press, 1987), chapter 13.

50. Raina, "Note on Language," 293.

51. Sonntag, "Political Saliency," 10-11.

52. For an argument that the lower-caste rural middle peasantry in North India is just one more faction of the ruling bourgeois elite, see Achin Vanaik, *The Painful Transition: Bourgeois Democracy in India* (New York: Verso, 1990), 79-85.

53. K. Srinivasulu, "Centrality of Caste: Understanding UP Elections," *Economic and Political Weekly*, 22 Jan. 1994, 159-60.

54. Francesca Orsini, "Why Tulsi?," *Seminar* 432 (Aug. 1995): 58.

55. Personal observation, Lucknow, Nov. 1993.

56. Krishna Kumar, interviewed by author, New Delhi, 19 Jan. 1994.

57. Nalin Verma, "English or no English, controversy rages," *Hindustan Times* (Patna), 1 Aug. 1993, 7.

58. Kailash S. Agarwal, "English, Laloo: a Bihari story," *The Independent* (Bombay), 23 Sept. 1993.

59. About 5 percent—of a billion people—know English in India.

60. As Pennycook has put it, "Counter-discourses can indeed be formed in English." Alastair Pennycook, "English in the world/The world in English," in *Power and Inequaliity in Language Education*, ed. James W. Tollefson (New York: Cambridge University Press, 1995), 55.

61. See Braj B. Kachru, *The Indianization of English: the English Language in India* (Delhi: Oxford University Press, 1983).

62. Ranjan Yadav, "An Essential Knowledge," *Hindustan Times* (Patna) (Sunday-spread), 15 Aug. 1993, II.

63. See Bishwanath Lal, "English stokes row in Bihar," *Tribune* (Chandigarh), 23 Sept. 1993.

64. Verma, "English or no English," 7.

65. Verma, "English or no English," 7.

66. Sheth, "No English Please," 35.

67. R. Ahmed, communication with author at the XVIII South Asian Language Analysis Roundtable, Jawarharlal Nehru University, New Delhi, 6-8 Jan. 1997.

68. See Binoy Prasad, "'Laloo Does It!' Consolidation of Backward Class Leadership in Bihar: An Analysis of 1995 Election to the State Legislature" (paper presented at the 24th Annual Conference on South Asia, Madison, Wisc., 20-22 Oct. 1995).

69. Walter Hauser, "Peasant Surprise," *The Telegraph* (Calcutta), 21 May 1996, 8.

70. The BJP government had been dismissed after the December 1992 razing of a mosque, the Babri Masjid, allegedly built over a Hindu holy site in Ayodhya, Uttar Pradesh. The razing by Hindu fanatics triggered communal riots throughout India (and indeed in neighboring Pakistan and Bangladesh as well).

71. Phoolan Devi remained on the hit list of her alleged rapists and was eventually assassinated in the late 1990s.

72. Sheth, "No English Please."

73. "Voices," *India Today* (North American Special Edition), 31 Mar. 1996, 10.

74. Rakesh Sharma, "Ideology—BJP's Achilles heel?" DH News Service, 4 Jan. 1998.

75. L. K. Advani, quoted in Jaffrelot, *Hindu Nationalist Movement*, 483.

76. Narayanan Madhavan, "India Hindu body denounces foreign firms, English," Reuters, 2 Oct. 1997 [India News Network Digest, server@INDNET.ORG (6 Oct. 1997)].

77. Sonntag, "Political Saliency," 18.

78. See Saba Naqvi Bhaumik, "Quiet Man Wields the Big Stick," *India Today*, 27 Oct. 1997, 16; Charu Gupta and Mukul Sharma, "Speaking in Tongues," *Himal South Asia* 9, no. 6 (Aug. 1996): 18-23.

79. Benjamin R. Barber, *Jihad Vs. McWorld* (New York: Ballantine Books, 1996), 191, 293.

80. Malaysia's tilt toward English is noted in "Malaysia: The Language of Progress," *Economist*, 15 Jan. 1994, 31; and reported by Jonathan Kent of the BBC World Service on radio on 2 Jan. 2003.

81. Alastair Pennycook, *The Cultural Politics of English as an International Language* (New York: Longman, 1994), 191.

Chapter 5

Language Politics in Democratic Transitions: Comparing South Africa and Nepal

In 1989, the world's attention was focused on Eastern Europe. The Berlin Wall came down and autocratic regimes crumbled. Countries in the region began their attempt to democratize. The following year, but with much less international fanfare, Nepal went through a similar process: a mass-based "people's movement" triggered a transition from autocratic monarchy to multiparty democracy. That same year, South Africa released Nelson Mandela from prison and, in 1991, convened multiparty negotiations to end apartheid and establish majority-rule democracy.

The experiences of the South Africans and Nepalese have much in common that distinguishes them from those of the former communist countries. While communist autocrats did not hesitate to exploit ethnic and national differences, their regimes were not founded on a race-based or ethnicity-based ideology. For the communists, identity was malleable: ideally, communism would lead to the erosion of ethnic, regional, and subnational identities, resulting in the creation of the "Soviet man." In contrast, in South Africa, the apartheid regime treated race and ethnicity as immutable characteristics that defined and justified a rigid social and political hierarchy.[1] Similarly, in Nepal, a Hindu monarchy justified hierarchy and exclusion on the basis of caste, a natal ascription imposed on both Hindus and non-Hindus to categorize the diversity in the kingdom.[2] In the early 1990s, the upheaval and regime-change in both South Africa and Nepal entailed a radical break with official State ideologies that had reified primordial identities.

The nature of this radical break is apparent in changes in the language policy of both countries. Language can be an overt, easily identifiable marker of ethnicity. In the old South Africa, language was the primary marker of "nations," a code-word for racial and tribal groups, with Whites divided into English- and Afrikaans-speaking peoples and Blacks into numerous tribes, each with its own "homeland."[3] Each of the South African "nations" allegedly had its own distinct culture, identified by language.[4] In Nepal, language had also become the official marker of group identity (for example, in the census).[5] Language was used to include and exclude: Nepali-speakers were either upper-caste Brahmins and Chhetris (Kshatriyas) or those lower in the hierarchy who had "Sanskritized," that is, emulated the upper castes in cultural values and customs. Language thus differentiated these groups from *matwali* (impure) Tibeto-Burman-speaking groups. In both apartheid South Africa and monarchical Nepal, the official language of the State was the mother tongue of the group identified as innately superior to others: Afrikaans (and English) in South Africa and Nepali in Nepal. In both countries, the transition to democracy has entailed the adoption of a multilingual language policy in an attempt to breakdown the exploitative status hierarchy of the *ancien régime*.

The Nepalese and South African experiences, along with Eastern Europe and the former Soviet Union, have in common the historical timing of their attempted transitions to democracy. They seem to be further evidence of a global wave of democratization in the last decades of the twentieth century.[6] Many have attributed the wave to the end of the Cold War. Others point to a larger, more systemic cause: globalization. Influential commentators, such as Thomas Friedman and Francis Fukuyama, have suggested that democratization results from economic liberalization and globalization.[7] However, others, such as Benjamin Barber, are much more cautious about the implications of globalization for democracy. Globalization, Barber argues, embodies both McWorld and Jihad, i.e., cultural homogenization resulting from "universalizing markets," and fragmentation based on "parochial ethnicity," neither of which are conducive to democracy.[8]

Language politics during the South African and Nepalese democratic transitions provide a window through which to view the nebulous relationship between democratization and globalization. Many would contend that the transition to official multilingualism in both countries represents linguistic democratization. However, global English has also been a factor influencing the nature of the transition. Its impact on any linguistic democratization must also be assessed. The differing role of global English in the two countries provides a discriminating lens for our analysis: In terms of the typology presented in chapter 1, South Africa is part of Kachru's outer circle, an "official English" country, whereas Nepal is categorized as a "marginal English" country. In South Africa, English was and is an official language, with contradictory overtones of hegemony and resistance. In Nepal, global English has been and remains a foreign language. Although marginal to Nepali linguistic hegemony, global English nevertheless has featured in the process of democratization.

We thus have the opportunity for a provocative comparative analysis in which South Africa and Nepal display many similarities in terms of their linguistic democratic transition but differ in terms of the degree of the use and status of global English. Through this linguistic window, we will explore the relationship between democratization and globalization in each society. How do democrats view globalization? How is linguistic globalization linked to economic liberalization? What are the contending perspectives on global English during the democratic transition? Is global English perceived to be a democratic or hegemonic force—and by whom? What is the relation between multilingualism, democratization, and global English? We can search for answers in the local politics of global English in South Africa and Nepal.

South Africa

> Like the question of colour, the language question is one that confronts us in every sphere of life in South Africa.
>
> —Neville Alexander[9]

The paradox of the South African language question is well cast in the representation of the English language. On the one hand, English is the language of liberation and democracy in South Africa. It was the language of resistance to the apartheid regime and its policy of Afrikaanization, taking on an emancipatory function most explicitly and famously during the Soweto riots of the mid-1970s. On the other hand, English is the language of the elite; in South Africa, as much of the current literature on the country's language policy notes, English is hegemonic. Hegemonic and liberatory, elitist and democratic: the conflicted nature of the language question could not be more acute.

Language Politics during Apartheid

English became the "language of liberation" in response to the Bantu Education Act of 1953 and its enhanced implementation in the 1970s. The Act instituted mother-tongue education for Blacks in South Africa. Nominally, such a policy would be exalted: Adopted soon after the UNESCO appeal for mother-tongue instruction in developing countries, it had the pretense of enlightenment and progressivity.[10] However, despite being coincidental with the UNESCO policy, the principles motivating the Act were far different.[11] The Act had two objectives: to shut down missionary schools associated with British colonialism that used English as the medium of instruction, and to divide and rule the subordinate Black population.[12] The anticipated by-product of the Act, which was vigorously promoted in the 1970s, was the imposition of Afrikaans.[13]

The white Afrikaans speakers, the Boers, had resented and resisted British colonial rule. When the Afrikaners' National Party (NP) came to power in 1948, it began rigorously implementing apartheid, of which the Bantu Education Act was an integral part. "Apartheid" means keeping apart. By limiting educational opportunities for Blacks to poorly financed mother-tongue schools in their "homelands," the Afrikaners sought not only to separate Blacks from Whites, but also from each other: There was no "Black majority," only a series of segregated and distinct African nationalities or "tribes," identified by language. Even where it was very difficult to keep Blacks from "co-mingling,"—for example, in urban areas where workers concentrated—the apartheid regime established sections of Black townships "demarcated for and allocated to individual language groups."[14] Kogila Moodley succinctly sums up the ultimate aim of the Bantu Education Act in asserting that "[i]n apartheid South Africa multilingualism had been an instrument of African exploitation within the apartheid project."[15] The language policy of the apartheid regime explicitly fomented fragmentation based on parochial ethnolinguistic identity. However, instead of provoking linguistic tribalism, the apartheid policy merely incited Blacks to rally around global English as the language of resistance and protest. In adopting a language policy that attempted to assert Afrikaner national identity vis-à-vis the British while subjugating Blacks to Whites (both British and Afrikaners), the apartheid regime succeeded only in bringing Blacks and the English language together. Blacks saw English as "the tool to combat divisive Bantu Education and the imposition of Afrikaans."[16] In 1976, matters came to a head: Students, many of them inspired by the Black Consciousness Movement, took to the streets in the township of Soweto, protesting the "Afrikaanization" of their school curriculum. The police retaliated brutally, only to galvanize students in other townships to follow suit. After more than a year of protest and retaliation, the apartheid regime retreated from its language policy.[17]

Soweto was a galvanizing event not only for the liberation movement within South Africa, but also for those outside of South Africa, in the English-speaking world, who were sympathetic to the anti-apartheid struggle.[18] Black South Africans had regarded Afrikaanization as "an attempt to isolate them from the international community, where English is often used as a lingua franca."[19] As the language of liberation, English enabled apartheid resisters to communicate with and gain the support of a progressive international community.[20] A protest which had as its immediate objective access to the English language activated a transnational solidarity movement predicated on advocacy of human rights and democratization. Of course, Soweto was about much more than language. Indeed, it is frequently recognized as the beginning of the end of apartheid.

The espousal of English by the Black South African liberation movement, however, was not unproblematic. Kathleen Heugh, a current-day language researcher and activist in South Africa, acknowledges that "misconceptions about the role of English as a language of liberation and potential national lingua franca took root and flourished" during the liberation struggle.[21] The problem, according to Neville Alexander, was that "the language question was never treated more than superficially" by the liberation movement.[22] Hence, the spontaneous uprising in Soweto caught many of the movement leaders off-guard.[23] As they struggled to gain control of the uprising, Alexander argues, they missed a golden opportunity: "At the critical time when Bantu education was being imposed on the black people, the leadership of the liberation movement across the board made a *de facto* decision to oppose Afrikaans in favour of English."[24] Alexander attributes the movement leaders' cursory embrace of English to their class moorings: "The black middle class, true to its missionary origins, plumped for English and adopted an elitist and patronising attitude to the languages of the people."[25]

Alexander has the credentials to make this critique. His well-known anti-apartheid activism landed him an eleven-year jail stint on Robben Island beginning in 1963.[26] His expertise in language policy is also well established by his chairmanship of LANGTAG (Language Plan Task Group), which was established by the ANC government in 1995-96. The ANC, or African National Congress, was the best known component of the liberation movement, a movement which was multifaceted and at times deeply divided.[27] Alexander represented the trade-union segment of the movement. According to Patrick Harries, the trade-union view of intra-Black differences was distinct from the ANC view.[28] The former explicitly disavowed any tribal or ethnic differences among Blacks, while the latter astutely avoided the issue. Alexander's views included a preference for a cross-ethnic class-based strategy for resisting apartheid. This put him at odds with the BC (Black Consciousness) segment of the anti-apartheid movement, which was ideologically committed to a socially constructed "Blackness," explicitly spurning any association with Whites.[29]

These differences within the anti-apartheid movement indicated a range of linguistic policy preferences, even if they were not always fully articulated. The ANC espoused multiracialism, with a de facto preference for English. The BC Movement was explicitly racialist—that is, it denied a role to Whites in the liberation struggle. Given its understanding of Blackness (a category that included [mixed-race] Coloureds and Indians) as socially constructed by historical oppression, primordial linguistic loyalties to indigenous African languages were presumably eschewed. Thus the implicit language policy of the BC would be identical to the ANC: de facto preference for English as the language of liberation.

Although Black Consciousness was the most prominent segment of the anti-apartheid struggle when the anti-Afrikaans protests broke out in Soweto in 1976, it did not survive the severe repression by the apartheid regime following Soweto.[30] With the ANC surviving primarily in exile, there was a vacuum in the internal anti-apartheid movement partially filled by union activity, but more forcefully occupied by the UDF (United Democratic Front) beginning in the early 1980s. The trade union movement, of which Neville Alexander was a recognized leader, was tacitly wedded to the use of the workers' languages while publicly disavowing the tribal identities associated with these languages. However, the UDF, despite espousing principles similar to the trade-union movement (and eventually incorporating most of it under its umbrella), found itself fighting a virtual tribal war in the late 1980s, in the eastern coastal province of KwaZulu Natal. The UDF's opponent in this war was the Inkatha Freedom Party (IFP), a party limited to KwaZulu

Natal because of its exclusionary appeal to Zulus, the "tribe" that had originated from and been "assigned" to the province under the apartheid Bantustan policy. The IFP explicitly employed a "mobilizing discourse" of Zulu ethnicity (although less so of the Zulu language) while at the same time championing the liberation struggle.[31] This gave a tribal spin on the conflict, with the IFP representing Zulus and the UDF increasingly associated with the exiled ANC and its Xhosa leadership. The apartheid regime cultivated this tribal interpretation of the conflict and actively supported IFP reprisals against the UDF.

Hence, even in its dying throes, the apartheid regime was attempting to "divide and conquer" South African Blacks according to tribal differences that the ruling regime associated with language differences. In both response and defiance, during the anti-apartheid struggle, there was an unspoken linguistic consensus among Blacks, in spite of the different language policy preferences of the various segments of the liberation movement. During apartheid, "Black attitudes about language had largely been conceived in terms of protest and resistance,"[32] and English was the language of this protest and resistance.

Afrikaans Language Politics in the New South Africa

The dissolution of apartheid has led to a vigorous debate on language policy and a clearer articulation of policy preferences. Ironically, it is the renewed saliency of Afrikaans as an identity marker, after relative linguistic indifference on the part of Afrikaners during the waning years of apartheid,[33] that has sparked the debate.

It is frequently acknowledged that the post-apartheid policy of eleven official languages was the result of the ANC accommodating the demand that Afrikaans retain official language status.[34] The ANC leadership allegedly preferred English to be the sole official language in the new South Africa. But when the NP (the Afrikaner National Party) insisted that Afrikaans remain on par with English, the ANC countered by making all the Bantu languages official as well.

The unexpected consequence of the NP's insistence on Afrikaans has therefore been the new South African language policy of official multilingualism. In response to this new policy, unanticipated alliances have been formed within government and civil society. In the broadest of terms, the advocates of multilingualism are arraigned against those who see English as the portal to economic development. What is surprising is who now advocates multilingualism in the new South Africa.

Those championing multilingualism are indeed an assortment of strange bedfellows, at least in the terms of the old South Africa. Almost by default, some of the strongest supporters of multilingualism are those campaigning for Afrikaans. Their concern is that without Afrikaners in power, Afrikaans will diminish in both status and corpus, ending up once again as a "kitchen language" as it was at the turn of the century.[35] They do not pine for a return to White minority rule—many of today's Afrikaans advocates actively spoke out against apartheid. One of the most vocal liberal Afrikaner intellectuals during apartheid, Hermann Giliomee, remains critical of apartheid's language policy while currently being one of most influential defenders of Afrikaans. The problem with the apartheid language policy, Giliomee argues, is that it wrongly "transferred to the state the task of ensuring the survival of Afrikaners and Afrikaans . . . by means of a white political monopoly, compulsory mother tongue education, and the entrenchment of Afrikaans in many ways."[36] A liberal strategy—one Giliomee advocates for the post-apartheid South Africa—would empower individuals to group together and associate independent of the State. The State's job should be to guarantee rights (e.g., minority rights, rights to mother-tongue instruction) in the constitution. It is up to civil society "to ensure that these rights come into effect . . . by acting through . . . efficient non-political organisation[s]."[37]

Giliomee has been active in the Group of 63, formed in May 2000 and dedicated to "protect[ing] Afrikaans and other minority languages and cultures in South Africa."[38] The group's "building blocks" are (1) to seek common cause with other minority language demands; (2) to democratize Afrikaans culture (e.g., incorporate Afrikaans-speaking Coloureds); (3) to remain part of civil society rather than becoming a political party; and (4) to emphasize congruence of the group's objectives with international human rights trends.[39] Similar liberal agendas can be found in the Foundation for the Empowerment of Afrikaans and the *Afrikaanse Taal en Kultuur Vereniging* (ATKV).[40]

But some question whether these agendas really are liberal. Liberalism is more than a vibrant civil society independent of government. It is also about individual choices of the good life. These include cultural choices. "Post-modern liberals" predict cosmopolitanism as the cultural wave of the future, where the individual samples from a variety of cultural choices.[41] According to this view, Afrikaans advocates, instead of celebrating a "new multilingual cosmopolitan" South Africa, appear to exhibit "paranoid anti-modernity," "romanticiz[ing] a lost past and fear[ing] the future."[42] Their nostalgia resembles, to some of their critics, more of an emotional and reactionary response to globalization—a type of "linguistic Jihad"—than a liberal response. Though Afrikaans advocates are careful to invoke internationally sanctioned rhetoric about minority rights, their constant reference to "group rights," is further cause for concern.[43] Are they surreptitiously promoting conservative communitarianism, "a vision of a homogeneous, regimented group" feeding into the right-wing *Volkstaat* agenda?[44] Heribert Adam accuses Giliomee of risking this by advocating a return to an emphasis on primordial identities and cultural conformity within the community.[45] Giliomee has reacted to Adam's criticisms with an appropriate post-modern retort: "You are working with a false dichotomy: one is either cosmopolitan and modern or ethnic and traditional/reactionary and outmoded. Why cannot the group renew itself ideologically and culturally? Why can one not balance ethnic particularisms and universality?"[46]

The Giliomee-Adam debate demonstrates how difficult it is to determine the ideological underpinnings of the Afrikaans language cause today. While the Afrikaner right wing has clearly espoused the language cause, its influence has faded since the mid-1990s.[47] The old apartheid champions of Afrikaans seem worn down and defeatist today; they feebly endorse newer groups of "younger people" who are "not identified with the establishment," such as the Group of 63.[48] Perhaps the most anti-establishment Afrikaner to give an initial, albeit tepid, endorsement to the Group of 63 was the internationally renowned anti-apartheid poet, Breyten Breytenbach.[49] One of the charges lodged against Breytenbach by the apartheid regime was plotting to blow up the Afrikaans Language Monument built in the 1970s in the Western Cape, a plot that Breytenbach admitted sounded tempting given the abominable architecture and sociolinguistic arrogance of the monument.[50]

Other, lesser known, Afrikaner anti-apartheid resisters have also been reevaluating the Afrikaans language cause in the new South Africa. Chris Louw, a journalist currently with the South African Broadcasting Corporation (SABC) radio, has been described as the "young Turk" of the Afrikaans movement.[51] He gained his anti-apartheid credentials in the mid-1980s, when he met with and reported on the ANC leadership-in-exile while it was still illegal to do so. At that time, he thought the Afrikaans language would eventually die out. Given the language's association with apartheid values, he was perfectly happy with this prospect. He has since changed his mind. Louw clearly implicates the Afrikaner leaders during apartheid and during the democratic transition for failing to be honest with the Afrikaner people. He believes, though, that if the new Black government sincerely wants to be inclusive, it needs to communicate with Afrikaners in their own language. It needs to educate and liberate Afrikaner masses from the blinders imposed by apartheid's leadership. This needs to be done in Afrikaans, through, for example, quality programming on radio and television. But, at least at SABC, this is not being done, and Afrikaans programming is continually being undermined. When Louw voiced his concern about this, he was accused of promoting the *Volkstaat* agenda and was ostracized at SABC. It took the intervention of the offices of Thabo Mbeki, with whom Louw had become acquainted in the 1980s, to at least temporarily resolve the tension.[52]

Chris Louw's case illustrates the ambiguities of the Afrikaans language cause.[53] He is wary of the real agenda of the Group of 63, fearing its goal may be to secure special privileges for Whites. He is also reluctant to endorse Karl Prinsloo's Foundation for Empowerment for Afrikaans or Frits Kok's ATKV agenda because, he thinks, these are merely cowardly attempts of former elites to appear respectable and favorable to the new South African government. Still, Louw thinks that the Afrikaans language cause could play a progressive role in the new South Africa, not only in re-educating Afrikaners but also in challenging the new elite to keep its commitment to multiculturalism.

Louw clearly believes there is something to be gained by retaining an Afrikaner culture, albeit one that is non- or even anti-apartheid in its politics. In the current political climate, it is easier for an Afrikaner to appear apolitical and assimilate to English, which is what most Afrikaners are doing rather than fighting for their Afrikaner identity. Louw seems to believe that complacency, whether under apartheid or the ANC government, is a grave danger, and one that Afrikaner culture, with its "pioneer values," can tackle.

Clearly Chris Louw, or even Hermann Giliomee, is not projecting an "Afrikaans Jihad" in response to the continued advance of English in South Africa. But neither will they be "co-opted" by English, especially given the democratic "space" that is now available to voice their opinions and to organize. Indeed, Louw seems to feel a democratic obligation to stand up for language rights. At any rate, it is clear that Afrikaners are better situated to take advantage of the democratic opening than other language groups.[54] Because of the support Afrikaans language organizations received during apartheid, they now have the necessary organizational capacity to be active in civil society.[55] As often seems to be the case, those who benefited from the former authoritarian regime are well positioned to take advantage of the democratization process.

It remains unclear, then, whether the embrace of multilingualism and the rejection of global English by those espousing the Afrikaans language cause are reflective of democratic values. If only for practical political reasons, Afrikaners realize that "Afrikaans must stand shoulder to shoulder with other African languages" in the face of the spread of global English.[56] In this regard, linguistic globalization appears to provoke an inclusive multilingualism rather than a parochial and exclusive linguistic Jihad. The accompanying rhetoric is, for the most part, democratic. However, it is difficult to conclude whether globalization causes democratization, which in turn enables multilingualism, or whether the espousal of multilingualism is an astute political attempt to retain at least some of Afrikaans linguistic capital relative to the increasing value of global English capital in the new South Africa.

Indigenous African Language Politics

Political power in South Africa has shifted dramatically since the mid-1990s. Afrikaners no longer have a monopoly on power and the ANC has won handsome majorities in democratic elections. A parallel, but less dramatic, shift has occurred in language politics. Afrikaans no longer has the monopoly of linguistic capital, although, as we saw above, Afrikaans advocates still dominate civil society. But linguistic capital has not shifted to indigenous African languages, nor are demands for these languages frequently made. There is, however, one vociferous advocate for these languages: Neville Alexander. As is widely acknowledged by his supporters and detractors, Alexander has almost single-handedly kept the government from being complacent about language issues. As he sees it, the transition to democracy provides a unique opportunity for confronting and dealing with the language question in a politically progressive manner. Historically in South Africa, language politics "from below" have been directed against the State, as was the Soweto uprising.[57] In the new, democratic South Africa, the opportunity now exists for the State to work with "non-state elements," that is, civil society and non-governmental advocacy groups, to rationally plan multilingualism.[58]

Despite these new opportunities afforded by democracy, the ANC government must be prodded to overcome its tendency to complacently and implicitly neglect multilingualism. There is ample evidence of neglect. One hears repeatedly that the ANC lacks the political will to formulate and implement a coherent and feasible multilingual language policy.[59] The ANC was a latecomer to the language debate during the democratic transition and, as mentioned above, its initial commitment to the policy of eleven official languages was a sop to the NP's Afrikaans demand.[60]

Nor do the new constitutional provisions on language provide the government with a clear blueprint for action. The new constitution lists the eleven official languages and recognizes basic language rights: "Every person shall have the right to use the language of his of her choice."[61] According to these provisions, the State is indeed committed to multilingualism, but the guiding principle is individual rights. As Heugh points out, the result is tension between the constitutional provisions endorsing multilingualism and those regarding individual language rights.[62] In essence, the constitutional provisions constitute "a passive right in a liberal human rights framework."[63] The problem with this, Heugh suggests, is that it absolves the government of the responsibility of actively promoting multilingualism. It is, in effect, a laissez-faire policy.[64]

LANGTAG, the Language Plan Task Group set up in 1995 and chaired by Neville Alexander, was considered a positive step forward in terms of government action. Not long after the group issued its heralded report, though, the Department of Arts, Culture, Science and Technology (DACST), under which LANGTAG was commissioned, went through an upheaval that reflected the instability of KwaZulu Natal politics more than anything else.[65] The department (now Ministry) is one of three ministerial portfolios held by the IFP (Inkatha Freedom Party). The IFP was brought into government by the ANC as a compromise and resolution of the devastating conflict between the Zulu-based IFP and the ANC-supported UDF in KwaZulu Natal in the 1980s, as described earlier. That the ANC readily relinquished the DACST portfolio to its political opponent may very well indicate the relative unimportance of the language question for the ANC-dominated government. The upheaval at the department was caused by the replacement, by one of his fellow IFP members, of the rather well-liked and competent minister, Ben Ngubane. The fallout for the government's language policy was the shelving of LANGTAG's report and the diminution of the watchdog status of the Pan-South

African Language Board (PanSALB), the statutory body that oversees national language policy. PanSALB's independence was being curbed under the new IFP minister. In protest, Neville Alexander resigned from the Board.[66] Many supporters of multilingualism considered the whole episode as further indication of the government's lack of commitment to a progressive language policy on multilingualism. Ngubane eventually returned to the DACST, where he attempted to restart the language policy initiatives.

Alexander was called back into service by Ngubane to work on the drafting of a language policy bill which was then presented to the Cabinet for discussion in fall of 2000. The bill was sent back to DACST for further revision, most specifically for a thorough cost analysis. It took more than two years to receive cabinet approval,[67] probably further evidence of governmental foot-dragging on the language issue. The essence of the bill was to implement multilingualism in government administration and services through rotation of the eleven official languages. The eleven languages were grouped into four categories: (1) Nguni group (isiNdebele, isiXhosa, isiZulu and siSwati); (2) Sotho group (Sepedi, Sesotho, and Setswana); (3) Tshivenda and Xitsonga; and (4) Afrikaans and English. Government documents would be made available in one language in each of the four categories. The selection from each category would rotate among the languages within that category. The diminution of the status of English in this scheme, to one of two languages in one of four categories, was ultimately not accepted by the ANC-dominated Cabinet, resulting in Tshivenda, Xitsonga, Afrikaans, and English each having their own category, for a total of six categories overall.

The bill as originally presented to the Cabinet clearly had Neville Alexander's linguistic prints all over it. These prints were, however, marks of a political outsider. Although Alexander has continued to work in and with the new government, he has decidedly maintained his independence. He remains committed to civil society's role in the democratization process. In his view, civil society has an important part to play in promoting multilingualism: "Only conscious mobilization of the people by those who understand the economic, political, and cultural significance of a policy of multilingualism will allow us to get away from mere lip service [by the government for multilingualism] to a noble ideal."[68] Alexander's non-governmental organizations, in particular the National Language Project (NLP) and the Project for the Study of Alternative Education in South Africa (PRAESA), have lobbied the transitional and post-apartheid governments vigorously on the language question.[69] One tangible outcome of these efforts was Alexander's appointment as chair of LANGTAG. Presumably after his constant needling, the ANC decided it was easier to have him on board rather than outside the language policymaking process. According to Alexander, LANGTAG "is itself the culmination of various intersecting processes which had their origins in civil society and which go as far back as the Soweto uprising of June 1976. From this perspective LANGTAG is a direct result of the struggle for democracy in South Africa."[70]

In pursuing the civil society route, Alexander is wary of fomenting parochial ethnolinguistic identities. He argues against establishing separate ethnolinguistic organizations in civil society in order to avoid "deepening the trenches of future ethnic wars."[71] Given the legacy of apartheid, the only language-specific groups in civil society are those for Afrikaans and, according to Alexander, Afrikaners are the only community really passionate about their language.[72] The nine African indigenous languages recognized by the new constitution were those sanctioned under apartheid's Bantustan policy, hardly a community-building legacy. That these languages are now official may reflect government thinking based on convenience rather than serious engagement with the issue of indigenous African multilingualism. Nevertheless, there is some concern that official sanctioning may reify ethnolinguistic differences.[73]

Given the Bantustan legacy and the concern over reifying differences, many "progressive South Africans" remain opposed to multiculturalism.[74] Alexander himself is explicit in espousing an "anti-nationalist" and "antitribalist" multilingualism,[75] consistent with his position during the anti-apartheid struggle (as discussed previously). Most provocatively, Alexander argues that the indigenous African languages should be "harmonized" and standardized into two languages, a Nguni language (assimilating isiZulu, isiXhosa, isiNdebele, siSwati, and Xitsonga) and a Sotho language (encompassing North Sotho/Sepedi, Sesotho, Setswana, and Tshivenda).[76] These two groupings constitute two of the language categories of the language policy bill, discussed above. Clearly this proposal of Alexander reflects not only his faith in language planning,[77] but also a disavowal of the old South African ideology of ethnolinguistic identity as primordial and immutable.

Alexander's colleagues attribute his fervency for multilingualism to his commitment to the class struggle and pedagogical soundness.[78] In other words, Alexander tends to see language not as a cultural marker but as linguistic capital. As we saw above, his trade union movement during the anti-apartheid struggle implicitly favored the use of workers' languages for purposes of rank-and-file participation, not for purposes of tribal or ethnolinguistic identification. Alexander's current agenda appears to be to undermine the elite monopoly on linguistic capital by raising the value of the capital of indigenous African languages. Alexander's linguistics are clearly political and appear to be consistent with his ideology of working-class democracy. Even more so than in the case of Afrikaans language politics in the new South Africa, indigenous African language politics evokes multilingualism as an indication of democratization rather than a symptom of fragmenting parochialism. However, the problem for Alexander today remains remarkably similar to his problem during the liberation movement: his passion for multilingualism (or socialism in his trade-union days) on behalf of those he claims to speak for is not necessarily their priority. Alexander's conceptions, today and in the past, frequently seem too idealistic and distant from the everyday experience of those whose cause he so fervently espouses.[79]

The New Enemy: English Hegemony

The push for multilingualism by both Alexander and liberal Afrikaners is at least partly in response to a new common enemy: global English. Advocates for multilingualism believe that the ANC-dominated South African government needs to be prodded on the language issue precisely because of its implicit preference for English. The concern is that a policy of neglect or a liberal "laissez-faire" policy will lead to hegemony of English by default.

There are at least two components to the argument that English is the new enemy, which is made by the South African advocates for multilingualism. One is the class bias of the new ANC leadership that Alexander notes.[80] In the classical Gramscian sense of "hegemony," English is the language of the new South African ruling class.[81] It is used as a tool of domination, but it is also perceived by the ruled as preferable, desirable, and natural—very different from the language of the old South African ruling class. But then, as Njabulo Ndebele and Courtney Jung both note, the apartheid regime was not hegemonic.[82] Blacks were physically subjugated; there was no pretense of convincing them of the desirability of apartheid. In the old South African apartheid regime, English was the language of liberation; under the new regime, English is the language of hegemony. Ironically the linguistic results are the same: just as in the old South Africa, the majority of Blacks in the new South Africa, like many Afrikaners, prefer learning English.[83] This irony underlies the Afrikaners' alliance with advocates of indigenous language in support of multilingualism.

The second component of English hegemony noted by language scholars and activists in South Africa is its global spread.[84] It is not uncommon in South Africa to interpret "hegemony of English" as concomitant with globalization. For many, English represents McWorld, a linguistic homogenization indicative of cultural globalization.[85] Vic Webb describes this "problem of cultural domination" posed by global English as follows:

> Given the strong present-day forces of international assimilation and homogenisation (the power of international financing and trans-national corporations; the political control by the big nations; global communication; industrialisation, urbanisation, etc.) it is likely that the right to be what you are or want to be, will continue to be under threat, and that cultural and linguistic diversity may be similarly threatened.
>
> On the South African linguistic scene, English can easily become an instrument in a process of cultural assimilation and homogenisation.[86]

Webb's analysis reflects a marked change of tone in regard to English among progressive linguists.[87] During the anti-apartheid struggle, the English language represented globalization-from-below, as it facilitated transnational solidarity. Toward the end of the apartheid regime, there was talk of a transformative "People's

English" and "a democratic variety of South African/Azanian English."[88] But by the mid-1990s, such aspirations were dissolving and "a more critical view of the dominance of English" prevailed.[89] By the late 1990s, South African language scholars warned of a "constant danger" of globalization-from-above transmitted through the hegemony of global English.[90]

The danger, some feared, was accentuated by the lack of public awareness of the hegemony of English: Indeed, many Black South Africans seem to prefer English.[91] South African language activists therefore saw the need to convince South Africans that multilingualism is in their best interests. As Alexander wrote in the LANGTAG report, there is a need to "[e]stablish a process consisting of diverse events by means of which the problems connected with the hegemony of English, the dangers of language chauvinism and the benefits of multilingualism can be highlighted and embedded in the consciousness of all South Africans."[92] In advocating this approach, Alexander opens himself up to criticism like the following:

> All too often [language] planners are guided by ideological concerns rather than by the practical possibilities of their plans. One major hurdle, as Alexander himself points out, is that planners have to take into account the language attitudes of the people of South Africa. Unfortunately, what they think is not what Alexander wants them to think. He therefore feels that 'they have got to understand' both the history of the country's language situation and its plans for the future. Besides being patronising and potentially undemocratic, this task will be a very difficult one indeed.[93]

This is a particularly stinging critique for the language activists coming out of the anti-apartheid tradition. For these activists, as we saw above, "multilingualism is an integral element of democracy, both ideologically and practically."[94] It is this linkage between democracy and multilingualism that makes linguistic democratization a potentially powerful counter-hegemonic force to global English.

The conundrum for the language activists is that State promotion of multilingualism is not necessarily a demand of most South Africans.[95] There are indications that multilingualism *is* valued by Black South Africans in informal, private milieux.[96] But in the public arena, particularly in socioeconomic and educational environs, given complete freedom of individual choice, the majority of South Africans would likely opt for English. As Moodley notes, multilingualism "is the ideal, proposed and practiced by cosmopolitan citizens like Breyten Breytenbach, Hermann Giliomee, Neville Alexander, or Ngugi wa Thiong'o. Their noble concern for childhood tongues and neglected minority languages is affordable because they have already mastered the world languages. For most of their fellow Africans, however, upward mobility still depends on proficiency in the dominant language."[97]

The relation between linguistic democratization and linguistic globalization in the new South Africa is, to a certain degree, reflective of the tension between the ideal of pursuing a truly transformative South African political project and the reality of seeking improvement in the majority of South Africans' lives in an increasingly liberalized and globalized economy.[98] Progressive language scholars and activists argue that blindly jumping on the global English bandwagon will exacerbate rather than resolve this tension. On the other hand, from the perspective of the new South African elite in the governing ANC, the "democratic" demand for English by South Africans coincides with linguistic globalization, which South Africa can exploit to its advantage, given the historical role global English has played in the country. The political debate on linguistic democratization and globalization in South Africa is not yet over.

Nepal

Nepal's political situation is like that of South Africa . . . The Varnasram *[caste system] means also apartheid.*

—Gopal Gurung[99]

Nepal offers an interesting comparison to South Africa. As outlined at the beginning of this chapter, there are important similarities in these two cases: the legacy of ethnic ideologies, the timing of the transition to democracy, and a shift to multilingualism in State language policy. But there is an important difference. In Nepal, English never played the role that it did or currently does in South Africa. In South Africa, as we saw above, the "hegemony" of English is implicated as much by local historical circumstances as it is by globalization. In Nepal, which, unlike its giant neighbor to the south, India, was never directly colonized, English was historically marginal. Nevertheless, global English has been a feature of local language politics during Nepal's democratic transition. As in South Africa, the Nepalese democratic transition has ushered in a new multilingual language policy. However, in contrast to South Africa, advocates for multilingualism in Nepal are not forming alliances in opposition to global English. Instead, global English is perceived to be a facet of external support for democratization. In Nepal, democrats who advocate multilingualism also easily tolerate global English. By examining language politics during the democratic transition in Nepal, we can compare and contrast the combination of multilingualism advocacy and tolerance of global English with the very different language politics in South Africa, where multilingualism advocates actively resist global English.

Language Politics during the People's Movement

In Nepal, the demand for multilingualism featured in the Movement for the Restoration of Democracy (MRD), or "people's movement" (*jana andolan*), that toppled the autocratic monarchical regime that had wielded absolute power since 1960.[100] However, just as in the South African case, the demand was fairly inchoate during the actual struggle against autocracy.[101] The main parties to the MRD, the Nepali National Congress (NC) and the United Left Front (ULF), had cursorily embraced the demand as a reaction to the Nepali-only policy of the government, without thoroughly defining a position or policy on ethnolinguistic matters.[102] The perfunctory attention may have been at least partially due to the domination of the NC and ULF by Nepali-speaking upper castes (Brahmins and Chhetris), many of whom had been educated in India in English-language schools while in exile during the repression of the previous regime.[103] As one observer put it, "interplay between high-caste leadership and a minority ethnic response became an internal contradiction of the democracy movement. The Brahman and Chhetri leaders of the Congress and the communist parties wanted democracy, but by their mere leadership they upheld the political dominance of an elite."[104]

It was not until the drafting of a new democratic constitution by the interim government (made up primarily of the NC and the ULF) in late 1990 that the degree of ambivalence of the movement's position on language issues became apparent. Numerous requests were made to the Constitution Commission on the language issue. However, "[r]ather than attempting to accommodate these [demands], the commission and the interim government . . . virtually dismissed them out of hand," considering them "peripheral issues."[105] The result was that the new constitution presented "a somewhat ambiguous position on the question of language."[106] Article 4 of the constitution recognizes Nepal as a "multilingual" country, an acknowledgment that was never countenanced by the previous regime. While retaining the former constitution's designation of Nepali as the *rashtra bhasa* (official/State language), the new constitution now recognized all the other languages of Nepal as *rashtriya bhasa* (national languages). Also new to the constitution was the right of "each community" to "preserve and promote its language, script and culture" and operate schools at the primary level in the child's mother tongue.[107] This was a distinct change from Nepali as the sole medium of instruction in the former autocratic regime. The linguistic dogmatism of the previous regime had resulted in Nepali being understood by about 70 percent to 80 percent of the population (whereas it is the mother tongue of about 50 percent).[108] The Nepali-only policy of the former regime had also been ruthlessly enforced, with defiance potentially resulting in jail time.[109]

The source of ambiguity regarding the new constitutional provisions on language was the murky distinction between *rashtra* and *rashtriya* languages. It was unclear what, if any, were the statutory implications of this distinction. The presumption was that the terms were adopted to appease linguistic minorities without affronting the Nepali-speaking upper castes.[110] Furthermore, the provision for mother-tongue instruction was merely that: Mother-tongue instruction was allowed, but not necessarily funded or supported, let alone required. It was a passive right a community could exercise, not an obligation of the government.

As in the South African case, there was little development of the language provisions of the constitution during the initial phase of democratic transition. The interim government, dominated as it was by high-caste Nepali speakers, tended to revert to the exclusionary rhetoric of the previous regime. In response, "the period of the interim government saw an upsurge of ethnic assertiveness, with demands for mother-tongue education and for an end to disadvantaged status particularly prominent."[111] Despite this assertiveness, the new government elected in 1991 continued to be inactive on the language issue.[112]

The Sanskrit Controversy

The inertia might have been prolonged indefinitely if the proverbial match had not been lit by a controversy over Sanskrit in the summer of 1992. In the early 1970s, Sanskrit had been dropped as a mandatory subject from the Nepalese school curriculum. In mid-1992, seventy-six Members of Parliament (nearly all Brahmin) signed a petition urging the National Education Commission to include compulsory Sanskrit for primary and secondary grade levels in its recommendations for the up-coming education bill to be presented to Parliament. The controversy reverberated far beyond the issue of language *per se*. Sanskrit, a "dead" Indo-Aryan language, is associated with Hindu scriptures. Making it a compulsory subject in school is akin to promoting Hinduism as the State religion, according to Sanskrit detractors. Nepalese Buddhists, many of whom are speakers of minority languages, felt particularly affronted. The old regime's tactics of using language to designate and differentiate the *matwali* (low-caste Tibeto-Burman-speaking groups) from the Indo-Aryan Brahmin and Chhetri castes seemed to be resurfacing. For many linguistic minorities, the Sanskrit controversy reflected "the domination of the Brahmins" and "racial sentiment" directed against Tibeto-Burman peoples.[113] The issue of mandatory Sanskrit hit deep raw nerves in the nascent democratic body politic because of the association, rightly or wrongly, of Sanskrit with Hinduism and the Hindu caste system, the latter serving as the moral justification given for the institutionalization of Brahmin-Chhetri dominance.

With emotions running high, the Sanskrit controversy galvanized activists into pressuring the government to take action on the constitutional provisions for multilingualism.[114] Initial pressure brought to bear resulted in several MPs, in particular those on the left, recanting and withdrawing their signatures from the original petition urging the Education Ministry to adopt mandatory Sanskrit. In the end, the government "compromised," making Sanskrit mandatory only at the lower secondary, and not the primary, level. Perhaps more importantly, the government was finally goaded into forming language policy commissions to advise it on how to proceed with constitutional provisions for multilingualism. Two commissions were formed: one for language policy in education, composed mainly of non-political language experts; and one for implementing multilingual broadcasting, with a much more political composition.[115] Most innovative were the criteria both bodies used to decide which of Nepal's many languages would receive priority as media of instruction and broadcasting. Not only were number of speakers and development of the language taken into account, but also whether the language was "Nepal-centered," i.e., indigenous to Nepal, or mostly spoken outside of Nepal (such as in North India or Tibet).[116] Priority was also given to inclusion of Tibeto-Burman languages, given their neglect in the past.

Minority Language Activism

These efforts to implement multilingualism led to certain languages receiving recognition while others did not. For example, Sherpa was not included in the language policy recommendations for either education or broadcasting, despite the Sherpas' international reputation—their low numbers (and, perhaps, their language's closeness to Tibetan) precluded inclusion. Decisions about what dialect or variant of a language should be recognized have also been politically contentious. Unlike South Africa, where earlier missionary activity created standards of various African languages, in Nepal, there are often no existing standards of minority languages available.[117] This quandary of a lack of language standardization was resolved most democratically in Nepal: The language speakers themselves were to decide which dialect or variant should be elevated to constitute the standard. In practice, this meant fostering the involvement of civil society, for it was minority leaders and minority organizations that took a prominent role in these decisions.[118]

For the most part, minority leaders were acculturated urbanites. Many of their organizations had urban origins in university student "picnic societies" during the authoritarian regime, when political organizing was outlawed.[119] In this regard, Nepal differed from South Africa—there were, in Nepal, nascent minority language associations that could champion the language cause once the opportunity for freedom of association was provided by democratization. Indeed what was unusual and quite promising in the Nepalese case was the coming together of most of these associations under an umbrella federation, with apparently very little in-fighting.[120]

Although minority language activists championed the cause of the rural, isolated monolingual minority-language speaker, many possessed a quite global linguistic repertoire themselves.[121] In all my interviews with language activists in Nepal in 1994, only one did not speak English. And this individual wasn't a *minority* language activist, but a upper-caste native Nepali speaker who, as chair of the government language commission on broadcasting, was sympathetic to the cause of multilingualism (and also supportive of mandatory Sanskrit). For minority language activists, the target is not global English. In fact, one activist, Gopal Gurung of the Mongol National Organization, goes so far as to give preference to English as the potential medium of instruction in Nepalese schools—precisely because of its neutrality and global currency.[122]

Indeed, the appeals language activists in Nepal make on behalf of their ethnolinguistic brethren are frequently couched in global terms. For example, they cite the UNESCO report on mother tongue instruction in support of their call for multilingualism.[123] For many minority language activists, the United Nations Year of the Indigenous Peoples (1993) provided an international forum for articulating their demands. In demanding *samaan adhikaar* (equal rights) for all of Nepal's languages at the forum, they adopted a liberal, universal human rights framework and attempted to garner international support.[124] From the perspective of the language activists, the real threat is an obdurate government, which, in denying the legitimate democratic aspirations of ethnolinguistic minorities, might provoke the struggle to turn "communal."[125] A 1999 court decision in Nepal banning local governments from using two of the more prominent minority languages, Newari and Maithili, is the type of intransigence on the part of the ruling elite that constitutes a veritable threat.[126]

Some Western scholars have warned that the global liberal democratic outlook embraced by Nepalese minority activists comes at a cost. Inevitably accompanying this outlook, so the argument goes, is the seduction of Western consumption patterns, an open door for the intrusion of McWorld.[127] In Nepal, one of the poorest countries in the world, the source of globalization is less likely to be penetration of Western multinational corporations, the "villains" of McWorld, than penetration of Western NGOs (non-governmental organizations) involved in development projects.[128] Ramjee Parajulee argues that heavy dependence on international donors rendered the autocratic monarchy susceptible to international pressure to accede to the Movement for the Restoration of Democracy (MRD).[129] Similar to the transnational solidarity in the anti-apartheid struggle, many democratic activists in Nepal invited international NGO support, including that of international human rights organizations, and appreciated it when it came.[130]

Global English in Nepal

Given this global context of Nepal's transition to democracy, what are the implications for global English? English is "the second most widespread language in Nepal in terms of popularity, education, and use," Nepali being the first.[131] Is sending one's children to an English-medium school a form of protest against Nepali hegemony, or a capitulation to McWorld by imitating a Westernized elite?[132] There appears to be some evidence for both, according to Sonia Eagle: "[W]hile preference for education in English among non-Nepali speakers is understandable" as an alleged form of protest against Nepali-only, "it is also popular among Nepali speakers, including the elite."[133] She goes on to note that "[a]lthough English may be a privilege for high-caste Nepali speakers, it is a necessity for many other people," often learned by the latter in informal, non-institutional settings.[134] This is particularly true for those employed formally or informally in the global tourism industry, a critical sector of Nepal's economy.[135]

Elite reverence for global English is apparent in the report published by the new democratic government's education commission, which debated the English language issue extensively.[136] The commission's report argues that acquisition of English is the mark of "an educated person" living "in harmony with the national and international environment of today, without losing his identity."[137] This has evoked concern, expressed by the chair of the National Language Policy Recommendations Commission for education, that under the new linguistic regime, mother-tongue medium schools will be relegated to the very poor, further differentiating Nepalese society on the basis of class.[138] As one Nepali academician laments, the spread of global English in Nepal is indicative of an incipient class-based society of "haves" and "have-nots."[139]

The emerging position of global English in Nepalese society hints at a class-based struggle as the more likely future for Nepal than linguistic fragmentation and ethnolinguistic conflict. The recent and very serious Maoist insurrection seems to confirm this implication. It is extremely difficult to decipher the Maoist position on language and ethnolinguistic identity.[140] On the one hand, there have been reports of linkage between the Maoists and the ethnolinguistic activist Gore Bahadur Khapangi, who advocates *matwali* self-respect.[141] And indeed there are suggestions that at least some of the support for the Maoists comes from disaffected ethnolinguistic minorities.[142] On the other hand, the rhetoric of the Maoist movement is distinctly that of a class revolution, with little apparent deviation from the Maoist line. In this regard, it is very different from the liberal democratic outlook that we identified above as common to many of the urban language activists.

Conclusion: Comparing Democratic Transitions

In many ways, the seriousness of the Maoist threat highlights Nepal's inability to consolidate its transition to democracy.[143] Although some have voiced apprehension about South Africa's democratic potential,[144] recent years of democratic consolidation have proceeded more smoothly in South Africa than in Nepal, at least in terms of political stability. As Nepal lurches from one government crisis to the next, punctuated by political in-fighting and personal vendettas (most tragically in the form of the massacre of most of the royal family in the summer of 2001), social issues, including language policy, receive less and less attention. The latest installment in this on-going crisis is the dismissal of the elected government by King Gyanendra in October 2002 and the indefinite postponement of democratic elections. Unfortunately, the King's actions are in many ways reminiscent of his uncle's (King Mahendra's) actions in 1960 when he instated the autocratic monarchical regime that reigned for thirty years.

Despite the different outcomes of their democratic transitions, there are several similarities between the South African and Nepalese experiences in regard to language politics:

- In both cases, the movement pushing for democratization and regime change was relatively unconcerned with the language question (ANC in South African case; MRD in Nepalese case). It was after the democratization process was initiated that the language question was visibly raised.
- In both cases, there was a significant degree of ambiguity in new constitutional provisions regarding language. Both the new South African and Nepalese constitutions gave official recognition to multilingualism while relegating positive action on the part of the new democratic regimes to a commitment to liberal passive rights.
- In both cases, civil society was recognized as having an important and prominent role to play in raising the language question and in pushing forward government action on formulating language policies. Curiously, though, given the outcomes of their democratic transitions, language associations were more robust in Nepal than in South Africa.
- In both cases, the new democratic regime eventually institutionalized language-policy bodies committed to multilingualism.

There are a few tentative conclusions regarding democratization and multilingualism that can be drawn from these similarities. First, at least in these two cases, democratization seems to spur demands for multilingualism. Multilingualism then is an outcome or, at minimum, an accompaniment of democratic transitions, and not an instigator of democratization. Civil society appears to be the forum for voicing demands for multilingualism, but activism based on these demands does not appear to extend beyond previously mobilized groups. So while Gerardo Munck has argued that "[democratic] transitions are moments partly open to agency,"[145] it appears that subaltern agency is not necessarily engaged. Indeed, in the South African case, the demand for multilingualism appears to be confined to political activists. In Nepal, the voicing of demands, if not the demands themselves, has been made predominantly by urban-based activists.

Once multilingual demands are raised, they appear to become embedded in the democratization process. In other words, in these two cases, demands for multilingualism were not hijacked by anti-democratic forces or parochial forces not particularly wedded to democracy, as long as democracy was a viable option. Although one may raise questions about the Afrikaners' democratic motives, the more they voice their linguistic demands, the more they must buy into wedding those demands to an inclusionary linguistic democratization. In Nepal, it has been only with the disintegration of democratization that the Maoists, who are not committed to multi-party parliamentary democracy, have attempted to co-opt ethnolinguistic minority demands. Democratization seems to consolidate multi-lingualism. It is the hope of language activists in both South Africa and Nepal that multilingualism will help consolidate democracy.

In regard to global English, a few parallels between the two cases can also be drawn. Clearly, in both cases there is concern that the liberal commitment to democracy, in which individual preferences and rights are prioritized, is weakening the case for multilingualism and fostering the spread of global English. This concern has been further heightened in both cases by the lackadaisical promotion of multilingualism on the part of the new democratic governments. An unspoken fear in both cases seems to be that the price for replacing the primordial politics of the previous regimes with universal democratic ideals is increasing globalization, in terms of both economic liberalization and global English. So while both multilingualism and global English appear to be positively correlated with democratization (in the sense that democratization opens up space for both), they seem to be negatively correlated with each other. That is, at least from the perspective of many activists, particularly in South Africa, multilingualism and global English are perceived to be incompatible.

Concern over global English is clearly more palpable in South Africa than in Nepal. In South Africa, the hope is that "indigenous languages can be a refuge away from the manipulative impersonality associated with corporate English language acquisition,"[146] without becoming the basis for a reversion to the primordial politics. In Nepal, global English clearly has class implications for Nepalese society, as it does in South Africa. But in Nepal, global English is perceived more in terms of a by-product of an appeal to global standards and less in terms of linguistic capital. In this regard, then, global English is more likely to be seen as a democratic rather than hegemonic force in Nepal, compared to South Africa. The irony is that South Africa has been more successful at democratization than Nepal. It has also been more successful at formal, governmental institutionalization of multilingualism. Yet the de facto spread of global English is by all accounts probably greater in South Africa. The explanation for this difference is most likely found in the historical role of English and the degree of global integration in each case. Nepal remains marginal in terms of both linguistic and economic globalization.

Are the provisional conclusions drawn from these two cases applicable to other cases of democratic transition? The comparative cases that may be most relevant are the multilingual states of the former Soviet Union. In many regards, the politics of language in the former Soviet Union on the eve of democratization were similar to those in both South Africa and Nepal. The language of the established elite, Russian, was imposed on non-Russian speakers throughout the periphery of the Soviet Union.[147] But there was an important difference. Ethnolinguistic minorities were not necessarily stigmatized according to a primordial hierarchy as was the case with race in South Africa or caste in Nepal. When democratization was triggered in the former Soviet Union, non-Russians had resources, including mother-tongue linguistic capital, to draw upon in their attempts to reverse the hegemonic politics of Russification.

Mikhail Gorbachev's *glasnost* appeared to unleash linguistic (and other) demands in the Soviet periphery. In this sense, the situation paralleled South Africa and Nepal, where democratization (or *glasnost*) has spurred ethnolinguistic demands, i.e., demands beyond the initial purview of the initiators of democratization. Many of the newly emerging popular fronts, which sprouted up throughout the Soviet Republics and signaled in the late 1980s a democratization process no longer under Gorbachev's control, presented linguistic demands.[148] However, the language policy they, and the newly democratic regimes they supported into power, advocated was not multilingualism. Instead, their new language policies were tinged with linguistic chauvinism—that is, a reversal of Russification by marginalizing Russian-speakers, economically and politically, through the implementation of local language competency requirements for citizenship and employment. In the case of the former Soviet Union, multilingualism did not accompany democratization, although demands for local languages (to the exclusion of Russian, the dominant language) did.

The central feature of language politics in the former Soviet Union republics has been, then, opposition to the former dominant language, Russian. Despite increasing globalization, there seems to be little concern about global English hegemony. As was the case with Nepal, this tolerance of global English may be a consequence of the marginal role English has historically had in these societies. On the other hand, in terms of degree of global integration, the former Soviet republics, at least those in the western part of the former Soviet Union, are more similar to South Africa than Nepal. Despite this similarity in degree of global integration, it is not apparent that these newly independent countries (such as the Baltic republics) see a trade-off between linguistic globalization and linguistic democratization, as appears to be the case in South Africa. In South Africa, many language activists want linguistic democratization but not the linguistic globalization that seems to accompany democratization. In the Baltic Republics, the preference seems to be for linguistic globalization without any accompanying linguistic democratization. Western European countries have voiced concerns that the chauvinistic language policies initially adopted in the Baltic Republics were detrimental to their consideration for admission into the European Union.

The comparative cases of the former Soviet Union do not, then, mirror the conclusions we drew from the South African and Nepalese cases. We should not expect them to. We found differences between Nepal and South Africa in terms of the relationship between democratization, multilingualism and global English. We explained those differences by acknowledging that these two countries differed in terms of the status and historical role of English and degree of global integration, our typological categories developed in chapter 1. We can see how the former Soviet Union republics also differ, according to these categories, from both Nepal and South Africa. Nepal is a "marginal English" country and marginally globalized. South Africa is an "official English" country and at least more globally integrated than Nepal. Like South Africa, the western-most former Soviet republics are increasingly globally integrated; but like Nepal, global English has been marginal. However, all three types of cases share in common immersion in the wave of democratization and economic liberalization that washed the globe in the early 1990s.

Democratic transitions in multilingual countries appear to provide opportunity for a reversal of linguistic hegemonic practices of previous regimes. Whether global English is associated with hegemony in the past, present or future in democratizing countries appears to depend of the historical role of English in terms of status and usage, and the current degree of global integration. In cases where both are minimal (e.g., Nepal), global English tends to be positively associated with democratization. In cases where status and usage of English has been hegemonic and there is a fair degree of (economic) global integration (e.g., South Africa), linguistic democratization and global English appear to be inimical. In cases where historically English is marginal but there is a high potential for (economic) globalization (e.g., former Soviet republics), linguistic democratization seems to suffer. Global English, then, is clearly related to linguistic democratization, but the resulting pattern is dependent on local language politics.

Notes

1. Heribert Adam, "The politics of ethnic identity: comparing South Africa," *Ethnic and Racial Studies* 18, no. 3 (July 1995): 457-75; Courtney Jung, *Then I Was Black: South African Political Identities in Transition* (New Haven, Conn.: Yale University Press, 2000), 13; Anthony W. Marx, *Lessons of Struggle: South African Internal Opposition, 1960-1990* (New York: Oxford University Press, 1992), 15.

2. Nancy Levine, "Caste, State, and Ethnic Boundaries in Nepal," *Journal of Asian Studies* 46, no. 1 (1987): 71-87.

3. Jean Benjamin,"Language and the struggle for racial equality in the development of a non-racial Southern African nation," in *African Languages, Development and the State*, eds. Richard Fardon and Graham Furniss (New York: Routledge, 1994), 97, 106.

4. Kathryn A. Manzo, *Creating Boundaries: The Politics of Race and Nation* (Boulder, Colo.: Lynne Rienner, 1996), 84.

5. Richard Burghart, "The Formation of the Concept of Nation-State in Nepal," *Journal of Asian Studies* 44, no. 1 (1984): 121.

6. Samuel P. Huntington, *The Third Wave: Democratization in the Late Twentieth Century* (Norman: University of Oklahoma Press, 1991).

7. Thomas L. Friedman, *The Lexus and the Olive Tree* (New York: Anchor Books, 2000); Francis Fukuyama, *The End of History and the Last Man* (New York: Penguin, 1992). Also see chapter 1.

8. Benjamin R. Barber, *Jihad Vs. McWorld* (New York: Ballantine Books, 1996), 6-7.

9. Neville Alexander, *Language Policy and National Unity in South Africa/Azania (an Essay)* (Cape Town: Buchu Books, 1989), 28.

10. See Benjamin, "Language and the struggle."

11. Nigel T. Crawhall, *Negotiations and Language Policy Options in South Africa* (Salt River, South Africa: National Language Project, 1993), 7; Kathleen Heugh, "From unequal education to the real thing," in *Multilingual Education for South Africa*, eds. Kathleen Heugh, Amanda Siegrühn, and Peter Plüddemann (Johannesburg: Heinemann, 1995), 42-43; Nkonko M. Kamwangamalu, "Multilingualism and education policy in post-apartheid South Africa," *Language Problems and Language Planning* 21, no. 3 (1997): 234-53.

12. Elizabeth de Kadt, "McWorld Versus Local Cultures: English in South Africa at the Turn of the Millennium," in *World Englishes 2000*, eds. Larry E. Smith and Michael L. Forman (Honolulu: College of Languages, Linguistics and Literature, University of Hawaii, 1997), 150.

13. Baruch Hirson, "Language in Control and Resistance in South Africa," *African Affairs* 80, no. 319 (Apr. 1981): 219-37.

14. Nhlanhla P. Maake, "Dismantling the Tower of Babel: In search of a new language policy for a post-apartheid South Africa," in *African Languages, Development and the State*, eds. Richard Fardon and Graham Furniss (New York: Routledge, 1994), 113.

15. Kogila Moodley, "African Renaissance and language policies in comparative perspective," *Politikon* 27, no. 1 (2000): 104.

16. Moodley, "African Renaissance," 108.

17. Alexander, *Language Policy*, 38; Benjamin, "Language and the struggle," 100; de Kadt, "McWorld," 151. See also Kathryn A. Manzo, *Domination, Resistance, and Social Change in South Africa* (Westport, Conn.: Praeger, 1992), 218.

18. Marx, *Lessons*, vii.

19. Russell H. Kaschula, "South Africa's language policy in relation to the OAU's language plan of action for Africa," *International Journal of the Sociology of Language* 136 (1999): 66.

20. Mubanga E. Kashoki, "Some Thoughts on Future Language Policy for South Africa," *African Studies* 52, no. 2 (1993): 148. See also Kamwangamalu, "Multilingualism."

21. Kathleen Heugh, "Disabling and enabling: implications of language policy trends in South Africa," in *Language and Social History*, ed. Rajend Mesthrie (Cape Town: David Philip, 1995), 342.

22. Alexander, *Language Policy*, 28.

23. See Marx, *Lessons*.

24. Neville Alexander, "Language Policy and Planning in the New South Africa," *African Sociological Review* 1, no. 1 (1997): 83.

25. Alexander, *Language Policy*, 28.

26. Marx, *Lessons*, 116-17.

27. See Marx, *Lessons.*

28. Patrick Harries, "Exclusion, Classification and Internal Colonialism: The Emergence of Ethnicity Among the Tsonga-Speakers of South Africa," in *The Creation of Tribalism in Southern Africa*, ed. Leroy Vail (Berkeley: University of California Press, 1989), 110.

29. See Marx, *Lessons.*

30. The well-known BC leader, Steve Biko, was killed in police custody in 1977.

31. See Jung, *Then I Was Black*, chapter 2.

32. De Kadt, "McWorld," 148.

33. See Jung, *Then I Was Black*, chapter 4.

34. Neville Alexander, Project for the Study of Alternative Education in South Africa, University of Cape Town, interview with author, Cape Town, 21 Nov. 2000; and Anne-Marie Beukes, Head of Language Planning, National Language Service, Department of Arts, Culture, Science and Technology, interview with author, Pretoria, 27 Nov. 2000. The eleven official languages (followed in parentheses by proportion of population speaking predominantly that language at home, according to 1996 census) are: English (8.6%), Afrikaans (14.4%), isiZulu (22.9%), isiXhosa (17.9%), isiNdebele (1.5%), Tshivenda (2.2%), Sesotho (7.7%), Sepedi (9.2%), Xitsonga (4.4%), Setswana (8.2%) and siSwati (2.5%).

35. Hermann Giliomee, "Being Afrikaans in the New (Multilingual) South Africa," *New Contree* 40 (Nov. 1996): 59-73. The "corpus" of a language refers to its lexicographical inventory. When language planners talk about "corpus planning," they are referring to efforts, often government-sanctioned, to develop the lexicography of the language so that it can function in "modern" domains, such as science, technology and international trade.

36. Giliomee, "Being Afrikaans," 61.

37. Giliomee, "Being Afrikaans," 73.

38. Howard Barrell, "Fighting for cultural 'space,'" *Mail & Guardian*, 24 Nov. 2000, 18.

39. Barrell, "Fighting," 18.

40. For the former organization, see Karl Prinsloo, "Language of the State, Languages of the People: The Repositioning of the Afrikaans Language Community in a Changing South Africa" (paper presented at the 7th International Conference on Law and Language, San Juan, Puerto Rico, May-June 2000). Information on the ATKV was gathered from Frits Kok, Managing Director of *Afrikaanse Taal en Kultuur Vereniging* (ATKV), phone interview with author, 8 Dec. 2000, and susequent e-mail correspondence.

41. See Jeremy Waldron, "Minority Cultures and the Cosmopolitan Alternative," in *The Rights of Minority Cultures*, ed. Will Kymlicka (Oxford: Oxford University Press, 1995), 93-199.

42. Heribert Adam, "Cultural Pessimism or Genuine Multiculturalism: A Response to Giliomee," *New Contree* 40 (Nov. 1996): 76, 78.

43. Chris Louw, journalist and executive director of Monitor Spektrum, SABC radio, interview with author, Johannesburg, 8 Dec. 2000.

44. Adam, "Cultural Pessimism," 76. *Volkstaat* refers to an Afrikaner ethnic state that is territorial defined and self-governed. The right wing embraced this idea of an ethnic homeland in the mid-1990s (see Jung, *Then I Was Black*). For a comparative case of conservative communitarianism, see the discussion in chapter 2.

45. Adam, "Cultural Pessimism," 76.

46. Hermann Giliomee, "Being Afrikaans as a Presumed Identity: A Response to Adam," *New Contree* 40 (Nov. 1996): 81. It is worth noting that this debate between Adam and Giliomee is an intellectual one and not necessarily acrimonious. Adam and Giliomee are not only intellectual colleagues but long-time family friends.

47. See Jung, *Then I Was Black.*

48. Bernard Louw, Head of *Die Suid-Afrikaanse Akademie vir Wetenskap en Kuns* (Afrikaans Language Academy) and former Direcetor-General of the Department of National Education in the apartheid regime; interview with author, Pretoria, 27 Nov. 2000.

49. Although there was apparently an initial association of Breytenbach with the Group of 63, Breytenbach has since broke off any connections, particularly to the Afrikaans language cause. Chris Louw, interview with author.

50. Breyten Breytenbach, *The True Confessions of an Albino Terrorist* (New York: Harcourt Brace & Company, 1983), 242.

51. Beukes, interview with author.

52. Chris Louw, interview with author.

53. See also Vic Webb and Mariana Kriel, "Afrikaans and Afrikaner nationalism," *International Journal of the Sociology of Language* 144 (2000): 43.

54. One indication of this is the fact that the amount of complaints received by the Pan-South African Language Board citing violation of Afrikaans language rights far exceeds that of any other language. According to the Pan South African Language Board, "[o]nly 9% of the complaints received to date have been lodged in relation to discriminatory treatment of the nine African languages recently afforded official status." See PanSALB/MarkData, *Summary of the findings of: A Sociolinguistic Survey on Language Use and Language Interaction in South Africa* (Pan South African Language Board, 2000), 61.

55. Hermann Giliomee, South African academic and intellectual, interview with author, Stellenbosch, South Africa, 20 Nov. 2000; B. Louw and Beukes, interviews with author.

56. Giliomee, "Being Afrikaans," 70; Kok, interview with author. At the time of my interview with Giliomee (Nov. 2000), he supported the Democratic Alliance (DA), an amalgamation of the old Liberal Party and the New National Party, as an alternative to the ANC government (the DA has since split apart). In appealing to liberal Afrikaners, Tony Leon, the head of the DA and an English-speaking liberal, has argued that "Afrikaans is a tough and adaptable language, spoken by tough and adaptable people . . . Part of this [Afrikaans language] planning must be to include other African languages in the fight against the hegemony of English." Tony Leon, *Hope & Fear: Reflections of a Democrat* (Johannesburg: Jonathan Ball Publishers, 1998), 62.

57. Alexander, "Language Policy and Planning," 86. See also Benjamin, "Language and the struggle," 104.

58. Neville Alexander, "Overview, Recommendations and Executive Summary," in Language Plan Task Group, *Towards a National Language Plan for South Africa*, report presented to the Minister of Arts, Culture, Science and Technology (Pretoria, South Africa: Department of Arts, Culture, Science and Technology, 8 Aug. 1996), 11.

59. Alexander, interview with author.

60. Theo du Plessis, "South Africa: From Two to Eleven Official Languages," in *Multilingualism and Government*, eds. Kas Deprez and Theo du Plessis (Pretoria, South Africa: Van Schaik, 2000), 103-4.

61. Quoted from the constitution in Language Plan Task Group, *Towards a National Language Plan*, 155.

62. Heugh, "Disabling and enabling," 341.

63. Heugh, "Disabling and enabling," 331.

64. Kathleen Heugh, "Tongues Tied," *Bua!* [formerly *Language Projects' Review*] 8, no. 3 (Sept. 1993): 27-30.

65. Kathleen Heugh, Researcher at PRAESA, University of Cape Town, and member of PanSALB, interview with author, Cape Town, 21 Nov. 2000; Beukes, interview with author.

66. Alexander remained active throughout on the language board of the Western Cape. Although beyond the scope of the current study, language policy and politics on the provincial level in South Africa are increasingly noteworthy.

67. Beukes, communication with author, and information from DACST website.

68. Neville Alexander, "Multilingualism for empowerment," in *Multilingual Education for South Africa*, eds. Kathleen Heugh, Amanda Siegrühn, and Peter Plüddemann (Johannesburg: Heinemann, 1995), 38.

69. Ken Hartshorne, "Language policy in African education: a background to the future," *Language and Social History*, ed. Rajend Mesthrie (Cape Town: David Philip, 1995), 315; Heugh, "Disabling and enabling," 346; Heugh, interview with author.

70. Alexander,"Overview, Recommendations," 10.

71. Neville Alexander, "Afrikaner Identity Today: A Response to Giliomee," *New Contree* 40 (Nov. 1996): 85.

72. Alexander, interview with author.

73. The accusation that the ANC unreflectively reinforces apartheid categories is a somewhat familiar one. For example, "Charterists" (i.e., those supporting the ANC's Freedom Charter during the anti-apartheid struggle) claimed that their recognition of distinct racial and ethnic groups was practical given the South African circumstances. In contrast, the Black Consciousness (BC) advocates argued that such a position reified primordial identities. See Marx, *Lessons*, 125.

74. Susan Mathieson and David Attwell, "Between Ethnicity and Nationhood," in *Multicultural States*, ed. David Bennett (New York: Routledge, 1998), 112.

75. Kas Deprez, Theo du Plessis, and Kristin Henrard, "Introduction," in *Multilingualism and Government*, eds. Kas Deprez and Theo du Plessis (Pretoria, South Africa: Van Schaik, 2000), 11.

76. Neville Alexander, "The Political Economy of the Harmonisation of the Nguni and the Sotho Languages," *Lexikos* 8 (1998): 269-75; see also Alexander, *Language Policy*.

77. Paul Walters, "A Response to the Paper 'Language Policy and Planning in the New South Africa'," *African Sociological Review* 1, no. 1 (1997): 93.

78. Beukes, interview with author.

79. In *Lessons*, Marx reaches a similar conclusion regarding the practicality of Alexander's politics during the anti-apartheid struggle, compared to, say, the UDF's.

80. See note 25.

81. It is interesting to note that in the glossary of the LANGTAG report, both "hegemony" and "hegemony of English" are glossed, with specific reference to Gramsci. See Language Plan Task Group, *Towards a National Language Plan*, 216.

82. Njabulo S. Ndebele, "The English Language and Social Change in South Africa," in *From South Africa*, eds. David Bunn and Jane Taylor (Chicago: University of Chicago Press, 1987), 224; Jung, *Then I Was Black*, 13.

83. Nkonko M. Kamwangamalu, "A new language policy, old language practices: Status planning for African languages in a multilingual South Africa," *South African Journal of African Languages* 20, no. 1 (2000): 55; Giliomee, "Being Afrikaans," 66; Chris Louw, interview with author.

84. Crawhall, *Negotiations*, 9; Heugh, "From unequal education"; Ndebele, "English Language and Social Change"; Kamwangamalu, "New language policy," 57.

85. See de Kadt, "McWorld"; Moodley, "African Renaissance"; Alexander, "Language Policy and Planning."

86. Vic Webb, "English and Language Planning in South Africa: the Flip-side," in *Focus on South Africa*, ed. Vivian de Klerk (Amsterdam: John Benjamins, 1996), 180.

87. Hartshorne, "Language policy in African education."

88. See Bronwyn Norton Pierce, "People's English in South Africa," *Language Projects' Review* 5, no. 1 (Apr. 1990): 7-9 [Extracted from Pierce, "Toward a Pedagogy of Possibility in the Teaching of English Internationally: People's English in South Africa," *TESOL Quarterly*, 23, no. 3 (Sept. 1989)]; National Language Project, "Historical Development of the National Language Project," *Language Projects' Review* 4, no. 4 (Jan. 1990): 22-23; Kathleen Heugh, "Language Policy and Education," *Language Projects' Review* 5, no. 3 (Nov. 1990): 15-17.

89. Daryl McLean and Kay McCormick, "English in South Africa 1940-1996," in *Post-Imperial English*, eds. Joshua A. Fishman, Andrew W. Conrad, and Alma Rubal-Lopez (Berlin: Mouton de Gruyter, 1996), 321.

90. De Kadt, "McWorld," 164.

91. De Kadt, "McWorld," 164; see also note 83.

92. Alexander, "Overview, Recommendations," 6.

93. Gary P. Barkhuizen, "A comment on Neville Alexander's 'Language Policy and Planning in the New South Africa,'" *African Sociological Review* 1, no. 1 (1997): 96.

94. Crawhall, *Negotiations*, 27.

95. In a recent language survey commissioned by PanSALB and conducted by Mark-Data (Pty) Ltd., questions regarding policy preferences were rephrased from preferred medium of instruction to a choice between mother-tongue instruction plus learning of English equally well and English-only instruction. According to Peter Titlestad, a vocal advocate of enhancing the status of English and former head of the English Language Academy, this survey was essentially a political document because it recast the data to suggest that the majority preference was *not* for English. See PanSALB/MarkData, *Summary of the*

findings; Peter Titlestad, Head of Department of English, University of Pretoria, interview with author, Pretoria, 29 Nov. 2000.

96. Stanley G.M. Ridge, "Mixed Motives: Ideological Elements in the Support for English in South Africa," in *Ideology, Politics and Language Policies: Focus on English*, ed. Thomas Ricento (Amsterdam: John Benjamins, 2000), 151-72; Sarah Slabbert and Rosalie Finlayson, "'I'm a cleva!': the linguistic makeup of identity in a South African urban environment," *International Journal of the Sociology of Language* 144 (2000): 119-35. Indeed, the work of Slabbert and Finlayson shows us that the complexity of informal multilingualism in South Africa, particularly in urban settings, appears to be engendering new linguistic identities.

97. Moodley, "African Renaissance," 114.

98. See Peter Hudson, "Liberalism, democracy and transformation in South Africa," *Politikon* 27, no. 1 (2000): 93-102.

99. Gopal Gurung, President of the Mongol National Organization, interview with author, Kathmandu, 8 Apr. 1994.

100. Michael Hutt, "Drafting the Nepal Constitution, 1990," *Asian Survey* XXXI, no. 11 (1991): 1030.

101. Martin Hoftun, "The Dynamics and Chronology of the 1990 Revolution," in *Nepal in the Nineties*, ed. Michael Hutt (Delhi: Oxford University Press, 1994), 23.

102. Kanak Dixit, editor of *Himal*, interview with author, Patan, Nepal, 20 Apr. 1994; see also Kamal P. Malla, "Language and Society in Nepal," in *Nepal: Perspectives on Continuity and Change*, ed. Kamal P. Malla (Kirtipur, Nepal: Centre for Nepal and Asian Studies, Tribhuvan University, 1989), 462.

103. The similarities with South Africa are striking here. As in Nepal, much of the current leadership in South Africa was educated in exile, in English.

104. Hoftun, "Dynamics," 24.

105. Hutt, "Drafting," 1028.

106. Hutt, "Drafting," 1036.

107. Article 18 of the 1990 Consititution. His Majesty's Government, *The Constitution of the Kingdom of Nepal 2047 (1990)* [English Translation] (Kathmandu, Law Books Management Board, Mar. 1992), 13-14.

108. Sonia Eagle, "The Language Situation in Nepal," *Journal of Multilingual and Multicultural Development* 20, nos. 4 & 5 (1999): 289.

109. See Selma K. Sonntag, "Ethnolinguistic Identity and Language Policy in Nepal," *Nationalism & Ethnic Politics* 1, no. 4 (1995): 119.

110. Hutt, "Drafting," 1036.

111. John Whelpton, "The General Elections of May 1991," in *Nepal in the Nineties*, ed. Michael Hutt (Delhi: Oxford University Press, 1994), 66.

112. Sueyoshi Toba, "Counterpoint: Role of Languages in Nepal," *The Independent* (Kathmandu), 10 June 1992, 2.

113. Padma Ratna Tuladhar, opposition Member of Parliament, interview with author, Kathmandu, 22 Apr. 1994; Ratan Kumar Rai, "Truth Denied" [Letters], *Himal* 5, no. 4 (July/Aug. 1992): 2.

114. Suresh Ale Magar, "Encounter: We are Against Brahminism, Not Brahmins" [interview], *The Independent* (Kathmandu), 29 July 1992, 6; Suresh Ale Magar, minority language activist, interview with author, Kathmandu, 4 Apr. 1994.

115. Naharya Acharya, Member of Parliament (Nepali Congress Party) and chair of the commission on multilingual broadcasting, interview with author, Kathmandu, 17 Apr. 1994; Til Bikram Nembangh, Chair of National Language Policy Recommendations Commission and renown poet, interviews with author, Kathmandu, Mar.-May 1994.

116. Sonntag, "Ethnolinguistic Identity," 111.

117. On South Africa, see Alexander, *Language Policy*; Harries, "Exclusion, Classification." Although lacking the long history they have in South Africa, missionaries nevertheless figure in the language politics of Nepal, albeit in relatively recent decades. See Sonntag, "Ethnolinguistic Identity," 119.

118. It has also meant that identifiable minorities without a distinct language may create or appropriate one (as in the case of Tharu) or a recognizable language with a diffuse community of speakers may trigger a greater sense of identity (as in the case of Tamang). Local linguistic identity has been a by-product of the democratization of language policy in Nepal. See Sonntag "Ethnolinguistic Identity."

119. Sonntag "Ethnolinguistic Identity," 110.

120. Mukta S. Tamang, "Democracy and Cultural Diversity in Nepal," *Himalayan Research Bulletin* XXI, no. 1 (2001): 22-25. The federation and the general movement it promotes are identified by the term "*janajati*," connoting marginalized subalterns as much as the "indigenous" gloss usually cited, given the dubiousness of autochthonous claims of many Tibeto-Burman groups. See Rajendra Pradhan, "A Native by Any Other Name . . .," *Himal* 7, no. 1 (Jan./Feb., 1994): 41-45.

121. See Laura M. Ahearn, "'We Were Kings Here Once': Gendered Constructions of Magar Ethnicity in a Speech by Gore Bahadur Khapangi," *Himalayan Research Bulletin* XXI, no. 3 (2001): 7; and M. Tamang, "Democracy," 23, for examples.

122. Gurung, interview with author.

123. National Committee for the International Year for the World's Indigenous Peoples, Nepal, *Country Paper on Indigenous Peoples of Nepal* (prepared on the occasion of UN's World Conference on Human Rights in Vienna, Austria, 14-25 June 1993); Tuladhar, interview with author.

124. See Parshuram Tamang, Suresh Ale Magar, and Nanda Kandangwa, eds., *Karyashaala-goshTi: Nepalmaa Bhashik Samasya ra Nirakarankaa Upayharu [Conference Proceedings: Linguistic Problems in Nepal and Solutions for Overcoming Them]* (Kathmandu: Nepal Janajati Mahasangh, 29-30 Asoj [Sept.-Oct.] 2050 [1993]); M. Tamang, "Democracy," 23.

125. William Raeper and Martin Hoftun, *Spring Awakening: An Account of the 1990 Revolution in Nepal* (New Dehli: Viking, 1992), 166.

126. "Supreme Court Failed to Recognise Local Language," *Kathmandu Post*, 14 June 1999 [forwarded to The Nepal Digest listserv, 16 June 1999].

127. See Mark Liechty, "Consumer Culture and Identities in Kathmandu: 'Playing with Your Brain'," in *Selves in Time and Place*, eds. Debra Skinner, Alfred Pach III, and Dorothy

Holland (New York: Rowman & Littlefield, 1998), 131-54; Lauren Leve and Vincenne Adams, "Situating and Historicizing Religion and Human Rights in Democratic Nepal" (paper presented at the 28th Annual Conference on South Asia, Madison, Wisc., Oct. 1999).

128. See Ramesh C. Chitrakar, *Foreign Investment and Technology Transfer in Developing Countries* (Brookfield, Vt.: Avebury, 1994).

129. Ramjee P. Parajulee, *The Democratic Transition in Nepal* (Lanham, Md.: Rowman & Littlefield, 2000).

130. Parajulee, *Democratic Transition*. The international positioning of the opposition was not lost on the government: Early on in the upheaval, the King employed the British public relations firm, Saatchi & Saatchi, to generate Western support the regime. See "King Birendra and his trouble and strife," *Economist,* 5 May 1990, 44.

131. Eagle, "Language Situation," 302.

132. Much of the imitation is poor. Many Nepal watchers and Nepalese have commented on the mediocre quality of the proliferating English medium schools. See Eagle, "Language Situation"; Deepa Pradhan, "Plight of English teaching in Nepal" [Letters], *Rising Nepal* (Kathmandu), 27 Mar. 1994, 4; National Education Commission, *Report of the National Education Commission, 1992* (Kathmandu: Keshar Mahal, National Education Commission, 1992), 3.

133. Eagle, "Language Situation," 306.

134. Eagle, "Language Situation," 308.

135. Rebecca Harding, "How a Language Dies," *Kathmandu Post*, 15 Dec. 2000, 3.

136. Ramawatar Yadav, linguist, academic, and member of the National Education Commission, interview with author, Kathmandu, 13 Mar. 1994.

137. National Education Commission, *Report*, 10, 16.

138. Nembangh, interview with author.

139. Dilli Ram Dahal, Professor, Department of Anthropology, Tribhuvan University, interview with author, Kirtipur, Nepal, Apr. 1994.

140. Mahendra Lawoti, "The Maoist Insurgency and Minorities: Overlap of Interests or the Case of Exploitation?" unpublished manuscript (Graduate School of Public and International Affairs, University of Pittsburg, 2002).

141. Raeper and Hoftun, *Spring Awakening*, 169; Suman Pradhan, "Nepalese minorities threaten revolt," InterPress Service, 30 July 1999 [forwarded to Nepali Digest listserv, 26 Aug. 1999]. *Matwali* is the "impure" label designated to the Tibeto-Burman groups in Nepal by the Hindu upper castes. In regard to initiating a self-respect movement, Khapangi sounds like a Nepali version of Steve Biko. But it is important to note that Khapangi, and virtually all language activists in Nepal, unlike Biko and many others in the South African case, do not question the primordial nature of linguistic identity. See also Ahearn, "We Were Kings."

142. Li Onesto, "Dispatches: Report from the People's War in Nepal, Part 16: Magar Liberation," *Revolutionary Worker* (USA), 12 Dec. 1999, 10-11; Lawoti, "Maoist Insurgency."

143. Shyam Shrestha, "Nepali Cart Before Horse," *Himal South Asia* (Sept.-Oct. 1997): 14-16.

144. For example, Pierre du Toit, *State Building and Democracy in Southern Africa* (Washington, D.C.: United States Institute of Peace Press, 1995).

145. Gerardo L. Munck, "Review Article: Democratic Transitions in Comparative Perspective," *Comparative Politics* 26, no. 3 (1994): 371.

146. Ndebele, "English Language and Social Change," 233.

147. See Rasma Karklins, *Ethnic Relations in the USSR* (Boston: Allen & Unwin, 1986).

148. Selma K. Sonntag, "Elite Competition and Official Language Movements," in *Power and Inequality in Language Education*, ed. James W. Tollefson (New York: Cambridge University Press, 1995), 106.

Chapter 6

Understanding Linguistic Globalization

We have looked at the local politics of global English in the United States, France, India, South Africa, and Nepal. What have we learned from these case studies? What kind of generalizations can we make about linguistic globalization based on these cases? There are at least two conclusions we can draw. First, there appears to be a correlation between globalization and local language politics regarding global English. The more globalization, the more the issue of global English is politicized locally. The second conclusion is that global English is a defining characteristic of linguistic globalization and, furthermore, linguistic globalization is an important dimension of globalization. On the surface, neither of these two generalizations seems earth-shaking. However, in arriving at these conclusions through comparing our cases, we will find that they hold true in some rather surprising ways.

Globalization and the Local Politics of Global English

In chapter 1, we noted how our cases vary according to the degree of global integration of the country, primarily conceived in economic terms, and also according to the usage and status of English. Nepal has a poorly globally integrated economy, India and South Africa are moderately integrated countries, and the United States and France are highly integrated globally. France and Nepal are in the same "marginal English" category, India and South Africa are again together in the category of "official English" countries, and the United States is a core English country.

Although France and Nepal are both "marginal English" countries, the local politics of global English differ significantly between the two countries, as we saw in the case studies. Whereas global English is more or less welcomed by most actors involved in language politics in Nepal, it is vehemently rejected and resisted in France. The global English issue is clearly more politically salient in France than in Nepal. This comparison does not hold for all language issues, however. In both France and Nepal, the State has vigorously promoted internal linguistic hegemony. This has triggered resistance to that hegemony, since the French Revolution in France, and more recently in Nepal. This similarity between these two "marginal English" countries disappears when the focus shifts from internal linguistic hegemony to the local politics of global English.

In many ways, the local politics of global English in France more closely resemble those of the United States than of Nepal. In both France and the United States, local politics of global English are geared toward attempting to enlist the State to protect the linguistic capital of elites. In the case of France, the threat to elite linguistic capital is global English itself. In the United States, the elites are reacting to a perceived threat to their linguistic capital posed by global immigration. While in the past the French State has been used to ensure internal linguistic hegemony (as is also the case in Nepal), it is now being entrusted with ensuring that global English does not undermine that hegemony. Similarly, the English-Only movement is attempting to bind the State to its hegemonic cause through legislation officializing English.

This suggests that global integration may be a better indicator of similarities in the local politics of global English than the usage-of-English categories. Obviously, global integration does not cause a particular pattern of local politics of global English, but there does seem to be a correlation with it. It may be that globalization heightens the mutual reinforcement of different types of elite capital, so that the increase in vulnerability of economic capital due to economic globalization enhances the saliency of other sorts of elite capital, including linguistic. We discussed, in chapter 2, Edward Cohen's argument that globalization has politicized the language issue in the United States.[1] We can extrapolate his argument about the U.S. case to also fit the evidence from our French and Nepalese cases: The higher degree of global integration, the more politicized the global English issue.

Our two other case studies, India and South Africa, offer further evidence. There is active resistance to global English in both countries, but this resistance is geared toward undermining the linguistic capital of domestic elites. In both of these cases, albeit for very different reasons, the State has, at least in the past, supported internal linguistic diversity. In the old South Africa, of course, this was a manipulative aspect of the apartheid agenda. In India, official multilingualism seems to have been a result of democratic politics with a fairly distinct subaltern voice being heard occasionally. There is, then, in our two case studies of moderately globally integrated countries, a similar outcome of local language politics both in regard to internal linguistic hegemony and to global English, at least at a very abstract level of generalization. Furthermore, in both cases the politics of global English is more a local debate than a global debate, compared to France, the United States, or even Nepal. However, the global dimension of language politics in both India and South Africa appears to have intensified as of late (i.e., under the BJP in India and since the end of apartheid in South Africa), concomitant with the on-going progression of the liberalization and global integration of these two countries.

Although the issue of global English is more politicized in countries with a high degree of global integration, this does not mean that subalterns are the primary agents of this politicization. In France, it is the elite and the State who resist global English, not subalterns. Indeed, those closest to fitting the "subaltern" category in France, such as Eric Bainvel and other young members of Emgann, are not necessarily against linguistic globalization and global English. Similarly in the United States, subalterns, such as Spanish-speaking immigrants, are not actively resisting English language hegemony; indeed, many embrace it. In this regard, they are strikingly similar to the majority of South Africans. In South Africa, there are intellectuals and activists (such as Neville Alexander) who are hoping to inspire subalterns to take up the global English challenge. But as of now, as was indicated in last chapter, the majority of poor, Black South Africans (as well as the underclass of Afrikaners) see global English as the ticket to upward mobility. It appears to be only in India, out of our five case studies, that subaltern resistance is directed toward global English. Yet, even in this case, as we saw in chapter 4, a positive view of global English as linguistic capital to be widely dispersed has featured in the strategies of some politicians, such as Laloo Prasad Yadav's appropriation of English for the masses. In Nepal, it seems that the goals of the struggle are still so basic—to democratize and to distribute more equally any kind of capital—that subaltern movements are far from considering challenging global English.

In his schema of concentric circles of English usage (as discussed in chapter 1), Braj Kachru is extremely ambiguous about South Africa. He hesitates to put it in the "outer circle" (what we have termed "official English" countries), for in many regards it is both core and marginal.[2] Under apartheid, South Africa could be considered a core country, where English, along with Afrikaans, was a language of power and privilege. But English was also the language of resistance to apartheid, as we saw in chapter 5. As the language championed by the disenfranchised, the language of subaltern solidarity, global English was at least symbolically a marginal language. In terms of numbers as well, English was marginal—few Black South Africans spoke it (as is still the case today). But with the drastic change in political power in South Africa, global English has acquired new dimensions. It seems that today South Africa would clearly belong to Kachru's outer circle and our "official English" category. Indeed, Neville Alexander looks to India as a model for South Africa.[3] While we may conclude that the politicization of global English is even greater in highly globally integrated countries than in moderately integrated ones, we must concur with Kachru that his outer circle is the most fascinating and most revealing. It seems to be in these countries that the increasing politicization of global English affords the greatest possibility for globalization-from-below—a different pattern of the local politics of global English from that of France and the United States.

Our comparisons reveal an important corollary to our generalization that globalization politicizes the global English issue. The State, in the sense of the officials, processes, and institutions at the national level where authoritative and allocative decisions are made, remains a critical actor and site of action in the relationship between globalization and the local politics of global English. The critical role of the State in national language politics has been established and analyzed in such seminal works as Eric Hobsbawm's *Nations and Nationalism since 1780*, Benedict Anderson's *Imagined Communities*, and Ernest Gellner's *Nations and Nationalism*.[4] These authors suggest that although economic forces such as industrialization and print capitalism were critical in the spread and standardization of vernaculars, it was the State that organized the boundaries and status of that spread. It was the State that authorized the transformation of a particular vernacular into a national and official language and allocated the resources to back this transformation. The extrapolation from the age of nationalism to the age of globalization fits our comparative evidence. Although global economic integration is correlated with the local politics of global English, it is the State that appears to be critical in determining the boundaries and status of the spread of global English. Hobsbawm's comment that "English has become [the] global language, even though it supplements rather than replaces national languages" confirms our extrapolation.[5] Just as the State used language to define national boundaries in the age of nationalism, so is the State negotiating global boundaries through language politics.[6] At the end of chapter 2, we posed the question of what the new global map will look like in the wake of linguistic globalization. Our corollary suggests that the new map will not look radically different from the current one. Although borders and boundaries may be less definite, the contours will still be determined by States.

The State is not a passive victim of linguistic globalization but an active participant, regardless of whether it is a core, official English, or marginal English country. This is a central theme in Cohen's book: "[G]lobalization over the past decades has been the *product* of the actions of the state and the use of its sovereign authority, not the cause of its demise."[7] This is not necessarily an argument that is widely accepted among globalization scholars. There has been an on-going debate about the role of the State in globalization, with some characterizing globalization as an independent, external force impinging on the State and undermining national sovereignty, and others, such as Cohen, arguing that the State is an active accomplice in globalization.[8] Although the arguments presented in this book tend toward Cohen's side of the debate, we have noted, particularly in our case study of the local politics of global English in France, that the State has become an increasingly amorphous and shifting target under the impact of globalization. In negotiating global boundaries through language politics, the State inevitably negotiates its own definition and that of civil society as well.

Global English and Linguistic Globalization

Our second generalization is that global English is a defining characteristic of linguistic globalization. Although this may seem obvious and in many ways has been a basic assumption throughout this book, it is not taken for granted by everyone. Barbara Wallraff's article, "What Global Language?," was featured on the cover of the November 2000 issue of the *Atlantic Monthly*, with the teaser "Don't bet on the triumph of English." Wallraff identifies two key variables to back up her argument: "demographics and technology."[9] In terms of number of native speakers, for example, English lags far behind Chinese. And technology has the potential to augment this global multilingualism. The combination of these two potent variables featured in a provocative advertisement for the international consulting firm, Accenture, which appeared several times in the *New York Times* in early 2001.[10] The full-page advertisement depicted a rural, idyllic Chinese background with a simulated newspaper clip in the foreground that read "Chinese to Become #1 Web Language by 2007." Underneath in light type and brackets was the comment, "Now it gets interesting." As Marwan Kraidy notes, there are, indeed, interesting technological trends that "point to a more fragmented linguistic landscape on the Internet."[11]

The notion of fragmentation as a characteristic feature of linguistic globalization finds support in the cultural studies literature on globalization.[12] For some cultural theorists of globalization, cultural and linguistic fragmentation seem to be "a 'natural' movement," "a natural drift."[13] This apolitical assessment should give us pause. Just as we dismissed the apolitical assessment of the spread of global English in chapter 1, so should we be wary of a similar explanation for barriers to the spread of global English. In our case study analyses, we have seen repeatedly that political agency is central to understanding linguistic globalization. If global English is *not* a defining characteristic of linguistic globalization, as Wallraff and others seem to suggest, then we should look to politics and political agency to understand why this is the case and not just to demographics, technology, or some kind of "natural" trend.

Even when English fragments into multiple "English languages" or "World Englishes," we have seen that this has been the result of politics and political agency, not "alchemy."[14] The English appropriated by Indians was the result of anti-colonial and subaltern political struggles. South African English is the outcome of the anti-apartheid struggle. These local transformations of British and American English are encompassed in our notion of "global English." As Alastair Pennycook has emphasized and as we have seen in our case studies, resistance to global English hegemony can be in global English. Resistance to global English in global English is a political act.

In concluding that global English is a defining characteristic of linguistic globalization, we are pointing to evidence of political agency in our case studies. The political nature of linguistic globalization directs us to a corollary conclusion, that linguistic globalization is an important dimension of globalization. Linguistic globalization is about politics, and politics matter greatly in understanding globalization.

Why do politics matter in globalization? Because it is through politics that globalization is structured and reproduced. Hence it is through politics that the course of globalization can change. Politics are what structure globalization-from-above and what make possible globalization-from-below. The nature of politics and political agency determine both the reality and the possibilities.

As we saw in chapter 1, some globalization theorists contend that the possibility of globalization-from-below is dependent on participatory democracy. What can we conclude about linguistic globalization and democracy from our case studies? Three of our cases were well-established democracies (the United States, France, and India), while two were democratizing (South Africa and Nepal, with the former having more success than the latter). We concluded in the last chapter, on South Africa and Nepal, that the democratization process seems to precede and stimulate the politicization of language issues. In this regard, democratization is similar to, rather than in conflict with, liberalization (i.e., the economic process which usually leads to further global integration): An increase in democracy and an increase in global integration are both positively correlated with further linguistic politicization. In Nepal, linguistic globalization in the form of global English is seen as an accompaniment to democracy, not as a detriment. In the South African case as well, global English and global economic integration have accompanied democratization, although there is dispute over any casual connection. At any rate, most South Africans have not challenged global English hegemony under their new democratic banner (although some South African language activists do). In the United States, liberal democracy, with its emphasis on individual rights and private autonomy, seems to provoke assimilation rather than a challenge to global English hegemony. And, in France, democracy is appealed to from above to challenge global English. Even in India democratic politics seem more of a vehicle of opportunism than an ideological foundation for challenging global English.

Hence, the assumption that democracy is associated with globalization-from-below doesn't necessarily hold in the case of linguistic globalization. Democracy does not necessarily spur resistance to linguistic globalization-from-above, i.e., to global English hegemony. Nor is resistance to globalization-from-above necessarily democratic, as we derived from our discussion of Barber's thesis in chapter 1. Indeed, in several of our case studies, we saw that the most serious challenge to global English is frequently mounted by conservative communitarians. The Afrikaners in South Africa and the BJP in India have both resisted global English and both are accused of having affinities to conservative communitarianism. The language politics of some Afrikaners and the BJP may have more in common with the anti-democratic English-Only movement in the United States than they do with other resisters to global English within their own countries. As we saw in chapter 2, the English-Only movement has ideological links with conservative communitarianism.

It seems that we must tap something besides democracy for the fountain of globalization-from-below, or at least for linguistic globalization-from-below. Let us remind ourselves of the corollary to our first generalization above, that the State is a critical actor and site in linguistic globalization. Our case studies of the local politics of global English should point us to the relation *between* State and democracy to look for the possibility of a politics of globalization-from-below. Just as Cohen has argued that State-society relations are the input into globalization-from-above,[15] those relations will also be the input into globalization-from-below. In India, there has occasionally been a congruent relation between the State and grassroots or participatory democracy—these have been the brief moments of the ascendancy of subaltern politics. In South Africa, Neville Alexander wants to harness the State to democracy, but is finding it difficult to do so. The rapidly changing and precarious nature of the State during democratic transitions signals the *potential* of globalization-from-below—a missed opportunity perhaps in South Africa, and even more so in Nepal. In both cases, although civil society bore the brunt of politicizing language issues during the democratization process, it has been difficult to sustain that momentum subsequently, particularly in Nepal. It may well be that sustainment requires engaging the State. Successful engagement may in turn transform the State—this is part of the agenda of South African activists.[16] In France, the breaking up of the entrenched, centralized French State is the only way that some see to truly democratize language politics. In the United States, the democratic battle has been for structural incorporation of linguistic minorities—only then, when linguistic minorities participate fully in American democracy, will the nature of the State and hence State-society relations be transformed, to allow for a linguistic globalization-from-below. Our case studies clearly indicate that we must consider the State-democracy relationship in our attempts to understand the possibility of globalization-from-below.

This is why linguistic globalization is an important dimension of globalization. Linguistic globalization can help us understand the reality of globalization-from-above and the possibility of globalization-from-below. In turn, the local politics of global English can help us understand linguistic globalization. They confirm the adage "Think Globally, Act Locally"—local political agency helps us think about, and ultimately understand, (linguistic) globalization.

We have concluded, then, that global economic integration, the usual goal of liberalization, tends to politicize the global English question. This politicization involves the State as a major actor and site in the local politics of global English. Furthermore, we concluded that the global English is a feature of linguistic globalization and that the local politics of global English can tell us a lot about globalization. The politics of hegemony and resistance, elites and subalterns, and liberalization and democratization constitute the local politics of global English. Globalization, both from above and below, is a product of the local politics of global English. Linguistically, that product is manifested in both the homogeneity and diversity of the English language. Politically its manifestation is hegemony and fragmentation. If global English represents both homogeneity and diversity, hegemony and fragmentation, what are the implications for other languages?

The Global Politics of Local Languages

The *New York Times* recently carried a short piece on a recent UNESCO report on the disappearance of roughly half of the world's six thousand languages in the not-so-distant future. In that piece, both the United States and France were highlighted as countries where indigenous languages have become virtually extinct, while India was commended. "Multilingual policies in India help keep local languages alive," the article noted.[17] The concern of UNESCO, as well as many others, is that the loss of linguistic diversity is akin and related to the global loss of biodiversity.[18] Local languages are often encoded with information about the beneficial relations between plants and humans. When these local languages become extinct, it is a loss for global humankind. The UNESCO report and similar testimonies are a clear call to the reverse adage, "Think Locally, Act Globally." What are the global politics of local languages, and what can our study of the local politics of global English add to our understanding of this issue?

Above we argued that the relationship between the State and societal democracy is critical to understanding the local politics of global English. As we saw in chapter 1, there are some globalization theorists, such as David Held and John Dryzek, who argue that we need to move from the local to the global level of politics, in essence bypassing the State, to ensure the potential for globalization-from-below.[19] That is, only when participatory and deliberative democracy break out of the confines of the State and generate a global civil society, will the potential of globalization-from-below be realized. How do language issues figure into the politics of this global civil society?

For Held, language issues do not figure into his vision of a global civil society. Held only briefly mentions a "multiplicity of languages and discourses in and through which people interpret their lives and cultures," and suggests, without elaboration, that there must be a respect of difference in any democratic global order.[20] Like Held, those who advocate globalization-from-below through the nurturing of a global democratic civil society are, in general, sympathetic to multiculturalism and respect of difference.[21] However, the practicalities of this are seldom worked out. Given the evidence from our case studies, there is little to suggest that a global democratic order would inherently be favorable to the survival and support of local languages. Hence, all the more urgency for this issue to be addressed by advocates of a global civil society. We saw in our case studies how, in practice, global English is most often the language of global democracy. In the South African case, we saw how global English was a significant component of the democratic struggle against apartheid, precisely because it facilitated global solidarity. Likewise in Nepal, global English was positively associated with global democracy and human rights. In our analysis of the French case, we saw how the French State attempts to project the French language, in opposition to global English, as inherently universal and democratic, but with little success. If linguistic diversity is to be a product of global democracy, then methods to assure this must be developed.

We also concluded above that linguistic globalization is an important dimension of globalization because it so clearly demonstrates the significance of politics. Hence we shouldn't assume that there is any inherent tendency toward linguistic diversity in efforts to globalize-from-below, but rather that this must be a conscious, political goal to strive for. By making this a conscious goal, there is the possibility of breaking out of the globalization-from-above paradigm that tends to overwhelm any efforts at globalization-from-below and the nurturing of a global civil society.[22] Unfortunately, there is little recognition of the linguistic dimensions of globalization and even less consciousness-raising regarding global English hegemony. David Cooke has argued, for example, that the battle against the MAI (Multilateral Agreement on Investment) in the late 1990s, a high priority of global democracy activists, was ideologically compromised by the unwitting acceptance and dominance of English as the medium of activist communication.[23] In contrast, the international organization through which the MAI would have been implemented, the WTO (World Trade Organization), spends a quarter of its budget and staff on language services.[24] As another example, we can look at the recent 2002 People's Earth Summit in Johannesburg, South Africa—an alternative globalization-from-below forum to the UN Summit on Sustainable Development. At the World Sustainability Hearing of the Summit, funded by the MacArthur Foundation and the David R. Brower Fund, among others, the organizers initially budgeted for translation services to ensure participation by monolingual subalterns. However, according to one of the organizers, "money for translation quickly became lowered in priority as we got closer to the event." In the end, "almost every speaker presented in English (although some had tremendous difficulty doing so)."[25]

Of course, as we have argued repeatedly throughout this book, global English can be a counter-hegemonic medium. This was clearly the implicit intent of the activists in Johannesburg. But global English will only be counter-hegemonic if the language issue is consciously politicized and democratized. We have indicated that many of the English languages and World Englishes that fall under the rubric of global English have evolved through political struggles. More recently, Ngugi wa Thiong'o, who mounted one of the best known challenges to global English in the 1970s by abandoning a successful writing career in English and returning to writing in Kikuyu, is now "encourag[ing] writers to use English to 'enable and not disable' their native languages."[26]

Ngugi wa Thiong'o's efforts and the cases of the indigenization of global English are individual and local examples of politicizing and democratizing global English. What have been the institutional efforts at the global level to politicize and democratize global English? The United Nations, which is looked upon by some global democracy advocates, such as Held, as a possible model, has long grappled with the language issue, with no solution beyond further entrenchment of global English as the working language.[27] The Japanese linguist, Yukio Tsuda points to the United Nations Educational, Scientific, and Cultural Organization's (UNESCO) Universal Declaration of Language Rights, along with the TESOL (Teachers of English to Speakers of Other Languages) association's Resolution of Language Rights as examples of an alternative paradigm to the hegemony of English.[28] These examples, however, both adopt the rights discourse of liberalism that may be limited in providing a real counter-hegemonic challenge, as we saw in chapter 2.

Given the paucity of attention at the global level, where else can we look for success? The Council of Europe's European Charter for Regional or Minority Languages, which went into effect in 1998, has certainly raised some hopes, particularly for formal institutional support of indigenous languages that are barely surviving the onslaught of linguistic hegemony and globalization in Europe. It may well be that it is the incorporation of States—in a collective, regional forum—that has allowed the hope of success in this case. As Jean Laponce argues, "minority languages best able to resist the pressure of more powerful competitors [such as global English] are those having government as their champion."[29] The global politics of local languages must engage governments, individually or collectively in intergovernmental organizations, whether in regional groupings, such as the Council of Europe, or global groupings, such as the United Nations and its agencies (for example, UNESCO). Likewise, NGOs (Non-Governmental Organizations) must also engage States rather than bypass them, as is the current tendency. This is what we concluded from our case studies: the State is an important actor in linguistic globalization, be it the local politics of global English or the global politics of local languages.

Conclusion

Toward the end of chapter 1 we posed a series of questions about global English. Is global English the linguistic feature of an insidious global hegemony or a medium for transmitting democratic values? Are local linguistic demands fervid parochial reactions to global English or democratic reflections of cultural and linguistic subaltern resistance? Is global English a tool for accessing economic and technological resources or a weapon in the arsenal of a hegemonic elite? And, finally, in summing up, does global English represent globalization-from-above or could it facilitate globalization-from-below? We have now, at the end of the concluding chapter, arrived at an answer to at least the last rendition of the questions: Global English represents globalization-from-above, but it also contains the possibility for globalization-from-below, most plausibly in terms of a democratic subaltern resistance to linguistic hegemony. Globalization pushes forward global English hegemony, but in doing so it creates its own antithesis: Globalization politicizes the language issue and hence "potentializes" a reaction. The burden is to ensure that the potential of this reaction is linguistically democratic.

This should point us in new directions of thinking, research, and dialogue. Political scientists and scholars of language have much to offer one another. In addition to case studies of the type presented in this book, both linguists and political scientists can make collaborative contributions to a whole host of salient issues on language politics at the global and local levels. For example, what are the politics of international versus local terminology for use in global negotiations or development efforts?[30] How do different political configurations, such as federalism or regionalism, affect local linguistic varieties of global English? How can we distinguish, politically and linguistically, counter-hegemonic English from global English-from-above?

There is a single point of consensus in the debate on globalization: Whatever it is, it is complex and full of nuances. We therefore have to complicate our analysis of globalization. One way is to cross disciplinary boundaries. By looking at both language and politics in this book, we have crossed those boundaries. Hopefully, most of us will also cross language boundaries many times.

Notes

1. Edward S. Cohen, *The Politics of Globalization in the United States* (Washington, D.C.: Georgetown University Press, 2001), chapter 6.

2. "Countries such as South Africa and Jamaica are difficult to place within the concentric circles. In terms of the English-using populations and the functions of English, their situations are rather complex." Braj B. Kachru, "Teaching World Englishes," in *The Other Tongue*, ed. Braj B. Kachru (Urbana: University of Illinois Press, 1992), 362.

3. Neville Alexander, interview with author, Cape Town, South Africa, 21 Nov. 2000.

4. Eric J. Hobsbawm, *Nations and Nationalism since 1780* (Cambridge, U.K.: Cambridge University Press, 1990); Benedict Anderson, *Imagined Communities* (London: Verso, 1991); Ernest Gellner, *Nations and Nationalism* (Ithaca, N.Y.: Cornell University Press, 1983).

5. Hobsbawm, *Nations*, 39.

6. Patricia Goff makes a similar argument in regard to culture. She argues that States are using negotiations involving the cultural industry (e.g., the "cultural exemption" clause in the Uruguay round of GATT negotiations) to establish "invisible" national borders in the

age of globalization. See Patricia Goff, "Invisible Borders: Economic Liberalization and National Identity," *International Studies Quarterly* 44, no. 4 (Dec. 2000): 533-62.

7. Cohen, *Politics of Globalization*, 80.

8. The view that globalization is a force of its own can be found among those who see globalization as benevolent as well as those who see it as malevolent. For the former, see Thomas L. Friedman, *The Lexus and the Olive Tree* (New York: Anchor Books, 2000); for the latter, see William Greider, *One World, Ready or Not* (New York: Simon & Schuster, 1997). For an additional version of Cohen's argument that the State is instrumental in globalization, see Alan Scott, "Introduction—Globalization: Social Process or Political Rhetoric?," in *The Limits of Globalization*, ed. Alan Scott (New York: Routledge, 1997), 1-22. For a more conventional view of the continuing importance of the role of the State in the contemporary era of globalization, see Linda Weiss, *The Myth of the Powerful State* (Ithaca, N.Y.: Cornell University Press, 1998).

9. Barbara Wallraff, "What Global Language?," *Atlantic Monthly*, Nov. 2000, 55.

10. Accenture was the new incarnation of Andersen Consulting, a part of Arthur Andersen that had broken off and attained autonomy before the Enron-Arthur Andersen scandal hit the press. The point of the advertisement was to gain name recognition for this new incarnation.

11. Marwan M. Kraidy, "From Imperialism to Glocalization: A Theoretical Framework for the Information Age," *CyberImperialism? Global Relations in the New Electronic Frontier* (Westport, Conn.: Praeger, 2001), 36. See also "Tongues of the Web," *Economist,* 16 Mar. 2002, 26-28.

12. See, e.g., Mike Featherstone, *Undoing Culture* (London: Sage, 1995), 86; John Tomlinson, *Globalization and Culture* (Chicago: University of Chicago Press, 1999), 84-85.

13. Sol Yurick, "The Emerging Metastate Versus the Politics of Ethno-nationalist Identity," *The Decolonization of Imagination,* ed. Jan Nederveen Pieterse and Bikhu Parekh (London: Zed, 1995), 208.

14. See chapter 1, regarding "English languages" and "World Englishes." Braj Kachru refers to "the alchemy that English uses for changing itself," claims that "English has caused transmutation of languages," and contends that English is "used as an alchemy for language modernization and social change." Braj B. Kachru, *The Alchemy of English* (New York: Pergamon, 1986), 13-14. Wimal Dissanayake, in wedding Kachru's "World Englishes" to cultural studies, contends that "World Englishes, the object as well as the concept, emerged as a consequence of the complex processes of globalization," again an agentless causal account, though Dissanayake subsequently brings up political factors. Wimal Dissanayake, "Cultural Studies and World Englishes," in *World Englishes 2000*, ed. Larry E. Smith and Michael L. Forman (Honolulu: College of Languages, Linguistics and Literature, University of Hawaii and East-West Center, 1997), 136.

15. Cohen, *Politics of Globalization*, 40.

16. This transformation through State engagement is noted by Anne Phillips: "When countries officially redefine themselves, for example, as multicultural or multi-ethnic societies, this implies more than a new settlement between public and private domains. It actively transforms what are understood as the shared premises of the society." Anne

Phillips, "The Politicisation of Difference: Does this Make for a More Intolerant Society?" in *Toleration, Identity and Difference*, ed. John Horton and Susan Mendus (New York: St. Martin's Press, 1999), 140.

17. "World Briefing: Esperanto, Anyone?," *New York Times* (21 Feb. 2002): A6.

18. Luisa Maffi (ed.), *On Biocultural Diversity: Linking Language, Knowledge, and the Environment* (Washington, D.C.: Smithsonian Institution Press, 2001); Daniel Nettle and Suzanne Romaine, *Vanishing Voices: The Extinction of the World's Languages* (Oxford: Oxford University Press, 2000).

19. David Held, *Democracy and the Global Order* (Stanford, Calif.: Stanford University Press, 1995), part IV; John S. Dryzek, *Democracy in Capitalist Times* (Oxford: Oxford University Press, 1996), 83-91. Dryzek in particular is intent on the need to bypass the State.

20. Held, *Democracy*, 125.

21. See, e.g., Iris Marion Young, *Inclusion and Democracy* (Oxford: Oxford University Press, 2000), chapter 7.

22. For a discussion of the overpowering of globalization-from-below efforts, see Mustapha Kamal Pasha and David L. Blaney, "Elusive Paradise: The Promise and Peril of Global Civil Society," *Alternatives* 23, no. 4 (1998): 417-50.

23. David Cooke, "Contending Discourses and Ideologies: English and Agency," *Langauge & Communication* 19 (1999): 415-24.

24. "Tongue-tied," *Economist,* 7 Apr. 2001, 83. The same article notes that the World Bank, also a frequent target of globalization-from-below activists, provides services in 56 different languages, through a decentralized communication structure that is fairly cost-efficient.

25. Personal communication with a co-organizer, Aaron Lehmer, Director, Grassroots Globalization Network, Earth Island Institute, San Francisco.

26. Catherine E. Shoichet and Piper Fogg, "Peer Review," *Chronicle of Higher Education* (26 July 2002): A10. Based on an interview with Ngugi wa Thiong'o. For a fuller exposition of Ngugi wa Thiong'o's language politics, see his *Decolonizing the Mind: The Politics of Language in African Literature* (Portsmouth, N.H.: Heinemann, 1986).

27. See C. E. King, *The Implications of Additional Languages in the United Nations System* (A/32/237) (Geneva: United Nations, General Assembly, 1977).

28. Yukio Tsuda, "Hegemony of English vs. Ecology of Language: Building Equality in International Communication," in *World Englishes 2000*, ed. Larry E. Smith and Michael L. Forman (Honolulu: College of Languages, Linguistics and Literature, University of Hawaii and East-West Center, 1997), 21-31.

29. Jean Laponce, "Politics and the Law of Babel," *Social Science Information* 40, no. 2 (2001): 179.

30. Professor Emeritus Fred Riggs, at the University of Hawaii at Manoa, is a political scientist who has been working on terminology problems for some time now. See, e.g., Fred W. Riggs, *Interconcept Report: A New Paradigm for Solving the Terminology Problems of the Social Sciences* (Paris: UNESCO, 1981).

Bibliography

Achebe, Chinue. "English and the African Writer." Pp. 216-23 in *The Political Sociology of the English Language*, edited by Ali Mazrui. Paris: Mouton, 1975.

Adam, Heribert. "Cultural Pessimism or Genuine Multiculturalism: A Response to Giliomee." *New Contree* 40 (Nov. 1996): 75-78.

———. "The politics of ethnic identity: comparing South Africa." *Ethnic and Racial Studies* 18, no. 3 (July 1995): 457-75.

Ager, Dennis. "Language and Power." Pp. 146-80 in *Structures of Power in Modern France*, edited by Gino G. Raymond. New York: St. Martin's Press, 2000.

———. *Identity, Insecurity and Image: France and Language*. Clevedon, U.K.: Multilingual Matters, 1999.

Ahearn, Laura M. "'We Were Kings Here Once': Gendered Constructions of Magar Ethnicity in a Speech by Gore Bahadur Khapangi." *Himalayan Research Bulletin* XXI, no. 3 (2001): 7-10.

Alexander, Neville. "The Political Economy of the Harmonisation of the Nguni and the Sotho Languages." *Lexikos* 8 (1998): 269-75.

———. "Language Policy and Planning in the New South Africa." *African Sociological Review* 1, no. 1 (1997): 82-98.

———. "Overview, Recommendations and Executive Summary." Pp. 1-40 in *Towards a National Language Plan for South Africa* (Final Report of the Language Plan Task Group; presented to the Minister of Arts, Culture, Science and Technology, Dr. B. S. Ngubane). Pretoria: Department of Arts, Culture, Science and Technology, 1996.

———. "Afrikaner Identity Today: A Response to Giliomee." *New Contree* 40 (Nov. 1996): 83-85.

———. "Multilingualism for empowerment." Pp. 37-41 in *Multilingual Education for South Africa*, edited by Kathleen Heugh, Amanda Siegrühn, and Peter Plüddemann. Johannesburg: Heinemann, 1995.

———. *Language Policy and National Unity in South Africa/Azania (an Essay)*. Cape Town: Buchu Books, 1989.

Anderson, Benedict. *Imagined Communities*. London: Verso, 1991.

Annamalai, E. "Satan and Saraswati: The Double Face of English in India." *South Asian Language Review* 1 (Jan. 1991): 33-43.

127

Appleton, Andrew. "The New Social Movement Phenomenon: Placing France in Comparative Perspective." Pp. 57-75 in *The Changing French Political System*, edited by Robert Elgie. London: Frank Cass, 2000.

Austin, Granville. *The Indian Constitution: Cornerstone of a Nation.* Bombay: Oxford University Press, 1966.

Barber, Benjamin R. "Globalizing Democracy." *The American Prospect* 11, no. 20 (11 Sept. 2000).

———. *Jihad Vs. McWorld.* New York: Ballantine Books, 1996.

———. "Jihad Vs. McWorld." *Atlantic Monthly*, Mar. 1992, 53-63.

Barkhuizen, Gary P. "A comment on Neville Alexander's 'Language Policy and Planning in the New South Africa.'" *African Sociological Review* 1, no. 1 (1997): 96-98.

Baron, Dennis E. *The English-Only Question.* New Haven, Conn.: Yale University Press, 1990.

Benjamin, Jean. "Language and the struggle for racial equality in the development of a non-racial Southern African nation." Pp. 97-110 in *African Languages, Development and the State*, edited by Richard Fardon and Graham Furniss. New York: Routledge, 1994.

Berger, Suzanne. "Bretons and Jacobins: Reflections on French Regional Ethnicity." Pp. 157-78 in *Ethnic Conflict in the Western World*, edited by Milton J. Esman. Ithaca, N.Y.: Cornell University Press, 1977.

Bernstein, Basil B. *Class, Codes and Control, Volumes 1-4.* London: Routledge and K. Paul, 1971-1975.

Bernstein, Richard. *Fragile Glory.* New York: Alfred A. Knopf, 1990.

Berryman, Sue E., *et al. Foreign Language and International Studies Specialists: The Market-Place and National Policy.* Santa Monica, Calif.: RAND, 1979.

Bothorel, Jean. *Un terroriste breton.* Paris: Calmann-Levy, 2001.

Bové, José and François Dufour. *The World is Not for Sale: Farmers Against Junk Food.* New York: Verso, 2001.

Brass, Paul R. *The Politics of India Since Independence* [The New Cambridge History of India IV, 1]. New Delhi: Cambridge University Press, 1990.

———. *Language, Religion and Politics in North India.* London: Cambridge University Press, 1974.

Breton, Roland. "Solidité, généralisation et limites du modèle "jacobin" de politique linguistique face à une nouvelle Europe?" Pp. 81-94 in *The Regional Languages of France: an Inventory on the Eve of the XXIst Century*, edited by Philippe Blanchet, Roland Breton, and Harold Schiffman. Louvain-la-Neuve, Belgium: Peeters, 1999.

Breytenbach, Breyten. *The True Confessions of an Albino Terrorist.* New York: Harcourt Brace & Company, 1983.

Broudic, Fañch. *Qui parle breton aujourd'hui?* Brest, France: Brud Nevez, 1999.

Burghart, Richard. "The Formation of the Concept of Nation-State in Nepal." *Journal of Asian Studies* XLIV, no. 1 (1984): 101-25.

Canagarajah, A. Suresh. "Negotiation Ideologies through English: Strategies from the Periphery." Pp. 121-32 in *Ideology, Politics and Language Policies*, edited by Thomas Ricento. Amsterdam: John Benjamins, 2000.

Castro Feinberg, Rosa. "Bilingual Education in the United States: A Summary of Lau Compliance Requirements." *Language, Culture and Curriculum* 3, no.1 (1990): 141-52.

Chatterjee, Partha. *The Nation and Its Fragments*. Princeton, N.J.: Princeton University Press, 1993.

Chaudenson, Robert. *Mondialisation: la langue française a-t-elle encore un avenir?* Paris: Institut de la Francophonie, Diffusion Didier Eruditon, 2000.

Chitrakar, Ramesh C. *Foreign Investment and Technology Transfer in Developing Countries*. Brookfield, Vt.: Avebury, 1994.

Citrin, Jack, Beth Reinhold, Evelyn Walters, and Donald P. Green. "The 'Official English' Movement and the Symbolic Politics of Language in the United States." *Western Political Quarterly* 43, no. 3 (1990): 535-59.

Clayton, Thomas. "Decentering Language in World-System Inquiry." *Language Problems & Language Planning* 23, no. 2 (1999): 133-56.

Cohen, Edward S. *The Politics of Globalization in the United States*. Washington, D.C.: Georgetown University Press, 2001.

Cooke, David. "Contending Discourses and Ideologies: English and Agency." *Language and Communication* 19 (1999): 415-24.

Coulmas, Florian. *Language and Economy*. Oxford: Blackwell, 1992.

Crawford, James. *At War with Diversity*. Clevedon, U.K.: Multilingual Matters, 2000.

———. "What's Behind Official English?" Pp. 171-77 in *Language Loyalties*, edited by James Crawford. Chicago: University of Chicago Press, 1992.

Crawhall, Nigel T. *Negotiations and Language Policy Options in South Africa*. Salt River, South Africa: National Language Project, 1993.

Crystal, David. *English as a Global Language*. Cambridge, U.K.: Cambridge University Press, 1997.

———. *Cambridge Encyclopedia of the English Language*. Cambridge, U.K.: Cambridge University Press, 1995.

Das Gupta, Jyotirindra. *Language Conflict and National Development*. Berkeley: University of California Press, 1970.

Dasgupta, Probal. *The Otherness of English: India's Auntie Tongue Syndrome*. New Delhi: Sage, 1993.

De Kadt, Elizabeth. "McWorld Versus Local Cultures: English in South Africa at the Turn of the Millennium." Pp. 146-68 in *World Englishes 2000*, edited by Larry E. Smith and Michael L. Forman. Honolulu: College of Languages, Linguistics and Literature, University of Hawaii, 1997.

De Swaan, Abram. "The Emergent World Language System: An Introduction." *International Political Science Review* 14, no. 3 (1993): 219-26.

Deprez, Kas, Theo du Plessis, and Kristen Henrard. "Introduction." Pp. 1-13 in *Multilingualism and Government*, edited by Kas Deprez and Theo du Plessis. Pretoria, South Africa: Van Schaik, 2000.

Diraison, Lena. "Une bergère et trois commis." Pp. 33-66 in *Crachins, Nouvelles fraiches de bretagne*, edited by Gerard Allé. Paris: Baleine-le Seuil, 2001.

Dissanayake, Wimal. "Cultural Studies and World Englishes." Pp. 126-45 in *World Englishes 2000*, edited by Larry E. Smith and Michael L. Forman. Honolulu: College of Languages, Linguistics and Literature, University of Hawaii and East-West Center, 1997.

Donahue, Thomas S. "'U.S. English': Its Life and Works." *International Journal of the Sociology of Language* 56 (1985): 99-112.

Donahue, Thomas S. "Language Planning and the Perils of Ideological Solipsism." Pp. 137-62 in *Language Policies and Education: Critical Issues*, edited by James W. Tollefson. Mahwah, N.J.: Lawrence Erlbaum, 2002.

Drohan, Madelaine and Alan Freeman. "English Rules." Pp. 428-34 in *Globalization and the Challenges of a New Century*, edited by Patrick O'Meara, Howard D. Mehlinger, and Matthew Krain. Bloomington: Indiana University Press, 2000.

Dryzek, John S. *Democracy in Capitalist Times.* Oxford: Oxford University Press, 1996.

Du Plessis, Theo. "South Africa: From Two to Eleven Official Languages." Pp. 95-110 in *Multilingualism and Government*, edited by Kas Deprez and Theo du Plessis. Pretoria, South Africa: Van Schaik, 2000.

Du Toit, Pierre. *State Building and Democracy in Southern Africa.* Washington, D.C.: United States Institute of Peace Press, 1995.

Dua, Hans. *Hegemony of English.* Mysore, India: Yashoda Publications, 1994 .

Duyvendak, Jan Willem. *The Power of Politics: New Social Movements in France.* Boulder, Colo.: Westview, 1995.

Eagle, Sonia. "The Language Situation in Nepal." *Journal of Multilingual and Multicultural Development* 20, no. 4 & 5 (1999): 272-327.

Eloy, Jean-Michel. "Les débats parlementaires français sur la loi linguistique de 1994: actualité politique et permanence d'un modèle de langue à la française." Pp. 265-76 in *Linguistic Identities and Policies in France and the French-Speaking World*, edited by Dawn Marley, Marie-Anne Hintze, and Gabrielle Parker. London: Association for French Language Studies in association with the Centre for Information on Language Teaching and Research, 1998.

Fabian, Johannes. *Language and Colonial Power.* Berkeley: University of California Press, 1986.

Fantasia, Rick. "Fast Food in France." *Theory and Society* 24 (1995): 201-43.

Featherstone, Mike. *Undoing Culture.* London: Sage, 1995.

Fishman, Joshua A. "The New Linguistic Order." *Foreign Policy*, no. 113 (Winter 1998-1999): 26-40.

———. "Bias and Anti-Intellectualism: The Frenzied Fiction of 'English Only.'" Pp. 638-54 in *Language and Ethnicity in Minority Sociolinguistic Perspective*, Joshua A. Fishman. Clevedon, U.K.: Multilingual Matters, 1989.

Fishman, Joshua A., Robert Cooper, and Andrew Conrad, eds. *The Spread of English*. Rowley, Mass.: Newbury House, 1977.

Fixman, Carol S. "The Foreign Language Needs of U.S.-Based Corporations." *The Annals of the American Academy of Political and Social Science* 511 (Sept. 1990): 25-46.

Flaitz, Jeffra. *The Ideology of English: French Perceptions of English as a World Language*. Berlin: Mouton de Gruyter, 1988.

Friedman, Thomas L. *The Lexus and the Olive Tree*. New York: Anchor Books, 2000.

Fukuyama, Francis. *The End of History and the Last Man*. New York: Penguin, 1992.

Geertz, Clifford. *The Interpretation of Cultures*. New York: Basic Books, 1973.

Gellner, Ernest. *Nations and Nationalism*. Ithaca, N.Y.: Cornell University Press, 1983.

Giddens, Anthony. *Central Problems in Social Theory*. London: Macmillan, 1979.

Giliomee, Hermann. "Being Afrikaans in the New (Multilingual) South Africa." *New Contree* 40 (Nov. 1996): 59-73.

————. "Being Afrikaans as a Presumed Identity: A Response to Adam." *New Contree* 40 (Nov. 1996): 79-82.

Gills, Barry. "Democratizing Globalization and Globalizing Democracy." *The Annals of the American Academy of Political and Social Science* 581 (May 2002): 158-71.

Goff, Patricia. "Invisible Borders: Economic Liberalization and National Identity." *International Studies Quarterly* 44, no. 4 (Dec. 2000): 533-62.

Gonzalez, Arturo. "Which English Skills Matter to Immigrants? The Acquisition and Value of Four English Skills." Pp. 205-26 in *Language Ideologies: Critical Perspectives on the Official English Movement, Volume 1*, edited by Roseann Dueñas González with Ildikó Melis. Mahwah, N.J.: Lawrence Erlbaum, 2000.

González, Roseann Dueñas. Introduction in *Language Ideologies: Critical Perspectives on the Official English Movement, Volume 1*, edited by Roseann Dueñas González with Ildikó Melis. Mahwah, N.J.: Lawrence Erlbaum, 2000.

Graddol, David. *The Future of English?* London: British Council, 1997.

Graham, Bruce. *Hindu Nationalism and Indian Politics*. New York: Cambridge University Press, 1993.

Greider, William. *One World, Ready or Not*. New York: Simon & Schuster, 1997.

Grin, François. "English as Economic Value: Facts and Fallacies," *World Englishes* 20, no. 3 (Mar. 2001): 65-78.

Guha, Ranajit, ed. *Subaltern Studies, Volumes 1-6*. Delhi: Oxford University Press, 1982-1990.

Hardgrave, Robert L., Jr. and Stanley A. Kochanek. *India: Government and Politics in a Developing Nation*. New York: Harcourt Brace Jovanovich, 1986.

Hardt, Michael and Antonio Negri. *Empire*. Cambridge: Harvard University Press, 2000.

Harries, Patrick. "Exclusion, Classification and Internal Colonialism: The Emergence of Ethnicity Among the Tsonga-Speakers of South Africa." Pp. 82-117 in *The Creation of Tribalism in Southern Africa*, edited by Leroy Vail. Berkeley: University of California Press, 1989.

Harrison, Selig S. *India: The Most Dangerous Decades*. Princeton, N.J.: Princeton University Press, 1960.

Hartshorne, Ken. "Language policy in African education: a background to the future." Pp. 306-18 in *Language and Social History*, edited by Rajend Mesthrie. Cape Town: David Philip, 1995.

Harvey, David. "Capitalism: The Factory of Fragmentation." *New Perspectives Quarterly* 9, no. 2 (Spring 1992): 42-44.

Hauss, Charles. *Comparative Politics: Domestic Responses to Global Challenges,* 4th edition. Belmont, Calif.: Wadsorth/Thomson Learning, 2003.

Heath, Shirley Brice. "A National Language Academy? Debate in the New Nation." *International Journal of the Sociology of Language* 11 (1976): 9-43.

Held, David. *Democracy and the Global Order.* Stanford, Calif.: Stanford University Press, 1995.

Hélias, Pierre-Jakez. *The Horse of Pride: Life in a Breton Village.* New Haven, Conn.: Yale University Press, 1975.

Heugh, Kathleen. "From unequal education to the real thing." Pp. 42-52 in *Multilingual Education for South Africa*, edited by Kathleen Heugh, Amanda Siegrühn, and Peter Plüddemann. Johannesburg: Heinemann, 1995.

———. "Disabling and enabling: implications of language policy trends in South Africa." Pp. 329-50 in *Language and Social History*, edited by Rajend Mesthrie. Cape Town: David Philip, 1995.

———. "Tongues Tied." *Bua!* [formerly *Language Projects' Review*] 8, no. 3 (Sept. 1993): 27-30.

———. "Language Policy and Education." *Language Projects' Review* 5, no. 3 (Nov. 1990): 15-17.

Hing, Bill Ong. *To Be An American.* New York: New York University Press, 1997.

Hirson, Baruch. "Language in Control and Resistance in South Africa." *African Affairs* 80, no. 319 (Apr. 1981): 219-37.

Hobsbawm, Eric J. *Nations and Nationalism since 1780.* Cambridge, U.K.: Cambridge University Press, 1990.

Hoftun, Martin. "The Dynamics and Chronology of the 1990 Revolution." Pp. 14-27 in *Nepal in the Nineties*, edited by Michael Hutt. Delhi: Oxford University Press, 1993.

Holborow, Marnie. *The Politics of English.* London: Sage, 1999.

Hudson, Peter. "Liberalism, democracy and transformation in South Africa," *Politikon* 27, no. 1 (2000): 93-102.

Huntington, Samuel P. *The Clash of Civilizations and the Remaking of World Order.* New York: Simon & Schuster, 1996.

———. *The Third Wave: Democratization in the Late Twentieth Century.* Norman: University of Oklahoma Press, 1991.

Hutt, Michael. 1991. "Drafting the Nepal Constitution, 1990." *Asian Survey* XXXI, no. 11 (1991): 1020-39.

Inman, Marianne. "Foreign Languages and the U.S. Multinational Corporation." Pp. 247-310 in *President's Commission on Foreign Language and International Studies: Background Papers and Studies*. Washington, D.C.: U.S. Government Printing Office, 1979.

Jacob, James E. and David C. Gordon. "Language Policy in France." Pp. 106-33 in *Language Policy and National Unity*, edited by William R. Beer and James E. Jacob. Totowa, N.J.: Rowman & Allanheld, 1985.

Jaffrelot, Christophe. *The Hindu Nationalist Movement in India.* New Delhi: Viking, Penguin India, 1996.

Jones, Mari C. "Death of a Language, Birth of an Identity: Brittany and the Bretons." *Language Problems and Language Planning* 22, no. 2 (Summer 1998): 129-42.

Jung, Courtney. *Then I was Black: South African Political Identities in Transition.* New Haven, Conn.: Yale University Press, 2000.

Kachru, Braj B. "Teaching World Englishes." Pp. 355-65 in *The Other Tongue: English across Cultures*, edited by Braj B. Kachru. Urbana: University of Illinois Press, 1992.

———. *The Alchemy of English.* New York: Pergamon, 1986.

———. *The Indianization of English: the English Language in India.* Delhi: Oxford University Press, 1983.

Kachru, Braj B. and Larry E. Smith, eds. *World Englishes.* Oxford: Blackwell 1982-2002.

Kamwangamalu, Nkonko M. "A new language policy, old language practices: Status planning for African languages in a multilingual South Africa." *South African Journal of African Languages* 20, no. 1 (2000): 50-60.

———. "Multilingualism and education policy in post-apartheid South Africa." *Language Problems and Language Planning* 21, no. 3 (1997): 234-53.

Kaplan, Robert. "The Coming Anarchy: How Scarcity, Crime, Overpopulation, Tribalism, and Disease are Rapidly Destroying the Social Fabric of Our Planet." *Atlantic Monthly*, Feb. 1994, 44-76.

Karklins, Rasma. *Ethnic Relations in the USSR.* Boston: Allen & Unwin, 1986.

Kaschula, Russell H. "South Africa's language policy in relation to the OAU's language plan of action for Africa." *International Journal of the Sociology of Language* 136 (1999): 63-75.

Kashoki, Mubanga E. "Some Thoughts on Future Language Policy for South Africa." *African Studies* 52, no. 2 (1993): 141-56.

Kaviraj, Sudipta. "Capitalism and the Cultural Process." *Journal of Arts & Ideas* 19 (1990): 61-75.

Kelly, Christine. *Tangled Up in Red, White, and Blue: New Social Movements in America.* Lanham, Md.: Rowman & Littlefield, 2001.

Kibbee, Douglas A. "Legal and Linguistic Perspectives on Language Legislation." Pp. 1-23 in *Language Legislation and Linguistic Rights*, edited by Douglas A. Kibbee. Philadelphia: John Benjamins, 1996.

King, C. E. *The Implications of Additional Languages in the United Nations System* (A/32/237). Geneva: United Nations, General Assembly, 1977.

King, Christopher R. *One Language, Two Scripts: The Hindi Movement in Nineteenth Century North India.* Bombay: Oxford University Press, 1994.

King, Robert D. *Nehru and the Language Politics of India.* Oxford: Oxford University Press, 1998.

Kraidy, Marwan M. "From Imperialism to Glocalization: A Theoretical Framework for the Information Age." Pp. 27-42 in *CyberImperialism?: Global Relations in the New Electronic Frontier*, edited by Bosah Ebo. Westport, Conn.: Praeger, 2000.

Kumar, Krishna. "Foul Contract." *Seminar* 377 (Jan. 1991): 43-46.

———. "Quest for Self-Identity." *Economic and Political Weekly*, 9 June 1990, 1247-55.

Kymlicka, Will. *Multicultural Citizenship*. Oxford: Clarendon Press, 1995.

Labov, William. *Language in the Inner City*. Philadelphia: University of Pennsylvania Press, 1972.

Lainé, Noël. *Le droit à la parole*. Rennes, France: Terre de Brume, 1992.

Lang, Jack. "L'amour de Babel." Pp. 128-30 in *Langues: une guerre à mort*, edited by Guy Gauthier. Courbevoie, France: Panoramiques-Corlet, 2000.

Language Plan Task Group. *Towards a National Language Plan for South Africa* (Final Report; presented to the Minister of Arts, Culture, Science and Technology, Dr. B. S. Ngubane). Pretoria, South Africa: Department of Arts, Culture, Science and Technology, 1996.

Laponce, Jean. "Politics and the Law of Babel." *Social Science Information* 40, no. 2 (2001): 179-94.

Lawoti, Mahendra. "The Maoist Insurgency and Minorities: Overlap of Interests or the Case of Exploitation?" Unpublished manuscript (Graduate School of Public and International Affairs, University of Pittsburgh), 2002.

Le Coadic, Ronan. "Les Bretons au pays des merveilles." Paper presented at the "La Bretagne à l'heure de la mondialisation" colloquium, Institute d'Études Politiques de Rennes, Rennes, France, 7-9 Dec. 2000.

———. *L'identité bretonne*. Rennes: Terre de Brume, 1998.

Leibowitz, Arnold H. *Educational Policy and Political Acceptance: The Imposition of English as the Language in American Schools*. Washington, D.C.: ERIC, Clearinghouse for Linguistics, 1971.

Leon, Tony. *Hope & Fear: Reflections of a Democrat*. Johannesburg: Jonathan Ball Publishers, 1998.

Leve, Lauren and Vincenne Adams. "Situating and Historicizing Religion and Human Rights in Democratic Nepal." Paper presented at the 28th Annual Conference on South Asia, Madison, Wisc., Oct. 1999.

Levine, Nancy. "Caste, State, and Ethnic Boundaries in Nepal." *Journal of Asian Studies* 46, no. 1 (1987): 71-87.

Liechty, Mark. "Consumer Culture and Identities in Kathmandu: 'Playing with Your Brain.'" Pp. 131-54 in *Selves in Time and Place*, edited by Debra Skinner, Alfred Pach III, and Dorothy Holland. Lanham, Md.: Rowman & Littlefield, 1998.

Limaye, Madhu. *Birth of Non-Congressism*. Delhi: B.R. Publishing Corp., 1988.

Lohia, Rammanohar. *Language*. Hyderabad, India: Navakind, 1966.

Loughlin, John. "A New Deal for France's Regions and Linguistic Minorities." *Western European Politics* 8, no. 3 (July 1985): 101-13.

Lovecy, Jill. "Protest in Brittany from the Fourth to the Fifth Republics: From a Regionalist to a Regional Social Movement?" Pp. 172-201in *Social Movements and Protest in France*, edited by Philip G. Cerny. New York: St. Martin's Press, 1982.

Lyons, James J. "The Past and Future Directions of Federal Bilingual-Education Policy." *The Annals of the American Academy of Political and Social Science* 508 (1990): 66-80.

Maake, Nhlanhla P. "Dismantling the Tower of Babel: In search of a new language policy for a post-apartheid South Africa." Pp. 111-21 in *African Languages, Development and the State*, edited by Richard Fardon and Graham Furniss. New York: Routledge, 1994.

Maffi, Luisa, ed. *On Biocultural Diversity: Linking Language, Knowledge, and the Environment.* Washington, D.C.: Smithsonian Institution Press, 2001.

Malla, Kamal P. "Language and Society in Nepal." Pp. 445-63 in *Nepal: Perspectives on Continuity and Change*, edited by Kamal P. Malla. Kirtipur, Nepal: Centre for Nepal and Asian Studies, Tribhuvan University, 1989.

Manzo, Kathryn A. *Creating Boundaries: The Politics of Race and Nation.* Boulder, Colo.: Lynne Rienner, 1996.

———. *Domination, Resistance, and Social Change in South Africa.* Westport, Conn.: Praeger, 1992.

Marek, Yves. "The Philosophy of the French Language Legislation." Pp. 341-48 in *Language Legislation and Linguistic Rights*, edited by Douglas A. Kibbee. Amsterdam: John Benjamins, 1998.

Marx, Anthony W. *Lessons of Struggle: South African Internal Opposition, 1960-1990.* New York: Oxford University Press, 1992.

Mathieson, Susan and David Attwell. "Between Ethnicity and Nationhood." Pp. 111-24 in *Multicultural States*, edited by David Bennett. New York: Routledge, 1998.

McArthur, Tom. *The English Languages.* Cambridge: Cambridge University Press, 1998.

McDonald, Maryon. *'We are not French!' Language, Culture and Identity in Brittany.* New York: Routledge, 1989.

McLane, John R. "The Early Congress, Hindu Populism, and the Wider Society." Pp. 47-61 in *Congress and Indian Nationalism*, edited by Richard Sisson and Stanley Wolpert. Berkeley: University of California Press, 1988.

McLean, Daryl and Kay McCormick. "English in South Africa 1940-1996." Pp. 303-37 in *Post-Imperial English*, edited by Joshua A. Fishman, Andrew W. Conrad, and Alma Rubal-Lopez. Berlin: Mouton de Gruyter, 1996.

Minow, Martha. "Rights and Cultural Difference." Pp. 347-65 in *Identities, Politics, and Rights*, edited by Austin Sarat and Thomas R. Kearns. Ann Arbor, Mich.: University of Michigan Press, 1995.

Mishra, Girish and Braj Kumar Pandey. *Rammanohar Lohia: The Man and his Ism.* New Delhi: Eastern Books, 1992.

Mittelmann, James H. *The Globalization Syndrome.* Princeton: Princeton University Press, 2000.

Moïsi, Dominique. "The Trouble with France." *Foreign Affairs* 77, no. 3 (May-June 1998): 94-104.

Monnier, Jean-Jacques. *Le comportement politique des Bretons.* Rennes, France: Presses Universitaires de Rennes, 1994.

Moodley, Kogila. "African Renaissance and language policies in comparative perspective." *Politikon* 27, no. 1 (2000): 103-15.

Morgenthau, Hans J. *Politics Among Nations.* New York: Alfred A. Knopf, 1960.

Munck, Gerardo L. "Review Article: Democratic Transitions in Comparative Perspective." *Comparative Politics* 26, no. 3 (1994): 355-75.

National Committee for the International Year for the World's Indigenous Peoples, Nepal. *Country Paper on Indigenous Peoples of Nepal.* (Prepared on the Occasion of UN's World Conference on Human Rights in Vienna, Austria, June 14-25, 1993). Kathmandu: National Committee for the International Year for the World's Indigenous People, Nepal, 1993.

National Education Commission. *Report of the National Education Commission, 1992.* Kathmandu: Keshar Mahal, National Education Commission, 1992.

National Language Project (NLP). "Historical Development of the National Language Project." *Language Projects' Review* 4, no. 4 (Jan. 1990): 22-23.

Ndebele, Njabulo S. "The English Language and Social Change in South Africa." Pp. 217-35 in *From South Africa*, edited by David Bunn and Jane Taylor. Chicago: University of Chicago Press, 1987.

Nehru, Jawaharlal. *The Discovery of India.* Garden City: New York: Anchor Books, Doubleday & Company, Inc., 1960.

Nettle, Daniel and Suzanne Romaine. *Vanishing Voices.* Oxford: Oxford University Press, 2000.

Ngugi wa Thiong'o. *Decolonizing the Mind: The Politics of Language in African Literature.* Portsmouth, N.H.: Heinemann, 1986.

Nunberg, Geoffrey. "Afterword: The Official Language Movement: Reimagining America." Pp. 479-94 in *Language Loyalties*, edited by James Crawford. Chicago: University of Chicago Press, 1992.

———. "Linguists and the Official Language Movement," *Language* 65, no. 3 (1989): 579-87.

"'Official English': Federal Limits on Efforts to Curtail Bilingual Services in the States." *Harvard Law Review* 100, no. 6 (1987): 1345-62.

Ogden, C.K. *Basic English: International Second Language.* New York: Harcourt, Brace and World, Inc., 1968.

Omvedt, Gail. *Reinventing Revolution: New Social Movements and the Socialist Tradition in India.* Armonk, N.Y.: M.E. Sharpe, 1993.

Orsini, Francesca. "Why Tulsi?" *Seminar* 432 (Aug. 1995): 55-58.

PanSALB/MarkData. *Summary of the findings of: A Sociolinguistic Survey on Language Use and Language Interaction in South Africa.* Arcadia, South Africa: PanSALB, 2000.

Parajulee, Ramjee P. *The Democratic Transition in Nepal.* Lanham, Md.: Rowman & Littlefield, 2000.

Parakrama, Arjuna. *De-hegemonizing Language Standards.* New York: St. Martin's Press, 1995.

Parekh, Bhikhu. *Rethinking Multiculturalism.* Cambridge, Mass.: Harvard University Press, 2000.

Pasha, Mustapha Kamal and David L. Blaney. "Elusive Paradise: The Promise and Peril of Global Civil Society." *Alternatives: Social Transformation and Humane Governance* 23, no. 4 (1998): 417-50.

Patten, Alan. "Political Theory and Language Policy." Paper presented at the American Political Science Association Annual Meetings, Washington, D.C., Aug. 2000.

Pennycook, Alastair. "English in the world/The world in English." Pp. 34-58 in *Power and Inequality in Language Education*, edited by James W. Tollefson. Cambridge, U.K.: Cambridge University Press, 1995.

———. *The Cultural Politics of English as an International Language.* New York: Longman, 1994.

Petherbridge-Hernández, Patricia. "The Recatalanisation of Catalonia's Schools." *Language, Culture and Curriculum* 3, no. 2 (1990): 97-108.

Phillips, Anne. "The Politicisation of Difference: Does This Make for a More Intolerant Society?" Pp. 126-45 in *Toleration, Identity and Difference*, edited by John Horton and Susan Mendus. New York: St. Martin's Press, 1999.

Phillipson, Robert. *Linguistic Imperialism.* Oxford: Oxford University Press, 1992.

Pierce, Bronwyn Norton. "People's English in South Africa." *Language Projects' Review* 5, no. 1 (Apr. 1990): 7-9. [Extracted from Pierce, "Toward a Pedagogy of Possibility in the Teaching of English Internationally: People's English in South Africa." *TESOL Quarterly*, 23, no. 3 (Sept. 1989)].

Poche, Bernard. *Les langues minoritaires en Europe.* Grenoble, France: Presses Universitaires de Grenoble, 2000.

Pool, Jonathan. "The World Language Problem." *Rationality and Society* 3, no. 1 (Jan. 1991): 78-105.

Poppi, Cesare. "Wider Horizons with Larger Details: Subjectivity, Ethnicity and Globalization." Pp. 284-305 in *The Limits of Globalization: Cases and Arguments*, edited by Alan Scott. New York: Routledge, 1997.

Pradhan, Rajendra. "A Native by Any Other Name . . ." *Himal* 7, no. 1 (Jan./Feb. 1994): 41-45.

Prasad, Binoy. "'Laloo Does It!' Consolidation of Backward Class Leadership in Bihar: An Analysis of 1995 Election to the State Legislature." Paper presented at the 24th Annual Conference on South Asia, Madison, Wisc., 20-22 Oct. 1995.

Prinsloo, Karl. "Language of the State, Languages of the People: The Repositioning of the Afrikaans Language Community in a Changing South Africa." Paper presented at the 7th International Conference on Law and Language, San Juan, Puerto Rico, May-June 2000.

Puri, Balraj. "Politics of Ethnic and Communal Identities." *Economic and Political Weekly*, 7 Apr. 1990, 703-5.

Quéré, Anna. *Les Bretons et la langue bretonne.* Brest, France: Brud Nevez, 2000.

Raeper, William and Martin Hoftun. *Spring Awakening: An Account of the 1990 Revolution in Nepal.* New Delhi: Viking, 1992.

Rai, Amrit. *A House Divided: The Origin and Development of Hindi.* Delhi: Oxford University Press, 1984.

Raina, Badri. "A Note on Language, and the Politics of English in India." Pp. 264-97 in *Rethinking English*, edited by Svati Joshi. New Delhi: Trianka, 1991.

Reece, Jack E. *The Bretons against France.* Chapel Hill: University of North Carolina Press, 1997.

Ricento, Thomas, ed. *Ideology, Politics and Language Policies: Focus on English.* Amsterdam: John Benjamins, 2000.

Richards, I. A. *Basic English and Its Uses.* New York: W.W. Norton & Co., 1943.

Ridge, Stanley G. M. "Mixed Motives: Ideological Elements in the Support for English in South Africa." Pp. 151-72 in *Ideology, Politics and Language Policies: Focus on English*, edited by Thomas Ricento. Amsterdam: John Benjamins, 2000.

Riggs, Fred W. *Interconcept Report: A New Paradigm for Solving the Terminology Problems of the Social Sciences.* Paris: UNESCO, 1981.

Robertson, Roland. *Globalization: Social Theory and Global Culture.* London: Sage, 1992.

Rodriguez, Cristina M. "Accommodating Linguistic Difference: Toward a Comprehensive Theory of Language Rights in the United States." *Harvard Civil Rights-Civil Law Liberties Review* 36, no. 1 (Winter 2001): 133-233.

Rodriguez, Richard. "The Romantic Trap of Bilingual Education." Pp. 351-54 in *Language Loyalties*, edited by James Crawford. Chicago: University of Chicago Press, 1992.

———. *Hunger of Memory.* Boston: David R. Godine, 1981.

Rogers, Vaughan. "Cultural Pluralism under the One and Incorrigible French Republic: *Diwan* and the Breton Language." *Nationalism & Ethnic Politics* 2, no. 4 (Winter 1996): 550-81.

Rudolph, Lloyd I., and Susanne Hoeber Rudolph. *In Pursuit of Lakshmi.* Chicago: Chicago University Press, 1987.

Sadowski, Yahya M. *The Myth of Global Chaos.* Washington, D.C.: Brookings Institution Press, 1998.

Safran, William. "Politics and language in contemporary France: Facing supranational and infranational challenges." *International Journal of the Sociology of Language* 137 (1999): 39-66.

Said, Edward. *Orientalism.* New York: Vintage Books, 1994.

Sandel, Michael J. *Democracy's Discontent.* Cambridge, Mass.: Belknap Press of Harvard University Press, 1996.

Schmidt, Sr., Ronald. *Language Policy and Identity Politics in the United States.* Philadelphia: Temple University Press, 2000.

Schneider, Susan Gilbert. *Revolution, Reaction, or Reform: The 1974 Bilingual Education Act.* New York: Las Americas, 1976.

Scott, Alan. "Introduction—Globalization: Social Process or Political Rhetoric?" Pp. 1-22 in *The Limits of Globalization*, edited by Alan Scott. New York: Routledge, 1997.

Searle, John R. *Speech Acts: An Essay in the Philosophy of Language.* London: Cambridge University Press, 1969.

Secada, Walter G. "Research, Politics, and Bilingual Education." *Annals of the American Academy of Political and Social Science* 508 (1990): 81-106.

Servan-Schreiber, Jean-Jacques. *Le défi américain.* Paris: Denoel, 1967.

Shelly, Sharon L. "Une certaine idée du français: the dilemma for French language policy in the 21st century." *Language & Communication* 19 (1990): 305-16.

Shiffman, Harold. "Forward." Pp. 5-8 in *The Regional Languages of France: an Inventory on the Eve of the XXIst Century*, edited by Philippe Blanchet, Roland Breton, and Harold Schiffman. Louvain-la-Neuve, Belgium: Peeters, 1999.

Sheth, D. L. "No English Please, We're Indian." *Illustrated Weekly of India*, 19 Aug. 1990, 34-37.

Shrestha, Shyam. "Nepali Cart Before Horse." *Himal South Asia*, Sept.-Oct. 1997, 14-16.

Simon, Roger. *Gramsci's Political Thought.* London: Lawrence and Wishart, 1982.

Slabbert, Sarah and Rosalie Finlayson. "'I'm a cleva!': the linguistic makeup of identity in a South African urban environment." *International Journal of the Sociology of Language* 144 (2000): 119-35.

Smith, Anthony D. *Nations and Nationalism in a Global Era.* Cambridge, U.K.: Polity Press, 1995.

Sonntag, Selma K. "Ideology and Policy in the Politics of the English Language in North India." Pp. 133-49 in *Ideology, Politics and Language Policies: Focus on English*, edited by Thomas Ricento. Amsterdam: John Benjamins, 2000.

———. "Language Contact in the United States: Symbolism and Saliency." Pp. 356-64 in *Recent Studies in Contact Linguistics* (Plurilingua XVIII), edited by Wolfgang Wölck and Annick De Houwer. Bonn: Dümmler, 1997.

———. "The Political Saliency of Language in Bihar and Uttar Pradesh." *The Journal of Commonwealth & Comparative Politics* 34, no. 2 (July 1996): 1-18.

———. "Elite Competition and Official Language Movements." Pp. 91-111 in *Power and Inequality in Language Education*, edited by James W. Tollefson. New York: Cambridge University Press, 1995.

———. "Ethnolinguistic Identity and Language Policy in Nepal." *Nationalism & Ethnic Politics* 1, no. 4 (1995): 108-20.

———. "The US National Defense Education Act: Failure of Supply-Side Language Legislation." *Language, Culture and Curriculum* 3, no. 2 (1990): 153-71.

Sonntag, Selma K. and Jonathan Pool. "Linguistic Denial and Linguistic Self-Denial: American Ideologies of Language." *Language Problems and Language Planning* 11, no. 1 (Spring 1987): 46-65.

Souaiaia, Mohamed. "Language, Education and Politics in the Maghreb." In *Language, Culture and Curriculum* 3, no. 2 (1990): 109-23.

Srinivasulu, K. "Centrality of Caste: Understanding UP Elections." *Economic and Political Weekly*, 22 Jan. 1994, 159-60.

Steger, Manfred B. *Globalism: The New Market Ideology.* Lanham, Md.: Rowman & Littlefield, 2002.

Stein, Jr., Colman Brez. *Sink or Swim: The Politics of Bilingual Education.* New York: Praeger, 1986.

Storing, Herbert J. *What the Anti-Federalists Were For.* Chicago: University of Chicago Press, 1981.

Subramanian, Narendra. *Ethnicity and Populist Mobilization: Political Parties, Citizens and Democracy in South India.* New York: Oxford University Press, 1999.

Sullivan, William M. *Reconstructing Public Philosophy.* Berkeley: University of California Press, 1986.

Tamang, Mukta S. "Democracy and Cultural Diversity in Nepal." *Himalayan Research Bulletin* XXI, no. 1 (2001): 22-25.

Tamang, Parshuram, Suresh Ale Magar, and Nanda Kandangwa, eds. *Karyashaala-goshTi: Nepalmaa Bhashik Samasya ra Nirakarankaa Upayharu [Conference Proceedings: Linguistic Problems in Nepal and Solutions for Overcoming Them].* Kathmandu: Nepal Janajati Mahasangh, 29-30 Asoj 2050 (Sept.-Oct. 1993).

Tannen, Deborah. *You Just Don't Understand.* New York: William Morrow and Company, Inc., 1990.

Tarver, Heidi. "Language and Politics in the 1980s: The Story of U.S. English." *Politics and Society* 17 (June 1989): 225-45.

Tatalovich, Raymond. *Nativism Reborn? The Official Language Movement and the American States.* Lexington: University of Kentucky Press, 1995.

Tatalovich, Raymond and Daynes, Byron W. *Social Regulatory Policy.* Boulder, Colo.: Westview Press, 1988.

Teitelbaum, Herbert and Richard Hiller. "The Legal Perspective." Pp. 1-64 in *Bilingual Education: Current Perspectives*, no. 1. Arlington, Va.: Center for Applied Linguistics, 1977.

Teune, Henry. "Global Democracy." *The Annals of the American Academy of Political and Social Science* 581 (May 2002): 22-34.

Tollefson, James W. "Introduction: Critical Issues in Educational Language Policy." Pp. 3-15 in *Language Policies in Education: Critical Issues*, edited by James W. Tollefson. Mahwah, N.J.: Lawrence Erlbaum Associates, 2002.

Tomlinson, John. *Globalization and Culture.* Chicago: University of Chicago Press, 1999.

Truchot, Claude. "The spread of English: from France to a more general perspective." *World Englishes* 16, no. 1 (1997): 65-76.

Tsuda, Yukio. "Hegemony of English vs. Ecology of Language: Building Equality in International Communication." Pp. 21-31 in *World Englishes 2000*, edited by Larry E. Smith and Michael L. Forman. Honolulu: College of Languages, Linguistics and Literature, University of Hawaii and East-West Center, 1997.

Vanaik, Achin. *The Painful Transition: Bourgeois Democracy in India.* New York: Verso, 1990.

Védrine, Hubert. *Les cartes de la France à l'heure de la mondialisation.* Paris: Fayard, 2000. [English translation: *France in an Age of Globalization.* Washington, D.C.: Brookings Institution Press, 2001].

Veltman, Calvin. "The Status of the Spanish Language in the United States at the Beginning of the 21st Century." *International Migration Review* 24, no. 1 (1990): 108-23.

Vernon, Raymond. *Sovereignty at Bay: The Multinational Spread of U.S. Enterprises.* New York: Basic Books, 1971.

Waldron, Jeremy. "Minority Cultures and the Cosmopolitan Alternative." Pp. 93-119 in *The Rights of Minority Cultures*, edited by Will Kymlicka. Oxford: Oxford University Press, 1995.

Wallerstein, Immanuel. *The Modern World-System II.* New York: Academic Press, 1980.

Wallraff, Barbara. "What Global Language?" *Atlantic Monthly*, Nov. 2000, 55-66.

Walters, Paul. 1997. "A Response to the Paper 'Language Policy and Planning in the New South Africa.'" *African Sociological Review* 1, no. 1 (1997): 93-95.

Waters, Sarah. "New Social Movement Politics in France: the Rise of Civic Forms of Mobilisation." *Western European Politics* 21, no. 3 (July 1998): 170-86.

Webb, Vic. "English and Language Planning in South Africa: the Flip-side." Pp. 175-90 in *Focus on South Africa*, edited by Vivian de Klerk. Amsterdam: John Benjamins, 1996.

Webb, Vic and Mariana Kriel. "Afrikaans and Afrikaner nationalism." *International Journal of the Sociology of Language* 144 (2000): 19-49.

Wedeen, Lisa. "Conceptualizing Culture: Possibilities for Political Science." *American Political Science Review* 96, no. 4 (Dec. 2002): 713-28.

Weiss, Linda. *The Myth of the Powerful State.* Ithaca, N.Y.: Cornell University Press, 1998.

Wexler, Leila Sadat. *Official English, Nationalism and Linguistic Terror: A French Lesson* (Working Paper No. 95-11-1). St. Louis: Washington University School of Law, 1995.

Whelpton, John. "The General Elections of May 1991." Pp. 48-81 in *Nepal in the Nineties*, edited by Michael Hutt. Delhi: Oxford University Press, 1993.

Widdowson, Henry G. "EIL, ESL, EFL: global issues and local interests." *World Englishes* 16, no. 1 (1997): 135-46.

Wiley, Terence G. "Continuity and Change in the Function of Language Ideologies in the United States." Pp. 67-85 in *Ideology, Politics and Language Policies: Focus on English*, edited by Thomas Ricento. Philadelphia: John Benjamins, 2000.

Wittgenstein, Ludwig. *Philosophical Investigations.* Malden, Mass.: Blackwell, 2001.

Wood, Gordon S. *The Creation of the American Republic, 1776-1787.* New York: W.W. Norton & Co., 1969.

Woolard, Kathryn A. "Sentences in the Language Prison: the Rhetorical Structuring of An American Language Policy Debate." *American Ethnologist* 16, no. 2 (1989): 268-78.

Young, Iris Marion. *Inclusion and Democracy.* Oxford: Oxford University Press, 2000.

Yurick, Sol. "The emerging Metastate versus the politics of ethno-nationalist identity." Pp. 204-24 in *The Decolonization of Imagination*, edited by Jan Nederveen Pieterse and Bhikhu Parekh. London: Zed, 1995.

Zentella, Ana Celia. "Who Supports Official English, and Why?: The Influence of Social Variables and Questionnaire Methodology." Pp. 160-77 in *Perspectives on Official English*, edited by Karen L. Adams and Daniel T. Brink. Berlin: Mouton de Gruyter, 1990.

Index